Francine Prince's
NEW JEWISH CUISINE

ALSO BY FRANCINE PRINCE

Francine Prince's
NEW JEWISH CUISINE

More than 175 recipes for
holidays and every day

Francine Prince

A PERIGEE BOOK

For Harold, always

Perigee Books
are published by
The Berkley Publishing Group
200 Madison Avenue
New York, NY 10016

First Perigee Edition 1992

Library of Congress Cataloging-in-Publication Data

Prince, Francine.
[New Jewish cuisine]
Francine Prince's new Jewish cuisine : more than 175 recipes for
holidays and every day / by Francine Prince.
p. cm.
Includes index.
ISBN 0-399-51755-3 (pbk.: alk. paper)
1. Cookery, Jewish. I. Title.
TX724.P76   1992   ·91-37490 CIP
641.5'676—dc20

Cover design by Mike McIver
Printed in the United States of America
5   6   7   8   9   10   11   12   13   14   15

This book is printed on acid-free paper.
∞

Contents

Introduction

JEWISH COOKERY YESTERDAY AND TODAY

Jewish cookery is an endearing and cherished folk cuisine. Like the Jewish mothers of my childhood in whose kitchens I formed a lifetime passion for it, Jewish cookery conjures feelings of warmth and security, of love—heaping platters of love—and of the wondrous joys of life. While it nurtures the body, Jewish cookery exalts the spirit.

That's a dazzling feat; and it happens, to my way of looking at it, because Jewish cookery is a gastronomy of symbols—hopeful symbols, happy symbols. Honey stands for the sweetness of the year ahead; stuffed foods, for abundance; fish, for fertility; wheat, for life's invincible continuity—and these are just a sparse and random harvest of foods that bespeak the eternal verities of the heart.

The very foundation of Jewish cooking, kashruth—the Bible's kosher nutritional imperatives—may be viewed as a symbol, an overarching symbol that unifies all the others. Kashruth stands for the sacredness of the human body and for the duty to treat it as a holy place so that foods "fit to be consumed" not only care for the physical being, but also elevate the spirit.

Which foods are "fit to be consumed"—that is to say, which foods are kosher—are ordained by the laws of kashruth.

The laws of kashruth, as pristine as the Ten Commandments, were interspersed among the first five books of the Old Testament (the Torah) some 3,300 years ago. Since then, those laws have been elaborated punctiliously by rabbinical scholars, yet the basics of kashruth have come down the long years to us virtually untouched.

The Basics of Kashruth: Permitted (Kosher) and Prohibited (Non-Kosher) Foods

- *Meat.* Permitted is the flesh of animals that have split hooves *and* chew their cud. Both characteristics are necessary to qualify as kosher. Accordingly, pork is prohibited as well as the meat of hares, badgers, horses and camels. Permitted is the meat of cows, goats, lambs and sheep; but hindquarters of these animals *are* prohibited unless the sciatic nerves and certain tendons have been removed. In my recipes, I use only permitted (kosher) cuts of meat.

- *Poultry.* Permitted are most species of domesticated birds, including chickens, Cornish hens, ducks, geese and turkeys. Prohibited are all birds of prey and scavengers.
- *Kashering.* Since all blood is strictly prohibited, every vestige of it must be removed from the animal or fowl before cooking. This is done by a ritual process that involves soaking the meat in water for several hours, draining, coating with kosher salt, letting stand for one hour, then rinsing well under hot water. (Fish need not be kashered.) Most commercial kosher meat and poultry have already been kashered (read the label). Prior to kashering, the animal is ritually slaughtered as rapidly and painlessly as possible by a trained and skilled technician, the shochet.
- *Fish.* Permitted are fish that have *both* fins and scales. These include cod, flounder, haddock, halibut, herring, mackerel, pickerel, pike, salmon, trout and whitefish. Prohibited are all shellfish, including clams, crabs, lobsters, oysters and shrimp; and fish that do not meet the criterion of possessing *both* fins and scales (a fish with one of those qualifications but not the other is non-kosher), such as dolphin and whale.
- *Dairy foods.* Permitted are dairy foods defined in the Jewish kitchen as milk and all foods containing milk or derived from milk, such as butter, cheese, cream, sour cream and yogurt.
- *Eggs.* Provided they are free from blood spots, eggs are permitted.
- *Other foods.* Fruits, vegetables, grains, nuts, oils, spices and herbs are permitted.
- *Food combinations.* All foods are, by kashruth tradition, divided into three categories: meat (fleishig), dairy (milchig) and foods that are neither meat nor dairy (pareve, pronounced PAHR-ev-uh). The combination of meat and dairy foods in the same dish, or even in the same meal, is prohibited. Pareve foods, permitted with either meat or dairy, include fruit, vegetables, grains, sugar, eggs, oil, pareve margarine, and fish.

The Many Nationalities of Jewish Cooking

Despite the universality of kashruth and of Jewish food symbols, there is no single Jewish cuisine. For millennia, the Jewish people have settled in new homelands throughout the globe; and wherever their kitchen fires glowed, they interwove the tastes, textures and redolences of the indigenous cuisines with the laws of kashruth; and accented their symbolic foods with the cooking styles of their new homelands.

A variety of Jewish cooking now spangles the globe. There is an Italian Jewish cookery, a Chinese Jewish cookery, a Mittel European Jewish cookery, an East European Jewish cookery, a Middle East Jewish cookery, even an Israeli Jewish cookery.

For categorical simplicity, geographers of gastronomics have divided the world of Jewish cookery into two broad divisions. One is Ashkenazic: European Jewish fare, particularly the robust dishes of Eastern Europe. The other is Sephardic, which originally signified the Jewish cookery of the Iberian peninsula, but now has been extended to encompass Middle East Jewish cuisine as well. Tangy, sometimes fruity, exotically spiced, propelling the gustatory imagination to cafés in faraway places with strange-sounding names, Sephardic is the very opposite of Ashkenazic.

Traditional American Jewish Cookery

Up to now, American Jewish cookery has been Ashkenazic, essentially the folk cuisine of the shtetls, those bucolic enclaves of the Jewish people that speckled the landscape of Eastern Europe—Russia, the Ukraine, Hungary, Romania, Latvia and Poland—at the turn of the century. Tevye of *Fiddler on the Roof* and his family and friends in the Russian shtetl Anatevka were nurtured on this cookery.

Shtetl cookery came to Ellis Island with the great waves of East European immigration in the late 1890s and early 1900s, took up residence in Manhattan's Lower East Side and in the Borscht Belt (those legendary Jewish Catskill Mountain resorts where you could eat all day and night and never spoil your appetite. The food tasted that good). Shtetl cookery, with minor modifications, became traditional American Jewish cookery.

It was as heavy as it was tasty. Rich in fat (even its star condiment was a fat, schmaltz) and packed with appetite stimulants sugar and salt, shtetl cookery was a dream cuisine for *fressers* (Yiddish for men and women incapable of pushing themselves away from a dining table). Portions were monumental.

Do you remember the quip about Chinese food: "Eat a Chinese meal and you're hungry again in three hours"? One of the nation's top humorists, remembering traditional American Jewish cookery, cracks, "Eat a Jewish meal and you're hungry again in three days."

But there's a new American Jewish cookery being born. To the ancient biblical imperatives of kashruth, I believe it would be prudent to add *The U.S. Surgeon General's Dietary Guidelines for Americans.* Putting the nutritional numerology aside, these guidelines are so simple that they can be expressed in a sound bite: *Cut down on the wrong foods. Step up on the right foods.* Wrong foods contain excess fats, saturated fats, cholesterol, salt and sugar. Right foods contain lower amounts of those pariah ingredients, and are likely to be high in fiber (which is good for you).

My New American Jewish Recipes

The recipes in this book are not just traditional American Jewish (Ashkenazic) recipes refashioned to current tastes, albeit I have concocted lighter variations of some enduring favorites (for some of those recipes, see Tradition, page 109). My New American Jewish recipes have been inspired as well by Sephardic cookery, and by expressions of Jewish cuisine from around the globe. In addition, drawing on the *tam* (Yiddish for "that special something") of Jewish cookery, and often using Jewish food symbols as my centerpieces, I have innovated dishes that you will be among the first to taste.

All my dishes—familiar and exotic, avant-garde and steeped in tradition—have this in common: They comply with the U.S. Surgeon General's recommendations. My creations are low*er* in fat, saturated fat, cholesterol, sugar and salt. Yet they are, as Jewish recipes always have been, among the highest in taste.

Doing without globs of banned tasteful ingredients and still bringing a tasteful dish to the table is the result of cooking-for-better-health tactics that I've developed over the past decade. Some are so simple that you'll say, "Why didn't *I* think of that?" Just one example: You cut salt way down, but you can't *live* without its strong tang. All you do is: Add half the cut-down amount of salt at the first step of the recipe, and add the other half at the last step. Or sometimes, add all the salt at the last step. Terrific taste!

Other tactics require some changes in your culinary mind-set—changes you'll *want* to make once you taste the difference. You'll find that seasoning with herbs and spices instead of just salt will open up a whole new world of flavor (salt can get so monotonous).

As you read through this book, you'll learn about the tactics for reducing amounts of the other ingredients on the Surgeon General's cut-down-on list—with no sacrifice of taste. Yes, you'll get sweetness with less sugar (and no chemical sweeteners), the taste of fat while slashing fat calories and the cooking/baking benefits of eggs while sharply reducing egg yolks (which are high in cholesterol).

You'll also get an extravagance of fruits, vegetables, legumes and whole grains—foodstuffs sans fats, saturated fats and cholesterol—combined in extraordinary taste patterns. This is the kind of Jewish cookery that, the work of some scholars suggest, could have been enjoyed at the tables of biblical times.

What you won't get in this book . . . Well, come back with me to my childhood and see for yourself:

My grandfather is about to prepare a dish, famous throughout the family—Grandpa's Fried Fish. He starts with thickly sliced flounder. *Not* filleted; *sliced* with skin and bones intact. He dips it into salted beaten eggs, then into salted matzoh meal, into eggs again and once more into the matzoh meal. He places the coated fish slices into a large frying pan containing an inch or more of hot fat and cooks until browned, turning once. Most of the fat is absorbed. Grandpa arranges a portion (huge) on a dinner plate and hands it to you. You taste it, and it's surprisingly—amazingly—delicious.

But you're not getting a recipe for Grandpa's Fried Fish in this book. The taste that was so delicious then was the taste of fat, and you can't cut down on fat appreciably and still duplicate that taste. So, good-bye to Grandpa's Fried Fish—and to several other fond recipes of years gone by that cannot be converted to today's lighter style. But you'll find the *New* American Jewish recipes even more appealing.

Celebrate the Holidays!

There are, including the Sabbaths, more than eighty well-observed Jewish holidays during the year, and more than a score of others. Why this abundance of holidays?

Rabbi Sam Seicol, a community chaplain in Phoenix, Arizona, theorizes that the author of the Bible, in which most of the holidays were originally decreed, "saw the miracle of God's presence in many different forms throughout the year, and felt the need and desire to commemorate and acknowledge this presence with . . . holidays."

Food symbolism, a leitmotif of all Jewish cookery, reaches a crescendo in holiday meals as chosen foods epitomize the significance of the holy days. In my New American Jewish cuisine, those foods are still revered at the holiday table—except that their preparation is new-style.

I may use less sugar and fewer egg yolks, but my gefilte fish is still gefilte fish. Or I may invent a new dish with the same holiday-linked symbolism as the traditional dish, but my version complies closely with contemporary nutritional doctrine.

Following is a lexicon of the most observed Jewish holidays and some of the foods traditionally associated with them in the United States. For my New American Jewish cuisine counterparts, turn to pages 23 to 28. (The holidays are arranged in the order of their appearance on the modern calendar, except Shabbat, which precedes all others.)

Promiment Jewish Holidays and Some of Their Traditional Foods

Shabbat (also known as Shabbes) is a weekly day (from Friday sundown to Saturday sundown) of relief from work and secular pressures. It is a day of rest, joy, prayer and the renewal of one's physical and spiritual self—a Sabbath. Shabbat foods by tradition include challah, chopped liver, chicken soup (with matzoh balls or kreplach, or as a broth), fish, cholent, chicken, pot roast, vegetable salad and honey cake.

Rosh Hashanah is the Hebrew New Year (which occurs in the fall). The foods that customarily grace the Rosh Hashanah table include challah, apples, honey and honey cake. The dominant culinary symbol is sweetness, expressing hope for a sweet life in the year ahead, and the table is resplendent with confections.

Yom Kippur is the time when you close your moral books for the preceding year with divine forgiveness for your misdeeds and get a clean slate and a fresh start for the New Year. On this solemn day of self-appraisal you are enjoined from eating or drinking. But, since this day is your gateway to a better and happier you, your pre-fast meal is festive. It customarily includes challah, chicken soup, a chicken or meat dish or stuffed cabbage, and an abundance of sweets. The fast is broken after sundown of the Yom Kippur day by foods that remind your palate of the joys of eating (pickled herring), foods that your empty stomach can accommodate without a struggle (challah, eggs, dairy soups) and desserts to satisfy the sweet tooth of hunger (blintzes and rice pudding).

Sukkoth, which celebrates the fall harvest, brings to your table a cornucopia of fruits and vegetables—a reminder of our indissoluble symbiosis with nature. Eggplant and squash dishes are longtime favorites. Fruits, such as peaches and plums, raw or transfigured into luscious pastries, satisfy the symbolic and gustatory yearnings for sweetness. As does mandelbrot, a crunchy cookie, wonderful with tea. The eight-day holiday is also a reminder of the journey of the ancient Hebrews as they followed Moses across a perilous desert where their shelter was only flimsy lattice-roofed booths and their faith in God. The booth, called sukkah, gives the holiday its name. To simulate the meals eaten in the sukkah, Jewish cooks over the years have created menus based on their local customs and available produce. Those Sukkoth meals now fixed by custom include, in this country, casseroles and stews, stuffed cabbage, kugels, kreplach, knishes and barley soup.

Chanukah keeps fresh a miracle that occurred in ancient Jerusalem. When rededicating the Temple, which had been desecrated by invading armies, the glorious Maccabees, who had recaptured that holy place, found that they had only one day's supply of sanctified olive oil to rekindle the eternal flame, and no shipment of oil could be expected for eight days. Yet that one-day supply burned for eight days, until the new shipment arrived. So frying food in cooking oil on this holiday became a way of commemorating the miracle of the rededication of the Temple to its holy purpose—the miracle of Chanukah. And what is, perhaps, the most delicious of Jewish fried foods? Latkes, those luscious pancakes. This is the reason the latke is the distinctive Chanukah food. (My New Jewish American cuisine latkes are sautéed in oil, not fried; that means less oil, but enough to satisfy symbolism and flavor.) To supplement latkes, Jewish foodlore has added over the centuries pea soup, chicken, tongue, vegetables, fruits, salads, noodles, kugels, pound cake, cheese strudels and cheesecake—altogether a "miraculous" feast to celebrate an ancient miracle.

Purim. The biblical book of Esther, on which this holiday is founded, is the story of how two heroic figures, Esther and Mordecai, thwart the plot of a high-ranking official of ancient Persia to kill all the Jews in his realm. This holiday, celebrating the victory of Esther and Mordecai over Haman, is one of exuberant joy. This is a holiday in the carnival spirit; and in that spirit, the distinctive food is the hamantaschen, a comic cookie-pastry rendering of Haman's three-cornered hat, which is filled with poppy seed or fruit jellies. Bolstering the holiday spirit is what amounts to a Top 5 of traditional Jewish cookery favorites from mushroom and barley soup to poppy-seed cake; and in between: chicken soup/chicken, pot roast and dried figs.

Passover (Pesach). Although it essentially commemorates the exodus—the liberation of the biblical Hebrews from bondage in Egypt and their trek to the Promised Land—Passover is a holiday that hallows the eternal return of spring, the unending quest for freedom, the obligation to care for those in need and the duty to regard the future with hope. The traditional foods of Passover, for the ritual Seders and other meals during the eight-day holiday, include gefilte fish with horseradish, boiled carp, chicken soup with matzoh balls, borscht, potato latkes, pot roast, lamb, applesauce, eggs, sponge cake, haroset, dried fruits and matzoh (which replaces bread; no leavening agents or regular flour are permitted).

Shavuot, a spring festival, exalts our deep-rooted attachment to nature. Accordingly, the food symbols for this holiday eschew meat, and are predominantly lacto-vegetarian (dairy, in terms of kashruth). From traditional Shavuot menus, you may choose dairy soups, cheeses, blintzes, strudels, knishes and rice pudding. Fish (pareve) is also a favorite.

To get a taste of how I adapt my New American Jewish cuisine to the culinary observance of a Jewish holiday, visit with me now, in your imagination, as a guest at my Rosh Hashanah—the Jewish New Year—dinner, which occurs in the fall.

You are welcomed with the greeting, *"Shanna Tova,"* as ritualistic as the sound of the shofar (the ram's horn) which heralded the New Year at the morning services in the synagogue. Dinner is almost ready, but first we sit down to kosher wine or its non-alcoholic surrogate, grape juice. Both beverages are symbols for joy; and that sets the mood for the dinner to come.

Traditionally, the table should be adorned with a round challah ("round" to symbolize perfection, the aim of all of us at the dinner party for the year ahead). But as you take your seat, you observe, not a round challah, but a platter of my round Challah Rolls, which I pass around. Each of us now has his or her own symbol of perfection (and the rolls approach nutritional perfection as well).

The first course traditionally is fish (a symbol for prosperity, among other joyous aspects of life). The fish tonight is my New American Jewish Baked Fish Mousse Balls, which add a contemporary gourmet touch to the repast.

Following a menu pattern hundreds of years old, chicken soup follows. But this is not the traditional Ashkenazic chicken soup (called *gildene yoich* for its yellow rings of fat). Instead, you are served my Chicken Broth, fat-free, enhanced with kreplach or matzoh balls.

The main course is customarily "a fat," which as a symbol holds the promise of a future of wealth, health and happiness. "A fat" has frequently been a roasted chicken, a fat one. But at my new-style dinner, it's a kind of chicken noted for its moderate fat—a Cornish hen.

The side dish is my Mixed Fresh Vegetable Salad—an Israeli favorite, which is traditional in that the Jewish New Year, coming in the fall, also celebrates the autumn harvest; but it is also new-style insomuch as a sharp restraint is clamped on the fat, sugar and salt content of the dressing.

But the distinctive theme of the dinner is joy in the year ahead, the symbol of which is sweetness. And now, as we reach the last course, the table rivals a dessert buffet at a fashionable restaurant. Traditionally, and at my table, honey is a favored sweet. At each place, there is a bowl of it, into which the diners dip slices of raw apple and snippets of challah, just as diners on Rosh Hashanah have done for centuries. On the table, too, is sliced honey cake, just as it might have been on a Rosh Hashanah table a long time ago—except it has been created in the new style. In my new style, also, is my contribution to the symbology of sweetness: my Banana/Carob Fluff. The dominant sweetener is not honey, but a favorite Jewish sweet dating back to biblical times, the carob (the sweetener of choice of many of the leaders of the recent nutrition revolution).

Coffee or tea is served with dessert. *Shanna Tova!*

Getting Ready to Cook My New American Jewish Cuisine

I cook in a typical New York apartment kitchen. It's just large enough for one cook at a time. Yet in it, I've developed and tested more than 1,500 published recipes while preparing a dizzying number of family and guest meals. A spacious kitchen is every cook's dream, but you can make dream recipes in any kitchen.

Most of the early Jewish immigrants cooked in cramped tenement quarters on coal stoves, preserving their foods in iceboxes or on window ledges (not fridges or freezers)—and these were the people, mostly women, who founded the great tradition of American Jewish cookery.

The formula for success in the kitchen is not its spaciousness or its equipment, but the loving spirit of the cook, her sense of daring and adventure and her joy of creation. Yet, modern technology has gifted today's kitchens with amazing tools that make cooking so much easier. You probably have many of them, but here are the few I regard as indispensable:

- *The food processor.* You won't believe how easy it is to make authentic challah rolls, piecrusts, dough wrappers for knishes and strudels, and sumptuous fruitcake, until you've followed my directions for making them with a food processor. It's also unsurpassed for chopping nuts and sticky fruits, and for fine-chopping raw meat, chicken and fish (you can now even chop your own fish for gefilte fish—easily). Great for making mousses, too.
- *The mixing machine with dough hook* (for bread making) and *with whisk attachment* (for beating egg whites to maximum volume).

In addition, an enamel-lined Dutch oven is favored for cooking pot roasts, cholents and other braised foods; nonstick skillets are mandatory for top-of-the-stove cooking using sharply reduced amounts of fat; and a well-seasoned iron skillet is a utensil I can't do without for top-of-the-stove-to-oven cooking (Grandma used the iron skillet). Turn to page 74 for instructions on preparing a well-seasoned iron skillet.

Also necessary in my kitchen are: a fine sieve (preferably a chinois) for eliminating cloudiness from stocks and sauces; a fat-skimming cup to separate the fat quickly from stocks and sauces; heavy-bottom saucepans to prevent liquid from boiling away too rapidly; and a mercury oven thermometer for accurate reading of oven temperature.

A word about three ingredients: The olive oil I favor does not have a strong olive taste. The butter/margarine blend I used in developing my recipes is composed of 60 percent corn-oil margarine and 40 percent sweet butter. The reduced-fat sour cream I used is called Light Choice.

When preparing your menus, look for the designations *"Meat," "Dairy"* or *"Pareve"* in the title. If you are an observer of kashruth, you'll want to be sure not to mix meat and dairy dishes. Pareve foods are neutral, and you can mix and match at will. Sometimes, the designation reads *"Dairy or Pareve."* That's when your choice of ingredients, as provided by the recipe, permits you to decide whether to make a dairy or pareve dish. For example, a recipe may call for sweet butter/margarine blend, which is dairy, or sweet pareve margarine, which is, obviously, pareve. Choose the former and the dish is dairy; choose the latter and the dish is pareve.

Ready Access Recipes

When you cut down on fat, sugar, salt and cholesterol foods, you take out tastes. When you take out tastes, you have to put tastes back in. That's the overriding principle of my cooking-for-better-health cuisines; and here, I've put that principle into practice with my Ready Access Recipes . . . basically, mixes you can keep on hand to add instant taste.

To acquaint yourself with these taste-boosters, read the Ready Access Recipes section before you begin to cook. In that section, you'll find:

- *Spice Mix.* A palate-pleasing combination of spices and dried herbs to be sprinkled over food *before* cooking.
- *Matzoh Meal Mix.* A rival to commercial shake-and-bake mixes, which I use as a second skin for skinned chickens (most of a chicken's fat is in and just under the skin), and as a crisp coating for meat and fish.
- *Mushroom-Tomato Sauce.* Use this versatile thick sauce to braise or skillet-sauté fish, meat or poultry; and as just the right companion to pasta and grains.
- *Stocks.* These highly concentrated clear broths are simply delicious ways to enrich soups, sauces and many other dishes. For my New American Jewish recipes, I use two stocks, a chicken stock (meat), and a vegetable stock (pareve).
- *Seasoned Olive Oil.* A replacement for Rendered Chicken Fat. It's not a taste-alike, but a new seasoning with an exciting taste of its own.

When any of these Ready Access Recipes are included in the list of ingredients, they are printed with a capital letter beginning each word, as in the following example: Spice Mix.

You Don't Have to Be Jewish . . .

. . . to enjoy my New American Jewish recipes. These are dishes rooted in an extravagant international culinary heritage, adapted to contemporary American eating style.

That style is "light." But this is not a diet book. My recipes are, for the most part, calorie-conscious, but they are not restrictive.

The contemporary American eating style is "healthful," and I've complied with current medical/nutritional guidelines for a healthful diet. I've selected most of my major ingredients for their high nutrient density (the amount of essential nutrients per unit weight); I've favored high-fiber foods; and, of course, I'm at my most parsimonious with fats, cholesterol, sugar and salt.

But there has been no skimping on taste. My New American Jewish recipes, fit to be consumed by healthy Americans who want to stay healthy, are replete with the joys of the table. *Enjoy them,* as the Jewish benediction goes, *in good health.* L'Chaim!

1

SELECTED MENUS

(Dairy and Meat)

Dairy

Cold Borscht
Baked Fish Mousse Balls
Coleslaw
Vegetable Cornbread
Luxurious Strawberry Cheesecake

Cucumber and Onion Salad
Challah Rolls
Layered Fish (A One-Dish Meal)
Carrot/Zucchini Puree
Peach Cake or Plum Cake

Mock Chopped Herring Hors D'Oeuvre
Cheese Blintzes
3-Fruit Sauce
Molly's Marble Cake

Onion Soup
Challah
Vegetable Loaf with Leek
Spicy Tomato Sauce
Mixed Fresh Vegetable Salad
Honey-Frosted Poppy-Seed Cake

Schav with Butternut Squash
Asparagus Latkes or Matzoh Brei Pancakes
Smooth-and-Sweet Applesauce
Cheese Strudel

The Following Menu Is Suitable for Passover

Pureed Watercress and Carrot Soup
Poached Lemon Sole with Horseradish Sauce
Asparagus Latkes
Coleslaw
Farfel and Fruit Candy

Meat

Challah
Light Chopped Liver
Friday Night Pot Roast
Kasha Varnishkes
Carrot/Date Condiment
Hamantaschen with Apricot/Prune Filling

Mushroom and Barley Soup
Sour Rye Bread
Turkey Cholent with Cranberries
Salad with 2 Herbs
Honey Cake

Cabbage Soup
Brown Rye Bread with 3 Seeds
Lamb Strudel or Vegetable Loaf with Leek
Lemon Sauce
Creamy Spinach (variation)
Banana/Carob Fluff
Carob-Sesame Cookies

Savory Poached Carp (Jelled)
Crusty Italian Bread
Chicken in a Pot
Tomato Kugel
Fig and Date Cake

The Following Two Menus Are Suitable for Passover

Matzoh Crisp
Gefilte Fish
Fresh Horseradish with Beets
Roast Stuffed Flank Steak
Hot Red Cabbage with Fennel
Pineapple/Nut Passover Sponge Cake

Light Chopped Liver
Matzoh
Festive Chicken or Baked Chicken with Sun-Dried Tomatoes
Potato Latkes
Smooth-and-Sweet Applesauce
Dried Fruit Tzimmes: A Dessert

2
SOME HOLIDAY FAVORITES
Traditional and New Style

Traditional	*New Style*
	SHABBAT
Round or braided challah	Challah (page 165)
Fish	Savory Poached Carp (page 97)
Cholent	Chicken and Lamb Cholent (page 49)
Chicken soup	Chicken in a Pot, Chicken Stock (or soup) (pages 52, 32)
Tzimmes	Yam and Cabbage Tzimmes (page 140)
Honey cake	Honey Cake (page 193)
Chopped liver	Light Chopped Liver (page 73)
Soups with meat	Vegetable Soup with Meat (page 45)
Vegetable salads	Carrot Salad (page 159)
Pot roast	Friday Night Pot Roast (page 75)
Roast chicken	Roast Chicken in a Pouch (page 61)

Traditional	*New Style*
	ROSH HASHANAH

Traditional	New Style
Round challah	Challah Rolls or Challah (pages 163, 165)
Fish	Baked Stuffed Fish (page 108) Baked Fish Mousse Balls (page 99)
Leek dishes	Vegetable Loaf with Leek (page 144)
Apples	Apple/Pear Pie (page 203)
Sweet potatoes	Baked Spiced Yam Slices (page 150)
Vegetable salads	Cucumber and Onion Salad, Mixed Fresh Vegetable Salad (pages 158, 155)
Dates and Figs	Fig and Date Cake (page 192)
Roast turkey, Cornish hens and chicken	Clay Pot Turkey, Cornish Hens with Couscous Stuffing, Roast Chicken in a Pouch (pages 64, 55, 61)
Apples	Smooth-and-Sweet Applesauce, Applesauce-Glazed Poppy-Seed Cake (pages 199, 200)
Stuffed fish	Flounder Paupiettes with Fennel and Dates (page 105)
Chicken soup with kreplach	Chicken in a Pot, Chicken Stock (or soup), Kreplach (pages 52, 32, 126)
Honey-sweetened desserts	Honey Cake, Banana/Carob Fluff, Fig and Date Cake (pages 193, 207, 192)
Vegetables	Spinach and Carrot Pie (page 147)
Tzimmes	Yam and Cabbage Tzimmes (page 140)
Sweet potatoes	See Tzimmes above and Shabbat

Traditional	*New Style*

YOM KIPPUR

Before the fast

Challah, sour rye bread	Challah, Challah Rolls, Sour Rye Bread (pages 165, 163, 168)
Chicken soup with matzoh balls	Chicken in a Pot, Chicken Stock (or soup), Matzoh Balls (pages 52, 32, 109)
Stuffed cabbage	Sweet-and-Sour Stuffed Cabbage (page 79)
Chicken	Baked Chicken Napoleon (page 60)
Meat	Potted Shoulder of Veal (page 91)
Fresh and dried fruits	Smooth-and-Sweet Applesauce, Dried Fruit Tzimmes: A Dessert (pages 199, 214)
Honey and honey-sweetened pastries	Honey Cake, Luxurious Strawberry Cheesecake (pages 193, 190)

After the fast

Chopped herring	Mock Chopped Herring Hors D'Oeuvre (page 98)
Challah, Rolls and other breads	Challah, Challah Rolls, Two-Grain Herb Loaf (pages 165, 163, 174)
Blintzes	Cheese Blintzes, Apple Blintzes (pages 122, 124)
Dairy soups	Cauliflower and Pea Soup, Pureed Watercress and Carrot Soup, Quick Fruit Soup (pages 42, 44, 37)
Rice pudding	Rice Pudding with Fruit (page 216)
Eggs	Rice Omelette (page 152)

SUKKOTH

Stuffed cabbage	Sweet-and-Sour Stuffed Cabbage (page 79)

Traditional	New Style
Eggplant	Eggplant Salad (page 156)
Knish	Lamb Knishes, Potato/Spinach Filling for Knish (pages 129, 131)
Squash	Carrot/Zucchini Puree (page 149)
Tzimmes	Tzimmes Condiment: Cranberry 1 and 2 (pages 180, 181)
Kugel	5-Fruit Kugel, Tomato Kugel (pages 121, 120)
Barley soups	Mushroom and Barley Soup, Hamburger Soup (pages 38, 39)
Fruit	Peach Cake and Plum Cake (page 195)
Chicken	Chicken with Caramelized Sugar, Cornish Hens with Couscous Stuffing (pages 62, 55)
Stews	Beef and Pepper Goulash (page 80)
Casseroles	Kibbeh (page 84)
Kreplach	Sautéed Kreplach (page 128)
Mandelbrot	Mandelbrot (toasted almond cookies) (page 212)

CHANUKAH

Latkes	Potato Latkes, Asparagus Latkes (pages 117, 118)
Chicken	Indonesian Chicken (page 68), and See Sukkoth
Tongue	Tongue with Juniper Berry Sauce (page 85)
Pea soup	Split-Pea Soup (page 41)
Vegetables	Stuffed Peppers (page 146)
Fruits	3-Fruit Sauce, Smooth-and-Sweet Applesauce (pages 184, 199)
Noodles	Noodle Dough (page 125)
Kugels	See Sukkoth

Traditional	*New Style*
Salads	Coleslaw, Eggplant Salad (pages 157, 156)
Pound cake	Apricot Pound Cake, Molly's Marble Cake (pages 215, 198)
Cheese strudel	Cheese Strudel (page 134)
Cheesecake	Luxurious Strawberry Cheesecake (page 190)

PURIM

Mushroom and barley soup	Mushroom and Barley Soup, Hamburger Soup (pages 38, 39)
Chicken	Orange Chicken with Fruit Stuffing (page 57)
Pot roast	Top-of-the-Stove Pot Roast (page 76)
Chicken soup	See Yom Kippur
Pomegranates	Pomegranate Chicken (page 54)
Dried figs	Fig and Date Cake (page 192)
Hamantaschen	Hamantaschen with Apricot/Prune Filling or Poppy-Seed Filling (pages 208, 210)
Poppy-seed cake	Honey-Frosted Poppy-Seed Cake, Applesauce-Glazed Poppy-Seed Cake (pages 201, 200)

PASSOVER

Gefilte fish	Gefilte Fish (page 95)
Horseradish	Fresh Horseradish with Beets (page 180)
Boiled carp	Savory Poached Carp (hot or jelled)(page 97)
Chicken soup with matzoh balls	See Yom Kippur
Borscht	Cold Borscht (page 35)
Potato latkes	Potato Latkes (page 117)

Traditional	New Style
Matzoh	Matzoh Brei Pancakes, Matzoh Crisp, Matzoh Stuffing (pages 132, 133, 124)
Pot roast	Top-of-the-Stove Pot Roast, Friday Night Pot Roast (pages 76, 75)
Lamb	Baked Lamb Shanks (page 81)
Roast chicken	Baked Chicken with Sun-Dried Tomatoes, Festive Chicken (pages 70, 66)
Applesauce	Smooth-and-Sweet Applesauce (page 199)
Egg salad	Farfel and Egg Salad (page 160)
Sponge cake	Pineapple/Nut Passover Sponge Cake (page 197)
Haroset	Haroset (page 194)
Dried fruits	Dried Fruit Tzimmes: A Dessert, Farfel and Fruit Candy (pages 214, 213)

SHAVUOT

Fish	Salmon & Rice Croquettes (or strudel), Halibut with Vegetable Marmalade (pages 102, 106)
Dairy soups	Quick Fruit Soup, Schav with Butternut Squash, Celeriac Soup (pages 37, 43, 40)
Cheese	Bagel Cheese Spread (page 187)
Blintzes	See Yom Kippur
Strudel	Lamb Strudel, Cheese Strudel, Apple/Cranberry Strudel (pages 116, 134, 135)
Knish	See Sukkoth
Rice pudding	Rice Pudding with Fruit (page 216)

3
READY ACCESS RECIPES

Spice Mix (Pareve)

Say good-bye to those frustrating kitchen moments when you scurry through your spice rack searching for the right seasonings—and come up blank. Keep this blend of herbs and spices on hand; and, before cooking, sprinkle over meats, fish, poultry and into soups and grains—and you'll never have to give a thought to what's the right seasoning for what. You may come to the same conclusion that I have: It's a mix you can't do without.

1 tablespoon ground ginger
2 tablespoons onion powder
1 teaspoon each allspice, cinnamon and cumin
½ teaspoon each dry mustard and salt

1 tablespoon each dried rosemary and oregano leaves, well crushed
1 tablespoon mild curry powder
⅛ teaspoon cayenne pepper

Combine all ingredients in small bowl. Spoon into covered container and shake several times. Store in a cool, dry place. Turn container upside down several times before using.

Yield: Scant ½ cup; recipe may be doubled

Matzoh Meal Mix   *(Pareve)*

In the spirit of "every day's a holiday," I created this storable mix to glorify meat, fish and poultry on Passover, and on any day for the rest of the year. The perk-up herbs and spices give the mix its *tam* ("that special something").

1½ tablespoons toasted sesame
    seeds, preferably unhulled
½ cup each matzoh meal and
    cake meal
¼ cup potato starch
1 tablespoon each dried
    rosemary and oregano,

    crushed
1 teaspoon each cinnamon and
    ground ginger
2 tablespoons onion powder
2 teaspoons mild curry powder
⅛ teaspoon cayenne pepper
¼ teaspoon salt (optional)

1. Place all ingredients in a bowl, stirring well to combine.

2. Spoon into a glass jar or container with lid, leaving a 2-inch space at the top. Shake or stir each time before using. Store at room temperature or refrigerate.

Yield: About 1⅔ cups; recipe may be doubled or tripled

Mushroom-Tomato Sauce   *(Pareve)*

Bright-tasting thick tomato sauce with multiple uses: excels over pasta or grains; use it to braise or skillet-sauté fish, meat or poultry. Keep in 1-cup measures in boilable bags for almost instant enjoyment.

1½ tablespoons Italian olive oil
2 large onions, minced
4 large cloves garlic, minced
1 large green bell pepper,
    seeded, coarsely chopped
½ teaspoon dry mustard
1 tablespoon Spice Mix
3 tablespoons minced fresh dill,
    or 1 teaspoon dried dill weed
½ teaspoon sugar

2 tablespoons white wine
    Worcestershire sauce
1 28-ounce can unsalted Italian
    plum tomatoes, coarsely
    chopped
½ pound snow-white fresh
    mushrooms, ends trimmed,
    damp-wiped
¼ teaspoon salt

1. Heat 1 tablespoon oil in a 2-quart heavy-bottomed saucepan until hot. Add onions, garlic and green pepper. Sprinkle in seasonings, dill and sugar. Sauté over moderate heat until softened (about 5 minutes), stirring often.

2. Add Worcestershire sauce. Cook for 1 minute. Then add tomatoes. Bring to a boil. Regulate heat to simmering; cover and cook for 45 minutes, stirring from time to time. Remove from heat.

3. Cut each mushroom in half, then crosswise into thin slices. Heat remaining oil in a nonstick skillet until hot. Add mushrooms, turning several times to coat. Sauté over medium-high heat, stirring often until all liquid evaporates and mushrooms begin to brown (about 6 minutes). Sprinkle with salt. Add to the sauce. Reheat to simmering and cook for 3 minutes.

Yield: About 5 cups; recipe may be doubled

Variation: Before adding mushrooms to sauce, stir 2 tablespoons dry sherry into browned mushrooms. Cook and stir until sherry evaporates.

Seasoned Olive Oil (a chicken-fat alternative) (Pareve)

My dear friend Josie Blumenfeld, a talented artist who has made healthful cuisine her avocation, has come up with this compromise for fat watchers who still love the taste of chicken fat. Here's olive oil, a monounsaturated fat—a "good" fat—with a hyped-up taste that makes it a candidate for chicken-fat lovers' approval. Use it in recipes calling for olive oil (except for baked goods) or for chicken fat. It's exceptional with Potato Latkes (page 117).

2 cups finely minced onion
2 cups good quality Italian olive
  oil

1. Combine onion and oil in a 2-quart heavy-bottomed saucepan. Bring to a boil over medium heat. Reduce heat to simmering. Partially cover and cook until onions begin to brown, stirring often to prevent onions from sticking to the bottom of the pan. Remove from heat, uncover and let stand to cool.

2. With wide bowl underneath, pour entire contents of saucepan through fine-meshed sieve, pressing out liquid. Store in tightly closed jar(s). Discard browned onions, or drain them on paper toweling and serve with Light Chopped Liver (page 73).

Yield: Scant 2 cups

Chicken Stock (or Soup)

(Meat)

A no-frills definition of chicken stock is: concentrated chicken soup. (A stock is a concentrated broth made by the patient simmering of a seasoned kind of food, such as meat, fish, poultry or vegetables.) But in Jewish cookery, chicken stock is the flavor-giving base of sauces and other soups, and the flavoring that imbues grains, matzoh balls and kreplach with stardom. The one dish that to me epitomizes the taste of Jewish cookery is matzoh balls cooked in chicken soup. Here is my version of chicken stock, so rich in natural seasonings that even an added trace of salt becomes superfluous.

Economy hint: When you purchase chickens for roasting or sautéing, save the necks and gizzards; rinse, dry and freeze them for your stockpot at another time. It's also a good idea to reserve the livers for Light Chopped Liver (page 73).

1 4-pound pullet or broiling chicken, skinned and halved, plus additional necks and gizzards
8 cups water
1 parsnip, peeled, trimmed, cut into 1-inch pieces
1 ¼-inch slice fresh ginger, cut in half
4 large cloves garlic, minced
3 ribs celery and leaves, cut into 2-inch slices
2 large carrots, peeled, trimmed,
cut into ½-inch rounds
3 large snow-white fresh mushrooms, ends trimmed, damp-wiped and halved
2 medium onions, coarsely chopped
½ cup 1-inch cubed and peeled yellow turnip (rutabaga)
½ peeled, cored and cubed apple
½ teaspoon each dried thyme, marjoram and peppercorns

1. Put chicken, giblets and water into a large Dutch oven. Bring to a rolling boil; then reduce heat to slow-boil. Cook for 10 minutes, periodically skimming foam from the surface as it accumulates. Add remaining ingredients except thyme, marjoram and peppercorns, and bring to a boil. Cook, uncovered, for 10 minutes, skimming surface often. Add thyme, marjoram and peppercorns. Reduce heat to simmering. Partially cover and simmer for 3 hours (1½ hours for soup).

2. Remove chicken and reserve for sandwiches, salads or kreplach. With large bowl underneath, pour contents of pot into a fine sieve, pressing out juices. Partially cool. Transfer to a large skimmer cup and let fat rise to the top for 15 minutes. Pour skimmed stock into a jar for use within 3 days, or freeze in 1-cup measures or ice-cube trays for soups or sauces.

Yield: About 1½ quarts

Vegetable Stock (or Consommé)   *(Pareve)*

Vegetable soups are a staple of Jewish cookery from Marrakech to Manhattan; and most great soups begin with a great stock. Often, the base for vegetable soup is meat or chicken stock, which displeases vegetarians and observers of the food-combining laws of kashruth. So, I've come up with this vegetable stock. Excitingly seasoned with a novel array of herbs and spices, it's so delicious you'll want to sip it as a consommé, and cook your kasha, rice, bulgur and other grains in it (you may never want to cook them in salted water again). Try this stock as a base for my Onion Soup (page 46) and Pureed Watercress and Carrot Soup (page 44).

2 carrots, ends trimmed and peeled
1 medium turnip, ends trimmed and peeled
¾ pound cabbage
6 cloves garlic, peeled
2 large firm onions, peeled
6 ribs crisp celery, including leaves

8 sprigs parsley, well rinsed
1 large bay leaf
2 teaspoons dried dill weed
4 whole cloves
3 tablespoons white wine Worcestershire sauce
7 cups water
2 tablespoons unsalted tomato paste

1. Cut first 6 ingredients into uniform pieces; break off florets from stems of parsley. Place ½ in workbowl of food processor that has been fitted with steel blade. Fine-chop, using on/off turns. Scrape into a 3-quart heavy-bottomed saucepan or Dutch oven. Repeat chopping with remaining vegetables.

2. Add bay leaf, dill weed, cloves, Worcestershire sauce and water. Bring to a boil. Reduce heat to simmering. Cover tightly and simmer for 45 minutes, adjusting heat when necessary to keep a steady simmer.

3. Stir in tomato paste. Re-cover and cook for 45 minutes longer. Uncover and let cool for 10 minutes. With bowl underneath, pour into a fine sieve (a conical chinois is excellent for this task) or a strainer lined with a piece of washed cotton cheesecloth, pressing out juices with large spoon.

4. Keep refrigerated in tightly closed jar(s) for up to 4 days; or pour into freeze-proof containers and freeze for up to 2 months.

Yield: About 1½ quarts

4

SOUPS

Cold Borscht (Dairy)

I fondly remember weekly luncheon visits to my grandmother and looking forward to her borscht, thick with beets, onions, fresh sour cream, sugar and lots of salt. It was never complete without crisp chopped cucumbers, scallions and radishes. It was memorably delicious. Here's my nineties' version of that fond memory.

1 large bunch beets with tops (about 7 beets)
1 large onion
2 large cloves garlic
3 large shallots
½ cup fresh lemon juice
4 cloves, crushed
5 cups water
2 tablespoons sugar
1½ tablespoons frozen apple juice concentrate

2 tablespoons honey
⅛ teaspoon cayenne pepper
1 large egg
½ teaspoon salt
¼ cup reduced-fat sour cream, plus ½ cup for garnish
2–3 tablespoons minced just-snipped fresh dill
Chopped scallions, cucumbers and radishes

1. Cut stems from beets (they're sandy) and rinse well. Break every 2 inches and peel back strings. Cut into 1-inch pieces and fine-chop in workbowl of food processor that has been fitted with steel blade (3 or 4 on/off turns). Scrape into 3-quart heavy-bottomed saucepan.

2. Rinse, peel and trim beets. Cut into 1-inch chunks. Place in workbowl with onion, garlic and shallots. Fine-chop in 3 or 4 on/off turns. Add to saucepan.

3. To saucepan add ¼ cup lemon juice, cloves, water, sugar and concentrate. Bring to a boil. Reduce heat to simmering. Cover and cook for 1 hour. Stir in remaining ¼ cup lemon juice, honey and cayenne pepper.

4. Beat egg with fork in 2-cup measure. Quickly stir in 1 cup soup and blend well. Pour back into simmering soup, stirring vigorously to prevent egg from congealing. Stir in ¼ teaspoon salt. Remove from heat and cool for 15 minutes. Briskly stir in sour cream. Refrigerate until well chilled.

5. When ready to serve, stir in remaining ¼ teaspoon salt. Put a teaspoon of dill in center of each serving bowl. Ladle borscht over it. Serve with side dishes of crisp chopped scallions, cucumbers, radishes and sour cream.

Yield: 6 to 7 servings

Cabbage Soup   (Meat)

I remember eating meat-enriched sweet-and-sour cabbage soup all year round—particularly during Chanukah, when our family spent holiday time at Catskill Mountain resorts. It was generally served with boiled potatoes on the side, which we would cut up and add to the soup. Although it was served as a first course, I usually made a meal of it, supplemented with the hotel's fresh-baked thick-sliced breads. My version, a true first course, will stay refrigerator-fresh for several days! And it freezes very well.

12 dried apricots, preferably
    unsulphured*
1 pound soup meat (flanken or
    lean chuck), cut into 1-inch
    chunks
1 cup water
1 pound cabbage
2 medium onions, peeled
4 large cloves garlic
2 tablespoons Italian olive oil
2½ tablespoons Spice Mix
2 tablespoons balsamic vinegar

3 cups Chicken Stock
½ cup fresh lemon juice
1 28-ounce can unsalted Italian
    plum tomatoes
2 tablespoons firmly packed
    dark brown sugar
⅓ cup dark seedless raisins
6 sprigs parsley, rinsed, tied into
    a bundle with white cotton
    thread
¼ teaspoon salt

*Available in health food stores and some supermarkets.

1. Put apricots in a strainer. Rinse under cold running water. Transfer to a small bowl. Add enough boiling water to barely cover. Let stand to soften.

2. In medium heavy-bottomed saucepan, combine meat with water. Bring to a boil. Reduce heat to slow-boil and cook for 5 minutes, skimming off foam as it rises to the top. Set aside.

3. Cut away tough outer leaves of cabbage. Shred or thin-slice cabbage by hand or in food processor. Fine-chop onions and garlic by hand. (Or cut onions into 2-inch chunks; cut garlic cloves in half. Place in workbowl of food processor that has been fitted with steel blade and fine-chop in 2 or 3 on/off turns.)

4. Heat oil in a large enameled Dutch oven until hot. Over medium-high heat, sauté onion and garlic until wilted without browning. Combine cabbage with mixture. Sprinkle with Spice Mix. Sauté, stirring often, until volume begins to decrease (about 5 minutes). Pour vinegar around sides of pot; then stir. Cook for 1 minute.

5. Add meat with cooking liquid, apricots with soaking liquid, and remaining ingredients (except salt). Bring to a boil; reduce heat to simmering. Cover and simmer for 3 hours, stirring from time to time.

6. Discard parsley bundle after pressing out juices. Stir in salt. Re-cover and let stand for 20 minutes before serving.

Yield: 8 servings as a main course

Quick Fruit Soup (Dairy)

A Hungarian Jewish prelude or finale to a dairy meal. I use canned sweet dark cherries (they're more easily found in supermarkets than sour cherries), and I include pomegranate juice for added tartness. Pineapples and apples complete the flavorsome medley that can be quickly prepared.

1 16½-ounce can sweet dark cherries
1 8-ounce can unsweetened pineapple tidbits or chunks, cut into small pieces
¾ cup pomegranate juice*
½ teaspoon cinnamon

3 tablespoons light brown sugar
1 large crisp sweet apple, such as Golden Delicious or Washington State, peeled, cored, coarsely chopped
½ cup reduced-fat sour cream, plus extra for garnish

*Available in health food stores and some supermarkets; or use juice from fresh pomegranates when available.

1. Drain juices from cherries into a medium heavy-bottomed saucepan. Drain juices from pineapple into a measuring cup. Set fruit aside. Add enough water to pineapple juice to equal ½ cup and pour into the saucepan. Stir in pomegranate juice, cinnamon and sugar. Bring to a boil; reduce heat to simmering. Partially cover and cook for 10 minutes.

2. Add canned fruit and apple to juices. Partially cover and cook for 10 minutes. Uncover and let cool for 20 minutes.

3. Pour about ¾ cup of juices into a 1½-quart covered bowl. Whisk in ½ cup sour cream until it's well blended. Stir in remaining contents of saucepan. Refrigerate until well chilled. Pour into a tureen. Float dollops of sour cream in soup (it makes a pretty display), or serve in individual soup dishes, each topped with a spoonful of sour cream.

Yield: 1 quart; 5 servings

Mushroom and Barley
Soup   (Meat)

Dried mushrooms and soup meat add an eloquent gustatory statement to this hearty and nutritious classic Jewish soupery.

*½ ounce imported dried
    mushrooms, preferably the
    dark variety**
*1 pound soup meat (flanken or
    lean chuck) cut into 4-inch
    chunks*
*2 beef bones that have not been
    cut with an electric saw*
1½ tablespoons Spice Mix
1 tablespoon Italian olive oil
*2 ribs celery with leaves,
    coarsely chopped*
*1 medium turnip, peeled and
    coarsely chopped*
*2 medium onions, coarsely
    chopped*
2 medium carrots, peeled and

coarsely chopped
*3 large cloves garlic, coarsely
    chopped*
2 tablespoons balsamic vinegar
2 cups water
*3 large sprigs dill and 1 bay leaf
    wrapped in doubled piece of
    cotton cheesecloth and tied
    with white cotton thread*
*2½ cups unsalted imported
    Italian plum tomatoes,
    chopped*
*¼ cup barley, rinsed and
    drained*
¼ teaspoon salt
Minced fresh dill or parsley

*Mushrooms are labeled "Imported Dry Mushrooms" and are available in supermarkets in see-through ½-ounce boxes.

1. Rinse mushrooms. Break up and put in a cup. Add enough water to barely cover and let stand.

2. Wash meat and bones thoroughly under hot running water. Dry with paper toweling. Rub with half the Spice Mix. Heat oil in an enameled Dutch oven until quite hot. Over medium-high heat, lightly brown meat and bones. Add coarsely chopped ingredients. Stir and cook until lightly browned.

3. Push mixture to the center of pot. Pour vinegar around sides of pot. Cook for 30 seconds; then combine with solids. Add water, dill bundle and remaining Spice Mix. Bring soup to a boil. Reduce heat to simmering; cover and slow-cook for 1 hour.

4. Stir in tomatoes, barley and mushrooms with soaking liquid. Return to simmering; then cover and simmer for 1½ hours longer.

5. Discard bones; press out juices from dill bundle and discard. Cut meat into bite-size pieces and return to soup (or serve large chunks on the side). Stir in salt. Simmer, uncovered, for 5 minutes. Sprinkle each serving with minced dill or parsley.

Yield: 6 servings

Hamburger Soup   (Meat)

This is an innovative mushroom-barley soup starring ground beef (hence the name) with a stellar cast of sautéed fresh mushrooms, seasonings, vegetables and chicken stock. That touch of mint or dill is a "wow" finish.

1½ tablespoons Italian olive oil
½ pound lean ground beef
¾ cup minced shallot or a combination of shallot and onion
1 tablespoon minced garlic
2 large carrots, peeled and thin-sliced
½ teaspoon each chili con carne seasoning and curry powder
1 tablespoon dried rosemary, crushed
1 tablespoon wine vinegar
1 28-ounce can unsalted Italian plum tomatoes, chopped
⅓ cup barley, rinsed and drained
2 cups Chicken Stock, or 1 cup each stock and water
6 sprigs parsley, 1 bay leaf and ¼ teaspoon dried thyme wrapped in double pieces of rinsed cotton cheesecloth and tied with white cotton thread
¾ pound snow-white fresh mushrooms, ends trimmed, damp-wiped and thin-sliced
¼ teaspoon salt
1 tablespoon fresh lemon juice
About 2½ tablespoons finely minced fresh mint or dill

1. Heat 1 tablespoon oil in a 3-quart heavy-bottomed saucepan or enameled Dutch oven. Add meat and sauté for 3 minutes, breaking up pieces with large spoon. Pour off any exuded water or fat. Add shallot, garlic and carrots; sprinkle with seasonings. Continue cooking and stirring for 2 minutes longer.

2. Nestle mixture to the center of pot. Pour vinegar around the sides and cook for 1 minute, combining all ingredients when vinegar bubbles up. Add tomatoes, barley, stock and parsley bundle. Bring to a boil; reduce heat to simmering. Cover and cook for 2 hours, stirring from time to time. Discard parsley bundle after pressing out juices.

3. Heat remaining oil in a large nonstick skillet. Over medium-high heat, sauté mushrooms until they brown and no liquid remains in skillet. Stir into soup along with salt. Simmer, uncovered, for 5 minutes. Stir in lemon juice. Pour into a warmed tureen or individual soup bowls. Sprinkle a teaspoon or more of mint or dill over soup and serve right away.

Yield: 8 servings

Serving suggestion: Any pareve breads or rolls featured in bread section (chapter 11).

Celeriac Soup (Pareve)

I've transformed a Sephardic combination of celeriac (knob celery) and carrots into a soup—thickened with Italian short-grain rice, sweetened with apple juice and sweet herbs and spices, brightened with tangy fresh ginger.

3¼ cups water	2 teaspoons minced fresh ginger
1½ tablespoons fresh lemon juice	¼ cup short-grain Italian rice (Arborio)
1 pound celeriac, ends trimmed, peeled, shredded or minced	2 tablespoons minced parsley
2 large carrots, ends trimmed, peeled, shredded or minced	1 tablespoon dried sweet basil
1 tablespoon minced garlic	2 teaspoons each sugar and frozen apple juice concentrate
1 cup minced onion	⅛ teaspoon cayenne pepper
	¼ teaspoon salt

1. Pour water and lemon juice into a 3-quart heavy-bottomed saucepan. Add celeriac as it's shredded or minced (your food processor does the most expedient job). Combine with carrots, garlic, onion and ginger.

2. Pour rice into a fine-meshed strainer and rinse under cold running water. Add to saucepan along with parsley, basil, sugar and cayenne. Bring to a boil. Reduce heat to simmering. Cover tightly and simmer for 30 minutes. Remove from heat and let stand for 20 minutes.

3. Pour into workbowl of food processor that has been fitted with steel blade and partially puree. Return to saucepan and slowly reheat. Stir in salt and serve.

Yield: About 1½ quarts

Variations:
   1. May be served as a side dish by cooking over moderate heat after returning to saucepan until most of liquid evaporates.
   2. When serving a dairy meal, sprinkle each serving with a teaspoon of freshly grated Parmesan cheese.

Split-Pea Soup (Meat)

Legumes, recently rediscovered for their nutritive value, were among the staples of the people of the Bible. The split pea, a superbly delicious and nutritious legume, is a prized soup ingredient among American Jewish cooks. Here is a split-pea soup for today to which the white meat of chicken contributes a special flavor. Together, the chicken and soup make a delicious and healthful complete meal.

2 cups split peas
1 2-pound chicken breast with bone, skinned
1½ tablespoons Italian olive oil
1 large onion, coarsely chopped
4 large cloves garlic, minced
2 ribs celery, strings pulled off, coarsely chopped
1 medium turnip, ends trimmed, peeled, coarsely chopped
2 carrots, ends trimmed, peeled, coarsely chopped

¾ teaspoon ground marjoram
½ teaspoon each curry powder and freshly grated nutmeg
¼ teaspoon crushed cloves
1 tablespoon dried basil, crumbled
5 cups water
6 sprigs parsley, tied into a bundle with white cotton thread
¼ teaspoon salt
Freshly ground black pepper

1. Put peas into a strainer and pick over. Rinse under cold running water. Turn into a bowl and cover with water. Let soak for 1 hour. Repeat procedure twice more. Drain.

2. Place chicken in 3-quart heavy-bottomed saucepan. Cover with water. Bring to a boil and cook for 5 minutes. Pour off water; rinse chicken under running water. Cut off a large double piece of white cotton cheesecloth. Place chicken in center of cloth and tie securely with white cotton thread. Set aside.

3. Wash and dry the pot. Place over medium-high heat with oil. When oil is hot, add onion, garlic, celery, turnip and carrots. Sauté for 2 minutes. Sprinkle with spices and basil. Stir and sauté until mixture begins to soften (do not brown).

4. Stir peas into mixture; cook for 1 minute. Add chicken, water and parsley bundle. Bring to a boil. Reduce heat to simmering. Cover, leaving just a crack open, and cook for 2½ hours, stirring from time to time. Remove from heat and let stand for 15 minutes.

5. Lift chicken out of soup. Open up cheesecloth and remove chicken from the bones. Cut into serving pieces to serve along with soup; or cut into bite-size pieces and return to soup. Sprinkle in salt and pepper. Simmer for 3 minutes and serve.

Yield: About 1 quart

Cauliflower and Pea Soup (Dairy)

Borscht Belt hotels of the thirties and forties featured for lunch dense dairy soups, so filling they hardly left room for the main course. Major seasonings were salt and cream. This delicate creation in the style of Borscht Belt lunch dairy soups derives its flavor from three vegetables (add carrots to those in the title). Combined with herbs, spices, Vegetable Stock and reduced-calorie sour cream, it does what a first course should do: It whets your appetite; it doesn't shut it down.

⅓ cup green split peas	*butter/margarine*
1¼ cups water	*1 cup coarsely chopped onion*
1 tablespoon white wine	*1 tablespoon minced garlic*
Worcestershire sauce	*1 tablespoon Spice Mix*
1 medium head cauliflower,	*2 tablespoons unbleached flour*
broken into small florets	*3 cups Vegetable Stock or water*
(about 4 cups)	*(see note)*
1 medium carrot, trimmed,	*⅓ cup reduced-fat sour cream*
peeled, cut into ⅜-inch slices	*¼ teaspoon salt (optional)*
2 tablespoons sweet	*Minced parsley or dill*

1. Put peas into a strainer. Pick over for any stones and rinse under cold running water. Transfer to a small bowl and soak for 1 hour. Drain. Add water to cover and soak overnight. Drain. Combine with 1¼ cups water and Worcestershire sauce in a 2- or 3-quart heavy-bottomed saucepan. Bring to a boil. Reduce heat to simmering. Cover and simmer until only solids remain and peas are tender (30 to 35 minutes), adding more water if necessary to complete cooking. Transfer to a bowl and set aside. Rinse and dry saucepan.

2. Steam cauliflower with carrot until tender but not oversoft. Transfer to workbowl of food processor that has been fitted with steel blade. Set aside.

3. Over low heat melt shortening in saucepan. Add onion and garlic; sprinkle with Spice Mix. Sauté until softened but not brown (about 5 minutes). Stir in flour and cook for 1 minute. Slowly add 1¼ cups stock, stirring until mixture thickens. Add cooked peas. Cover and simmer for 3 minutes. Pour into workbowl with cauliflower and carrot. Process until smooth. Return soup to saucepan.

4. While stirring over low heat, add remaining stock. Simmer, uncovered, until heated through. Whisk in sour cream and heat to simmering point. Taste for salt (I don't think you'll need it). Serve hot, sprinkled with parsley or dill.

Yield: 1½ quarts

Note: When using water instead of stock, increase Spice Mix to 1½ tablespoons.

Schav with Butternut Squash
(Dairy)

Schav is sour grass (the herb sorrel), plentiful in the Ukraine where schav (the soup) originated. A soup of transcendent sourness, it is here sweetened with butternut squash, which is also a natural thickener. So, for the first time—a sweetened-sour schav. Origin: the U.S.A.

2 cups ½-inch cubed and peeled butternut squash (about ¾ pound)
¼ teaspoon each cinnamon and ground coriander
½ teaspoon curry powder
4 tablespoons reduced-fat sour cream
2 large shallots

1 medium onion
½ pound sorrel, stems removed, well rinsed
1 quart water
3 tablespoons fresh lemon juice
4 teaspoons sugar
1 large egg
¼ teaspoon salt
Dash cayenne pepper

1. Steam squash until tender but not oversoft. Transfer to workbowl of food processor. Add spices and 2 tablespoons sour cream. Puree until smooth. Scrape into a bowl and set aside.

2. Cut shallots in half; cut onion into 1-inch pieces. Add to workbowl and mince in 1 or 2 on/off turns. Scrape into a heavy-bottomed 2- or 3-quart saucepan. Add sorrel to workbowl and fine-chop in 2 or 3 on/off turns. Combine with onion mixture.

3. Add water. Bring to boil. Reduce heat to simmering. Partially cover and cook for 20 minutes. Stir in pureed squash mixture. Bring to simmering point and cook, uncovered, for 10 minutes more. Stir in lemon juice and sugar.

4. Put egg into cup and beat lightly with a fork. Ladle ¼ cup hot soup into cup, stirring to combine. Pour mixture into saucepan. Stir in salt and pepper. Simmer for 5 minutes. Serve hot or chilled, with a teaspoon of sour cream atop each serving.

Yield: 6 servings

Pureed Watercress and Carrot Soup (Dairy)

A tempting smooth and savory prelude to a dairy meal. Vegetable Stock, curry and tarragon are the prime flavor boosters. Arborio rice (a short-grain Italian variety) is the natural thickener.

1 tablespoon Italian olive oil
1 large onion, minced
1-inch slice fresh ginger (about ¾ inch in diameter)
3 large cloves garlic, minced
¼ cup short-grain Italian rice (Arborio)
1 pound young carrots, trimmed, peeled and thin-sliced

2 cups loosely packed crisp watercress leaves, rinsed, dried and chopped
3½ cups Vegetable Stock
1 teaspoon each dried tarragon leaves, crumbled, and mild curry powder
1 tablespoon minced parsley
⅓ cup reduced-fat sour cream
¼ teaspoon salt

1. Heat oil in 3-quart heavy-bottomed saucepan. Sauté onion, ginger and garlic over moderate heat until softened without browning. Add rice, stirring to coat. Cook for 1 minute.

2. Add carrots and watercress and sauté for 1 minute.

3. Pour in stock. Stir in tarragon, curry powder and parsley. Bring to a boil. Reduce heat to simmering. Cover and simmer for 30 minutes, stirring once, midway. Uncover and let cool for 10 minutes.

4. Puree in food blender or processor fitted with steel blade. Pour soup back into saucepan and whisk in sour cream and salt. Slowly reheat without boiling. Serve at once.

Yield: 5 servings

Serving suggestion: Kasha/Grapenut Muffins (page 175).

Vegetable Soup with Meat *(Meat)*

M y mother's way: To a hand-cut assortment of vegetables she added the meat (flanken or brisket) and salt to taste. For added seasoning, ketchup was served at the table. In the years since, American Jewish tastes have undergone a revolutionary change: there's less chicken fat and more chic. So it is with *my* way of making vegetable soup with meat. The emphasis is on an abundance of seasonal vegetables and a just-right selection of herbs and spices to reach a new flavor peak. Ketchup, good-bye!

1½ pounds soup meat (flanken or chuck), well trimmed, plus 2 beef bones
5 cups water
2 teaspoons Spice Mix
1 teaspoon balsamic vinegar
4 sprigs parsley, 1 bay leaf, ¼ teaspoon dried thyme wrapped in a doubled piece of washed cotton cheesecloth and tied with white cotton thread
1 carrot, ends trimmed, peeled

2 ribs celery
1 large onion
Small wedge fennel (about 1 cup ½-inch chunks)
Small wedge cabbage (about 1 cup ½-inch chunks)
4 large cloves garlic
1 small zucchini, well scrubbed
¼ pound green beans
1 small turnip, peeled
1 tablespoon unsalted tomato paste
¼ teaspoon salt

1. Wash meat and bones under hot running water. If bones appear splintered (they're sometimes cut with an electric saw), securely wrap them in a doubled piece of washed cotton cheesecloth. Place them in a heavy Dutch oven (preferably enamel-lined). Add 4 cups water. Bring to a boil. Reduce heat to slow-boil and cook, uncovered, for 10 minutes, periodically skimming foam from the surface as it accumulates.

2. Stir in 1 teaspoon Spice Mix, vinegar and parsley bundle. Reduce heat to simmering, cover and cook for 1½ hours. Pour liquid into skimming cup to remove any fat. Return skimmed liquid to Dutch oven.

3. Fit food processor with steel blade. Coarse-chop carrot, celery, onion, fennel, cabbage and garlic. By hand, dice-cut into ⅜-inch pieces the zucchini, green beans and turnip (or cut each into 1-inch chunks and chop in food processor in 3 or 4 on/off turns). Add to Dutch oven with remaining 1 cup water, 1 teaspoon Spice Mix and tomato paste. Bring to a boil. Reduce heat to simmering; cover and cook until meat is tender (about 1½ hours). Discard parsley bundle after pressing out juices; discard bones. Stir in salt. Let stand for 15 minutes before serving (or refrigerate and reheat the next day).

4. Serve in one of the following ways: As a main course, remove meat, cut into serving pieces and serve on the side with the soup. As a starter, cut meat into small pieces and serve in the soup (portions are smaller than main course portions).

Yield: 6 or 7 servings as a main course; about 10 to 12 servings as a starter

Onion Soup   *(Dairy or Pareve)*

This borrowing from French cuisine is as low in salt as the Gallic original is high. It is based on a vegetable stock, not a beef stock as in France, which means it is pareve, giving the Jewish cook a greater latitude in developing her menus.

Its robust flavor is all its own, thanks in part to thin-slicing the onions and those auxiliary flavor-boosters, the shallots.

6 medium onions (about 1½ pounds)
6 large shallots
2 tablespoons Italian olive oil
1 tablespoon sweet pareve margarine or sweet butter/margarine
½ teaspoon chili con carne seasoning
About ⅛ teaspoon cayenne pepper
1 teaspoon sugar

1 tablespoon unbleached flour
1 teaspoon balsamic vinegar
4 cups Vegetable Stock
1 tablespoon unsalted tomato paste
6 slices Challah (page 165) or Crusty Italian Bread (page 170) or good quality commercial equivalent
¼ cup freshly grated Parmesan cheese (for Dairy)

1. Thin-slice onions and shallots by hand; or fit workbowl of food processor with thin-slicing blade and slice, using minimum pressure (you should have 7 cups). Heat oil and shortening in a large heavy-bottomed saucepan (a stainless-steel pot is suitable) until very hot. Over medium-high heat, sauté onions and shallots, stirring often, until volume decreases by ⅓.

2. Sprinkle with chili con carne seasoning, pepper (use less if you prefer), sugar and flour, stirring well to combine. Continue to sauté until onions turn golden and mixture reduces to about 1½ cups and begins to caramelize. (Stir continually and adjust heat when necessary to prevent burning.) Pour vinegar around sides of the pot; then combine with solids.

3. Whisk together the stock and tomato paste. Pour around sides of pot. Stir many times to combine. Bring to simmering point. Cover and simmer for 30 minutes, stirring from time to time.

4. Toast bread. Ladle servings into individual bowls. Float bread in soup. Sprinkle with Parmesan cheese (for dairy) and serve at once.

Yield: 6 servings

Variation: Hearty Fish Chowder (dairy or pareve): Prepare recipe through step 3, cooking for 15 rather than 30 minutes. Add ½–¾ pound 1-inch pieces of fish fillets (flounder, cod, scrod). Bring to a boil. Reduce heat to simmering. Cover and simmer for 15 minutes longer (cooking time will vary with thickness of fish). Sprinkle with cheese (dairy), if desired, and serve bread on the side. Makes 7 or 8 servings.

Chicken Soup

Recipes for chicken soup appear in the Poultry section (Chicken in a Pot, page 52), and in the Ready Access section (Chicken Stock or Soup, page 32).

5

POULTRY

Chicken and Lamb Cholent *(Meat)*

A cholent is a one-dish meal, usually a stew, baked at a low temperature all night before the Sabbath (because lighting a fire is prohibited on the Sabbath, while eating a hot midday meal is regarded as a duty).

This dish is a stew in the style of a cholent, intended for any day enjoyment. Bake it for 3 hours at your convenience. I also break tradition with my choice of ingredients: unusual combinations of meats and vegetables. They marry happily, though, to help create a robust winter meal. For an even more unusual modern cholent—made with turkey—see page 51. Both cholents reheat extremely well.

1 cup pinto beans, well rinsed
2 tablespoons white vinegar
1 10-ounce box frozen whole okra (or fresh)
2 chicken legs with thighs (about 1½ pounds), skinned and disjointed
2½ pounds lamb shoulder or koshered lamb shanks (about 2¼ pounds), trimmed of all visible fat
2 tablespoons Spice Mix
2 tablespoons Italian olive oil
3 medium onions, coarsely chopped

5 large cloves garlic, minced
¼ cup barley, rinsed and drained
¼ cup balsamic vinegar
3 tablespoons unsalted tomato paste
2½–3 cups Chicken Stock
¼ teaspoon salt
½ teaspoon freshly ground black pepper
2 tablespoons minced flat parsley or fresh coriander
2 medium red onions, coarsely chopped

1. Pour beans into a strainer. Pick over and rinse. Transfer to a bowl. Cover with water and let soak for 1 hour; drain, put back into bowl and add fresh water. Let stand for several hours or overnight. Pour into a strainer and rinse under cold running water. Preheat oven to 300°F.

2. Fill a 1-quart saucepan with water to which vinegar has been added; bring to a boil. Add okra, return to a boil and cook for 2 minutes to remove some of the dominant gelatinous properties of okra. Drain in a colander; rinse under cold running water. Set aside. (Steps 1 and 2 may be completed well in advance of cooking.)

3. Prick chicken and meat in several places with a sharp-pronged fork. Sprinkle and rub with Spice Mix. Heat oil in large Dutch oven (preferably enamel-lined) until moderately hot. Add chicken and meat and lightly brown. Transfer to a dish.

4. Add onions and garlic to the pot and cook until translucent (about 3 minutes), stirring often. Add barley. Cook and stir for 1 minute. Pour vinegar around the sides of pot. In bowl, whisk tomato paste with 2 cups of stock. Pour into pot. Combine beans and okra with mixture.

5. Return chicken and meat to the pot. Add enough of remaining stock to cover all. Bring to a boil. Reduce heat to simmering. Cover tightly and cook on top of stove for 5 minutes. Transfer to the center section of oven. Bake for 2½ hours; then stir. (Although cholent isn't traditionally stirred while cooking, I prefer to stir it after 2½ hours to check the absorption of liquid.) Most but not all of the liquid will be absorbed. Return pot to the oven for 30 minutes longer, checking after 15 minutes to see if more stock is needed. Blot any visible fat with paper toweling. Then stir. Finished cholent should remain moist with very little if any liquid remaining.

6. Lift out chicken and meat; discard bones. Re-cover pot to keep food warm. Cut the meat and chicken into chunks and return to cholent. Sprinkle with salt, pepper, and parsley or coriander; then fold into mixture. Cover and let stand for 15 minutes. If your Dutch oven is decorative, stand it on a trivet and serve directly from it. Or turn cholent into a warmed serving bowl and ladle out portions at the table. Serve with chopped onion on the side.

Yield: 6 to 8 servings

Serving suggestion: Mixed Fresh Vegetable Salad (page 155).

Turkey Cholent with Cranberries
(Meat)

1 cup navy beans, well rinsed
½ teaspoon each ground sage and cinnamon
2 turkey thighs (about 2½ pounds), skinned and boned (reserve the bones)
1½ tablespoons Italian olive oil
2 medium onions, coarsely chopped
4 large cloves garlic, coarsely chopped
1 green bell pepper, seeded and coarsely chopped
1 large sweet apple, such as Washington State, peeled, cored and coarsely chopped

¼ cup barley, rinsed and drained
1 tablespoon cider vinegar
¾ cup unsweetened apple juice
About 2 cups Chicken Stock
1 cup fresh cranberries, rinsed and picked over
1 tablespoon dried rosemary, crushed
6 parsley sprigs, tied into a bundle with white cotton thread
1 navel orange, peeled and sliced crosswise
¼ teaspoon salt

1. Follow directions for soaking beans in step 1 of recipe for Chicken and Lamb Cholent (page 49). Preheat oven to 300°F.

2. In cup, combine sage with cinnamon. Rinse and dry turkey. Prick in several places with sharp-pronged fork. Sprinkle and rub with spices. Heat oil in a large Dutch oven (preferably enamel-lined) until moderately hot. Add turkey and lightly brown on each side, scooping up with spatula to turn. Transfer to a dish.

3. To the pot add onions, garlic, pepper and apple. Stir and cook until mixture begins to brown. Combine barley with mixture. Stir and cook for 1 minute. Pour vinegar around the sides of pot and cook for 1 minute. Add ¼ cup apple juice, 1¾ cups stock, cranberries, rosemary and parsley bundle. Bring to a boil.

4. Return turkey to the pot, turning several times and spooning with some of the solids. Stir in drained beans and orange. Tightly cover and cook over moderate heat on top of stove for 5 minutes. Transfer to oven and bake for 1 hour. Uncover. Stir in remaining apple juice. Re-cover and bake for 1½ hours.

5. Lift out turkey; discard bones and parsley bundle after pressing out juices. Cut turkey into chunks and stir into cholent. Return to oven for about 15 minutes. (If mixture seems dry, stir in remaining stock.) When cooking is completed, sprinkle salt over cholent, then combine. Re-cover and let stand for 15 minutes before serving.

Yield: 4 or 5 servings

Chicken in a Pot   *(Meat)*

This is a one-dish meal of chicken and soup, prepared with just the right amount of vegetables. This fat-skimmed version (which doubles as a chicken stock) is flavored with a good measure of dill and celery, more than a pinch of caraway and ginger, plus other seasonings—all of which give the dish that special full-bodied taste that chicken-soup mavens will applaud.

1 3½–4-pound chicken,
*   including neck and gizzard,*
*   skinned and quartered*
6 cups water
2 ribs celery with leaves, cut
*   into ½-inch slices*
3 large cloves garlic, minced
3 medium carrots, trimmed,
*   peeled, cut into ½-inch slices*
2 medium onions, cut into
*   1-inch chunks*

1 medium turnip, peeled,
*   trimmed, cut into 1-inch*
*   chunks*
5 sprigs each fresh dill and
*   parsley*
½ teaspoon ground ginger
1 tablespoon caraway seeds,
*   partially crushed*
¼ teaspoon salt
Minced fresh dill

1. Put chicken and giblets into a large Dutch oven. Add water. Bring to a rolling boil; then reduce heat to slow-boil. Cook for 10 minutes, periodically skimming foam from the surface as it accumulates. Add all but last 4 remaining ingredients. Bring to a boil and repeat skimming procedure. When liquid looks clear, add ginger and caraway seeds. Cover and simmer for 2 hours.

2. Remove chicken pieces from pot. With bowl underneath, pour remaining contents of pot into a fine sieve. Pick out carrots and reserve. Press out juices from remaining vegetables and herbs. Rinse pot and dry. Pour soup back into pot and skim off any fat (there will be very little). Stir in salt and carrots.

3. Return chicken quarters to soup (or remove from bones and cut into bite-size pieces). To serve, place 1 teaspoon minced dill in each soup plate. Ladle in a serving of soup. If chicken is left in large pieces, serve as a main course following the soup.

Yield: 5 servings

Serving suggestion: Add 1 or 2 of the following: Matzoh Balls (page 109), Kreplach (page 126), rice or noodles.

Lemon Chicken (Meat)

I've left out the olives (too salty) in my version of this Sephardic dish. But a mixture of herbs and spices, carefully selected to please the American palate, preserves the exotic flavor.

1 4-pound chicken (or 2 legs with thighs and 1 large chicken breast with bone), skinned
3 tablespoons cornstarch
½ teaspoon each ground sage, ground marjoram and dry mustard
2 tablespoons Italian olive oil
2 teaspoons minced garlic
½ cup minced onion

½ cup Chicken Stock
½ cup fresh lemon juice
1 teaspoon minced lemon zest
½ teaspoon dried mint
1 tablespoon minced parsley
½ pound snow-white fresh mushrooms, ends trimmed, damp-wiped, quartered, then thin-sliced
3 tablespoons dry sherry
¼ teaspoon salt

1. Disjoint chicken legs; cut breast and bone in half. Rinse and dry completely with paper toweling. Prick all over with a sharp-pronged fork.

2. In a cup, combine cornstarch with sage, marjoram and mustard. Spread across a sheet of wax paper. Lay chicken atop mixture, pressing to adhere. Turn and coat on second side.

3. Heat 1½ tablespoons oil in a large well-seasoned iron skillet. Over moderate heat, lightly brown chicken on both sides (about 5 minutes), scooping up with tip of spatula to turn. Transfer to a plate. Add garlic and onion. Stir and cook until softened without browning. Pour stock and lemon juice around sides of skillet and combine. Add lemon zest, mint and parsley. Bring to a boil. Return chicken to pan, turning to coat. When liquid boils up again, reduce heat to simmering. Cover and cook for 40 minutes, turning and basting once, midway.

4. Heat remaining oil in a large nonstick skillet until hot. Add mushrooms and sauté until exuded liquid evaporates and mushrooms begin to brown. Remove from heat.

5. Uncover chicken; add sherry. Raise heat slightly and cook until sauce is reduced by ⅓, turning chicken pieces once. Transfer chicken pieces to a warm serving bowl; cover to keep warm. Stir salt and mushrooms into sauce. When sauce simmers, spoon it over chicken.

Yield: 4 servings

Serving suggestion: Extremely tasty with Matzoh Balls (page 109) and just-cooked green peas.

Pomegranate Chicken (Meat)

There is some scholarly evidence that the idea of pomegranate chicken originated in the ancient Holy Land where that fruit was a ubiquitous staple. But, except for the idea, this is a totally new recipe, utilizing mostly American products and developed for Americans with a taste for something different.

½ teaspoon each ground marjoram and curry powder
¼ teaspoon each allspice and cinnamon
1 3½–4-pound chicken, skinned, cut into eighths
2 tablespoons Italian olive oil
1½ cups minced onion
1 tablespoon minced garlic
About ¾ cup Chicken Stock
2 tablespoons honey
1½ tablespoons fresh lemon juice
*1 cup unsweetened pomegranate juice, fresh or bottled**
2 carrots, ends trimmed, peeled, thin-sliced
3 tablespoons minced parsley
½ cup dark seedless raisins
*½ cup whole-wheat couscous**
¼ teaspoon salt (optional)
Sliced fresh apricots or seedless grapes

*Available in health food stores and some supermarkets.

1. In a cup, combine and blend spices. Wash chicken under hot running water. Dry well with paper toweling. Prick all over with a sharp-pronged fork. Sprinkle and rub with spices.

2. Heat 1½ tablespoons oil in a large well-seasoned iron skillet or enamel-lined Dutch oven. Add minced ingredients. Over medium-high heat, cook, stirring often, until mixture is lightly browned (about 5 minutes). Transfer to a plate.

3. Add remaining oil to cooking vessel. Sear chicken on both sides (it will brown very rapidly). Return minced medley to pot. Combine stock with honey, lemon juice and pomegranate juice; pour around the sides of pot. Add carrots, half the parsley, and raisins. Bring to a boil. Turn chicken pieces to coat. Reduce heat to simmering and cook for 40 minutes, turning and basting chicken once, midway.

4. Sprinkle couscous into the liquid and stir. Re-cover and simmer for 5 minutes. Remove pot from heat and let stand for 10 minutes.

5. Taste sauce, adding salt if desired. Stir sauce over chicken (its texture should be thick and spoonable; add a bit more stock if it appears too thick). Reheat briefly. Arrange chicken on warmed individual serving plates surrounded with thick sauce. Sprinkle with remaining parsley and garnish with fresh fruit.

Yield: 6 servings

Serving suggestion: Cooked peas or green beans sprinkled with freshly grated nutmeg.

Cornish Hens with Couscous Stuffing (Meat)

Cornish hen is a distinctly American contribution to Jewish cookery. But it would have come as no surprise to biblical cooks, who often included small birds on their menus (quail, pigeon, partridge and doves, among others). Couscous is of Sephardic origin. So once again, a New American Jewish recipe takes shape from time, geography, the culinary preferences of here-and-now and a piquant measure of invention (dried fruits and crunchy nuts).

FOR THE MARINADE AND HENS:
3 large leeks, split, rinsed, tough end sections discarded
3 large cloves garlic, peeled
3 tablespoons balsamic vinegar
1 cup fresh orange juice
2 tablespoons dark brown sugar
1 teaspoon dry mustard
½ teaspoon each ground marjoram, dried thyme and cinnamon
3 Rock Cornish hens (1½ pounds each)

FOR THE STUFFING:
¾ cup combined water and fresh orange juice
½ cup whole-wheat couscous*
2 teaspoons Italian olive oil
⅓ cup leftover leek mixture
¼ pound snow-white fresh mushrooms, ends trimmed, coarsely chopped
3 tablespoons coarsely chopped blanched almonds
8 pitted prunes, cut into small pieces
1 tablespoon minced flat parsley
¼ teaspoon each ground marjoram and cinnamon
⅛ teaspoon each salt and cayenne pepper
½ large egg yolk (optional)

FOR THE BASTING SAUCE AND GRAVY:
Reserved marinade
2 tablespoons minced flat parsley
Remaining leek mixture (about ½ cup)
½ cup Chicken Stock
¼ teaspoon salt (optional)

*Available in health food stores.

1. Coarse-chop leeks (a processor does the best job); mince the garlic. Turn into a bowl. You will need 1 cup. Measure out 2 tablespoons and place in a large bowl. Set the remainder aside for the stuffing and the basting sauce. To the bowl add vinegar, orange juice, sugar, mustard and spices; stir to combine. Wash hens inside and out under hot running water. Dry well with paper toweling. Prick all over with a sharp-pronged fork. Bathe in marinade, turning several times to coat and spooning some into the cavities. Cover with plastic wrap and refrigerate for 4 hours or longer, turning at least once.

2. To prepare stuffing, bring combined water and juice to a boil in a heavy-bottomed saucepan. Stir in couscous. Reduce heat to simmering; cover and simmer for 3 minutes (all water will be absorbed). Fluff with a fork. Set aside.

3. Preheat oven to 350°F. Spread oil across a nonstick skillet. Over medium heat, sauté leek mixture with mushrooms until softened and no liquid remains in pan (about 10 minutes). Add to couscous. Stir in nuts, prunes, parsley and seasonings. Blend in egg yolk, if desired (the small amount improves flavor and binds the stuffing; stuffing may be prepared several hours ahead. Do not fill cavities until you're ready to roast them).

4. Drain hens; pour marinade into a saucepan. Stuff cavities. Secure openings with thin skewers and truss birds so that the legs and wings hug the body. Set on a rack in a roasting pan. Roast, uncovered, in center section of oven for 20 minutes.

5. While hens roast, prepare basting sauce and gravy. Heat marinade to boiling point with 1 tablespoon parsley and remaining leek mixture. Reduce heat to slow-boil; cook, uncovered, until mixture reduces to ½ cup. Stir in stock and simmer for 2 minutes.

6. Spoon hens with ¼ cup basting sauce. Cover the pan tightly with heavy-duty aluminum foil and roast for 1 hour. Baste with pan juices. Re-cover and roast for 30 minutes. Baste again with pan juices. Pour remaining juices from pan into a skimmer cup and return hens to the oven for 15 minutes longer. Pour defatted sauce into marinade. Then strain, pressing out juices; sauce will be thin. Stir in salt, if desired. Pour back into saucepan and reheat.

7. Place hens on carving board. Remove skewers and trussing. Cut each hen in half and arrange on heated individual serving plates. Spoon each serving with warm sauce. Sprinkle with remaining parsley, garnish with fresh fruit (pineapple, oranges or grapes) and serve at once.

Yield: 6 servings

Variation: Substitute dried apricots for prunes in the stuffing. Soak them in boiling water until softened. Squeeze out liquid and cut them into small pieces.

Orange Chicken with Fruit Stuffing

(Meat)

Chicken, a popular but too often prosaic American Jewish dish, here assumes a poetic personality with the addition of fruit juice and sherry and a date-sweetened bulgur stuffing. Because this chicken is roasted without the skin (to cut down on fat), be sure to follow basting directions to seal in delicious succulence.

FOR THE MARINADE AND CHICKEN:
1 tablespoon minced shallot
½ cup dry sherry
¼ cup frozen orange juice concentrate
1 tablespoon dried rosemary, crushed
1 teaspoon dry mustard
½ teaspoon allspice
¼ teaspoon dried thyme leaves
⅛ teaspoon cayenne pepper
1 tablespoon flavorful honey, such as thyme, dissolved in 1 tablespoon hot water
2 3-pound broiling chickens, skinned
¼ teaspoon salt (optional)
Orange sections for garnish

FOR THE STUFFING:
⅓ cup bulgur*
1 cup water, boiled
1 large rib celery, cut into 1-inch pieces
1 medium onion, cut into 1-inch pieces
14 pitted dried dates, halved
1 sweet crisp apple, cored, peeled and quartered
1 tablespoon Italian olive oil
3 cups 1-inch cubed Sour Rye Bread (page 168) or good quality commercial Jewish rye bread, toasted
¼ teaspoon each cinnamon, allspice, ground sage and salt
2 tablespoons minced parsley
½ cup Chicken Stock

*Available in health food stores and some supermarkets.

1. Prepare marinade by combining first 9 listed ingredients in bowl, beating with fork to blend. Let stand for 10 minutes before using. Rinse chickens inside and out under hot water. Dry well with paper toweling. Place in a large bowl. Prick all over with sharp-pronged fork. Pour marinade over birds, spooning some into cavities and turning several times to coat. Let stand at room temperature for 30 minutes. Cover tightly and marinate in refrigerator for six hours, or overnight, removing one hour before stuffing.

2. To prepare stuffing, place bulgur in medium bowl. Add boiling water; stir. Let stand for 1 hour. Preheat oven to 400°F.

3. Put celery, onion and dates in workbowl of food processor that has been fitted with steel blade. Medium-chop in 3 or 4 on/off turns. Cut each apple quarter in half; add to workbowl. Fine-chop everything in 3 on/off turns.

4. Heat oil in nonstick skillet until very hot. Scrape contents of work-bowl into skillet. Sauté over medium-high heat for 3 minutes, stirring continually. Remove from heat.

5. Put bread cubes into a large bowl. Sprinkle with spices, sage, salt and parsley. Stir in sautéed ingredients. Drain bulgur of any excess water (most of it will be absorbed). Add to bowl and combine. While stirring, drizzle in stock.

6. Drain chickens well, pouring marinade into a small saucepan. Fill each cavity with stuffing. Close cavities with small skewers and white cotton thread. Tie each bird so that legs and wings hug body. Place them, breasts up, on a rack in a roasting pan. Cover tightly with heavy-duty aluminum foil. Roast for 20 minutes. Reduce oven heat to 375°F.

7. Warm marinade over low heat. Spoon birds with ¼ of the marinade. Turn each bird on its side. Re-cover and return to oven for 20 minutes more. Repeat basting procedure once more, turning birds on their other side. Turn chickens on their backs. Pour off exuded juices and stir into the remaining marinade. Roast, uncovered, for 30 minutes longer, basting every 10 minutes.

8. Cut into serving pieces and arrange on warmed platter. Pour any exuded juices from pan into saucepan and reheat; ladle over chicken. Sprinkle with salt, if desired. Garnish with orange sections and serve.

Yield: 6 servings

Note: Try the stuffing on its own as a side dish. Add ¼ teaspoon salt, if desired, to mixture. Pile it into a greased covered casserole; strew with 2 teaspoons sweet pareve margarine cut into small pieces and bake in a preheated 375°F oven for 30 minutes. Serve with meat, vegetables or poultry.

Chicken with Red Cabbage

(Meat)

Cabbage is the unlikely natural thickener that transforms a simple chicken recipe into a dish that may be called a hybrid of chicken cacciatore and Hungarian chicken stew. Wonderful, garnished with Chicken Kreplach (page 126).

2 3-pound broiling chickens, skinned, cut into serving pieces (backs reserved for stockpot)
1½ tablespoons Spice Mix
2 tablespoons Seasoned Olive Oil or Italian olive oil
½ pound red cabbage
2 large cloves garlic

1 large onion
⅔ cup kosher dry red wine
6 tablespoons unsalted tomato paste
1 cup unsalted tomato juice
2 tablespoons minced dill
¼ teaspoon salt
2 tablespoons fresh lemon juice

1. Wash chicken under hot running water. Dry thoroughly with paper toweling. Prick all over with sharp-pronged fork. Place in a large bowl; sprinkle and rub with Spice Mix. Heat oil in a heavy enamel-lined Dutch oven or large well-seasoned iron skillet until moderately hot. Add chicken and cook over medium heat until lightly browned (about 10 minutes), scooping up with spatula to turn. Transfer to a plate.

2. While chicken browns, fine-chop cabbage, garlic and onion by hand. (Or cut cabbage into 1-inch chunks; place in workbowl of food processor that has been fitted with steel blade; chop in 2 on/off turns. Cut onion into 1-inch chunks; halve the garlic and add both to workbowl; fine-chop all in 2 or 3 on/off turns.)

3. Scrape mixture into hot Dutch oven or skillet after chicken has browned (no need for additional oil). Sauté over medium-high heat until cabbage is limp and onion and garlic begin to brown. Nestle mixture to center of pot. Pour wine around it. When liquid bubbles, stir it into solids and cook for 30 seconds. Combine tomato paste with tomato juice and add to medley. Bring to a boil.

4. Return chicken to the pot, turning several times to coat. Bring to simmering point. Cover and simmer for 50 minutes, turning and basting 4 times at equal intervals. With slotted spoon, transfer chicken to warmed serving platter; tent with foil to keep warm.

5. Turn up heat under sauce. Sprinkle in dill, salt and lemon juice. Cook until sauce is reduced to desired consistency. Ladle some over chicken. Serve remainder in gravy boat.

Yield: 6 servings

Baked Chicken
Napoleon   (Meat)

Layered dishes symbolize abundance and are popular in virtually all branches of Jewish cookery. Here is an original kind of layered dish based on an American favorite (adapted from the French), the napoleon. The filling, though, is not custard but alternating layers of chicken and a combination of vegetables (onions, mushrooms and asparagus). It makes a pretty presentation served hot, or cold (with reduced-fat mayonnaise, perked up with fresh dill and freshly ground black pepper).

1 medium onion, peeled, cut into 1-inch chunks
3 large cloves garlic, halved
14 slender asparagus spears, well rinsed, tough butt ends discarded, cut into 1-inch pieces
¼ pound snow-white fresh mushrooms, ends trimmed, damp-wiped and quartered
1 tablespoon Italian olive oil
½ teaspoon freshly grated nutmeg
1 teaspoon each curry powder and dried rosemary or basil,

crushed
¼ teaspoon salt
1¾ pounds boned and skinned chicken breasts, trimmed of any visible fat and cartilage
1 large egg
1 tablespoon fresh lemon juice
2 ripe plum tomatoes, cored, seeded and cut up
2 teaspoons minced parsley
2 teaspoons sweet pareve margarine
About 2 cups Mushroom-Tomato Sauce

1. Preheat oven to 350°F. Coarse-chop onion, garlic and asparagus by hand or use a food processor fitted with steel blade. Place onion and garlic in workbowl and coarse-chop in 2 or 3 on/off turns. Add asparagus and mushrooms. Process on/off in 2 or 3 turns to coarse-chop, taking care not to puree.

2. Heat oil in a nonstick skillet until very hot. Scrape mixture into skillet. Sauté over medium-high heat for 2 minutes, stirring continually. Combine seasonings; sprinkle mixture with half seasoning medley. Reduce heat and continue sautéing until onion and asparagus start to wilt and no liquid remains in pan (6 to 7 minutes). Set aside.

3. Cut chicken into 1-inch chunks. Add to workbowl of processor (no need to wash it out). Add egg, lemon juice, tomato, parsley and remaining seasoning medley. Process until chopped but not pureed. (Mixture may also be put through a grinder fitted with coarse blade.)

4. Grease an 8-inch loaf pan with ½ teaspoon margarine. Spread ¼ of chicken mixture across bottom of pan. Cover with ⅓ of sautéed vegetable mixture, smoothing out and pressing into chicken. Repeat layering procedure, finishing with chicken. Cut remaining margarine into pieces and strew across top layer. Cover tightly with sheet of heavy-duty aluminum foil.

5. Spread an ample-sided broiling pan with a dishcloth. Place loaf pan on cloth. Pour 2 inches of boiling water around the pan. Bake in center section of oven for 45 minutes. Remove from oven. Pour exuded juices off the napoleon into a saucepan. Re-cover pan; let stand for 10 minutes. Pour any lingering residue of juices into the saucepan.

6. Add tomato sauce to the saucepan and heat to simmering. Run a blunt knife around the sides of napoleon. Place a warmed serving plate over it and invert; a sharp rap to the bottom of the pan should loosen it. Spoon some sauce over the loaf. Cut into ¾- to 1-inch slices. Serve with remaining hot tomato sauce on the side.

Yield: 5 to 6 servings

Roast Chicken in a Pouch *(Meat)*

The pouch (oven cooking bag) means no basting and very little cleanup. Here, it also means a kind of chicken you would otherwise have to journey to the shores of the Mediterranean to savor. The fruit marinade makes it a winner.

1 recipe Dried Fruit Marinade (page 182)
4–6 legs and thighs from boiling chicken, skinned, legs disjointed (or 2 small broiling chickens, each cut into serving pieces, excluding backs)

¾ cup Chicken Stock
1 tablespoon minced parsley
1 tablespoon potato starch dissolved in 1 tablespoon water (see note 1)
¼ teaspoon salt (optional)
Minced fresh coriander

1. Prepare marinade using a large bowl. Wash chicken under hot running water and paper-dry. Prick all over with a sharp-pronged fork. Place in marinade, turning several times to coat. Cover and let stand for 1 hour at room temperature or refrigerate for several hours, returning to room temperature before roasting. Preheat oven to 375°F.

2. Open up a pouch bag (see note 2). Lift chicken out of marinade and place in the bag. Heat the stock with parsley and stir into the marinade that remains in the marinade bowl. Pour the mixture into the pouch and seal. Place in a large ovenproof casserole; cut vents following directions on the box, and cut away unfilled extended portions of the pouch beyond the closure. Place in center section of oven and bake for 1 hour (if chicken pieces are very meaty and thick, bake 15 minutes longer).

3. Make a small cut in the pouch and pour the sauce into a small saucepan. Re-seal the bag to keep chicken warm. Bring sauce to a boil. Cook over medium-high heat for 2 minutes, stirring so that solids don't stick to the saucepan. Prepare potato starch mixture. Reduce heat. While stirring, dribble into the sauce. Cook until thickened (about 3 minutes). Taste for salt, adding it if desired.

4. Arrange chicken in a warmed serving bowl. Top with some of the sauce; spoon remainder around chicken. Sprinkle coriander over all and serve at once.

Yield: 4 to 6 servings

Serving suggestion: Yam and Cabbage Tzimmes (page 140).

Notes:
  1. Potato starch is permitted for Passover.
  2. Reynolds oven cooking bags in various sizes are available in kitchen supply stores.

Chicken with Caramelized Sugar   *(Meat)*

Yes, there *is* a Chinese Jewish cuisine (there are kosher Chinese restaurants in major cities throughout the United States), and most American Jewish people I know are devotees of Chinese food—so why not a Chinese-influenced dish for my New American Jewish cuisine? (Particularly since I studied with a leading Chinese chef aided by an interpreter.) Serve with Potato Latkes to complete the Sino-American Jewish connection.

1 recipe Oriental Marinade 1 (page 183)	ginger
	1 tablespoon minced garlic
1 3½–4-pound chicken, skinned, cut into eighths	¾ cup minced onion
	1 tablespoon frozen apple juice
2 tablespoons peanut oil or Italian olive oil	concentrate
	1 tablespoon fresh lemon juice
2 tablespoons firmly packed dark brown sugar	¼ teaspoon salt
	1 tablespoon dry sherry
1 tablespoon minced fresh	(optional)

1. Prepare marinade. Rinse and dry chicken. Pierce all over with sharp-pronged fork. Add to marinade, turning several times to coat. Cover and refrigerate for 3 hours or longer.

2. Drain chicken, reserving marinade. Lay pieces on paper toweling.

3. In large well-seasoned iron skillet, combine oil with sugar. Set skillet over low heat. Cook for 4 minutes, stirring often, taking care not to burn. Mixture will be thick and very hot. Stir in ginger. Cook for 30 seconds. Add chicken pieces in 1 layer; lightly brown on both sides, scooping up with spatula when turning. Transfer to a plate.

4. Add garlic and onion to skillet and cook until mixture starts to brown. Pour reserved marinade around sides of skillet; add apple juice concentrate. Bring to a boil, scraping up solids that may stick to pan. Return chicken to the skillet, turning several times to coat. Set temperature to simmering. Cover and cook for 1 hour, stirring and turning 3 times at equal intervals. Using slotted spoon, transfer chicken to a serving bowl. Cover to keep warm.

5. Turn up heat under skillet and reduce sauce by half. Stir in lemon juice and salt and cook for 1 minute. Taste, adding sherry if desired. Cook an additional minute and spoon over chicken.

Yield: 4 servings

Easiest-Ever
Braised Chicken *(Meat)*

Keep my Mushroom-Tomato Sauce (page 30) or my Spicy Tomato Sauce (page 186) in your freezer, and you're equipped with quick-to-prepare-dinner insurance any day, any time of the year. In this recipe, one or the other tomato sauces brings a new taste experience to one of the oldest Jewish favorites—chicken.

This is a basic recipe. Use the ingredients and techniques with boned and skinned chicken breasts, or fillets of lamb or veal.

1 4-pound broiling chicken, skinned, wing tips removed, cut into eighths
1 tablespoon Spice Mix
1½ tablespoons Italian olive oil
2 tablespoons minced shallot
1½ cups Mushroom-Tomato Sauce (page 30) or Spicy Tomato Sauce (page 186)
2 tablespoons minced fresh dill, or 1 teaspoon dried dill weed

4 sprigs parsley, 1 bay leaf, ¼ teaspoon dried thyme wrapped into a bundle with double rinsed piece of cotton cheesecloth and tied with white cotton thread
¼ teaspoon salt
Minced fresh herb, such as dill, mint, parsley, basil or oregano

1. Wash chicken and dry well with paper toweling. Prick all over with a sharp-pronged fork. Sprinkle and rub with Spice Mix. Cover and let stand for 30 minutes or refrigerate for several hours.

2. Heat oil in a large well-seasoned iron skillet until hot. Spread shallot across skillet and cook without stirring for 1 minute over medium heat. Arrange chicken pieces atop shallot and cook until lightly brown all over, scooping up with spatula when turning.

3. Push chicken to center of skillet; pour sauce around the sides; add dill. When liquid bubbles up, combine it with the chicken; add parsley bundle. Cover and simmer until chicken is tender (45 to 50 minutes), turning and basting twice at equal intervals. With slotted spoon, transfer chicken to a hot serving platter; cover to keep warm.

4. Discard parsley bundle after pressing out juices. Turn up heat under skillet and reduce sauce by ⅓; stir in salt. Spoon it over and around the chicken. Sprinkle with fresh herb of your choice and serve at once.

Yield: 4 servings

Serving suggestion: For a taste-matched meal, serve with tomato kugel, which is also prepared with Mushroom-Tomato Sauce.

Notes:

  1. If you prefer a thickened sauce, do not reduce it in step 4. Instead, combine and blend 1 tablespoon yellow cornmeal, cornstarch or potato starch (for Passover) with 1 tablespoon water until smooth. With sauce bubbling, slowly stir in mixture and cook until lightly thickened.

  2. When using the basic recipe for boned and skinned chicken breasts or meat, cooking time and sauce measurement may vary with the thickness of the chicken or meat.

Clay Pot Turkey *(Meat)*

In my informed imagination, I see ancient Hebrews, like other people at the dawn of history, wrapping fowl in wet clay and placing the package on a glowing fire. The clay hardens, exuding moisture, which turns to steam, and the bird is simultaneously steamed and roasted, creating a hybrid flavor that's as irresistible as it is unusual. That's one reason wet clay cooking is resurgent, albeit in a contemporary form: *the clay pot,* which does everything fired wet clay once did, except shatter.

Consider these other advantages of the clay pot: The steamy atmosphere creates a nonstick utensil, which makes cutting down on fats and oils so much easier. Everything, including flavor, remains in the pot, which also is a peerless tenderizer. Finally, and to many cooks, most importantly, it's an effort-saving device. Just add the ingredients to be cooked, place your clay pot in the oven and forget about it—it's self-basting!—and the presentation is exquisite.

½ cup balsamic vinegar
3 tablespoons frozen orange
   juice concentrate
2½ tablespoons Italian olive oil
1 teaspoon each ground sage
   and chili con carne
   seasoning
2 tablespoons caraway seeds,
   partially crushed
¾ cup dry sherry
1 whole turkey breast (6–7
   pounds), bony back section
   of bone split
6–8 large shallots, peeled, each
   cut in half

4 large cloves garlic, peeled,
   each cut in half
2 large onions
2 large yams
1¼–1½ pounds white turnip
1 teaspoon each cinnamon and
   sugar
⅛ teaspoon cayenne pepper
⅓ teaspoon salt
2 tablespoons fresh lemon juice
3 tablespoons finely minced dill
1 tablespoon cornstarch
   dissoved in 1 tablespoon
   water (optional)

1. Prepare marinade in a large flat-bottomed bowl or Dutch oven: Combine vinegar, orange juice concentrate, 1 tablespoon oil, seasonings, caraway and ¼ cup sherry. Add turkey, turning several times to coat. Cover and refrigerate overnight.

2. Soak clay pot (including cover) in tepid water for 20 to 30 minutes.

3. Fit workbowl of food processor with steel blade and, with machine running, drop shallot and garlic clove halves through feed tube. Scrape into measuring cup. (You will need about ⅔ cup firmly packed mixture.) Gently separate skin from flesh of breast; push half the mixture under skin on each side of breast, smoothing out and patting down skin to distribute evenly. Cut away any surplus skin.

4. Fit food processor with slicing blade. Using gentle pressure, thin-slice onions. Slice peeled yams and turnip separately. Heat remaining 1½ tablespoons oil in large heavy-bottomed saucepan. Add onion and sauté over medium heat until onion begins to wilt (about 2 minutes). Add yams and turnip. Sprinkle with cinnamon and sugar. Continue sautéing until volume begins to diminish (about 8 minutes).

5. Spoon half the vegetable mixture over ridged bottom section of clay pot. Drain turkey, pouring marinade into a saucepan. Place turkey over vegetable mixture, bony side down. Spoon the remaining vegetable mixture over breast.

6. To marinade in saucepan add remaining ½ cup sherry, cayenne, salt and lemon juice. Heat until bubbly. Gently pour over turkey and vegetable mixture. Sprinkle dill over all. Cover pot securely.

7. Position oven rack in bottom third of oven. Set thermostat at 400°F. Place pot on rack in cold oven and bake for 2 hours. Remove from oven. Open cover just a crack and let steam escape for 10 minutes. Place turkey on large warmed serving platter. Tent with foil to keep warm.

8. Pour remaining contents of clay pot into colander with large skimming cup underneath. Drain well. Arrange vegetables around turkey. Re-cover while sauce is reheated and thickened, if desired.

9. Pour defatted sauce into saucepan (there will be about 2 cups). Over high heat, reduce to 1¼ cups. If adding thickener, dribble in cornstarch mixture and stir until lightly thickened. Spoon some gravy over turkey and vegetables; serve remainder in gravy boat.

Yield: 8 to 10 servings

Variation: Add ¾ cup fresh rinsed and picked-over cranberries when reheating marinade (step 4).

Note: The clay pot, which looks like a covered casserole, is available at many stores that sell kitchen utensils.

Festive Chicken   (Meat)

This skillet-to-oven recipe is my tribute to festive occasions. The chicken is first bathed in a mixture of honey, fruit juice and spices; it's then coated with flavor-promoting Matzoh Meal Mix and crisped before baking. Without culinary antecedent, this is an American Jewish original.

3 tablespoons honey
¼ cup frozen orange juice
    concentrate or a mixture of
    orange and pineapple
    concentrates
½ teaspoon each finely crushed
    cloves and paprika
1 3½–4-pound broiling chicken,
    skinned, cut into serving
    pieces
½–⅔ cup Matzoh Meal Mix
2½ tablespoons Italian olive oil
2 medium onions, coarsely
    chopped
5 large cloves garlic, minced
2 ribs celery, coarsely chopped
2 Granny Smith apples, peeled,
    cored, coarsely chopped
3 tablespoons minced parsley
¼ teaspoon salt
2 tablespoons fresh lemon juice
2 teaspoons prepared Dijon
    mustard (preferably
    unsalted)
Fresh sliced pineapple

1. Put 2 tablespoons honey in an 8-ounce measure. While stirring, add concentrate, cloves and paprika. Fill with water to 8-ounce mark and stir. Pour into a wide bowl.

2. Rinse and dry chicken. Prick all over with sharp-pronged fork. Add to bowl, turning several times to coat. Let stand at room temperature for 30 minutes.

3. Drain chicken, reserving marinade. Arrange pieces on large flat plate. Sprinkle with ¼ cup Matzoh Meal Mix, pressing to adhere. Turn. Sprinkle and press ¼ cup Mix into the chicken, adding more if needed to evenly coat each piece. Chill in freezer for 10 minutes.

4. Preheat oven to 375°F. Heat 1 tablespoon oil in a large well-seasoned iron skillet. In a bowl, combine onions, garlic, celery and apples. Strew ¼ cup across hot oiled skillet. Cook for 30 seconds over medium-high heat. Add half the chicken and lightly brown on both sides (about 5 minutes), scooping up and turning with sharp-edged spatula. Transfer chicken and browned particles to a plate. Add another tablespoon of oil. Strew ¼ cup chopped mixture across skillet. Repeat the browning, turning and transferring procedure.

5. Add remaining ½ tablespoon oil to skillet. Sauté balance of chopped mixture until lightly browned (about 3 minutes), scraping up crisp particles. Pour reserved marinade around sides of skillet. Add 2 tablespoons parsley and bring to a boil, stirring to combine.

6. Return chicken to pan, spooning with thick sauce. Cover and simmer on top of stove for 3 minutes. Baste. Place in center section of oven for 50 minutes, spooning with sauce once, midway.

7. Remove from oven. Sprinkle salt evenly over all. In cup, blend remaining tablespoon of honey with lemon juice and mustard. Pour over chicken. Re-cover and let stand for 5 minutes.

8. Drain chicken of sauce and arrange pieces on large warmed serving platter. Stir sauce and reheat briefly. Spoon some of it over the chicken. Cut each pineapple slice into thirds and arrange around sides of plate in a neat pattern. Serve immediately, sprinkled with remaining parsley; serve extra sauce on the side.

Yield: 4 or 5 servings

Serving suggestion: Hot Red Cabbage with Fennel (page 141).

Indonesian Chicken   (Meat)

Here is a dish that has traveled from Indonesia to South Africa (where it's a favorite among the Jewish community) and now, in my version, to the United States of America. In its country of origin and in South Africa, the satay is prepared with chicken breasts, cut into pieces, skewered and barbecued. Use dark meat as well as white, bake, then broil without skewers. The taste is not as unusual as the ingredients would seem to indicate; actually, it's a pleasing, albeit rare taste. Try the satay mixture with quartered and skinned Cornish hens as well for another adventure in the new and different American Jewish cookery.

1 ⅜-inch slice smooth-skinned fresh ginger (center cut)	1 tablespoon balsamic vinegar
2 large cloves garlic	½ teaspoon each ground curry powder and ground cumin
1 large onion	¼ teaspoon cayenne pepper
1 slice sour rye bread or challah, crust removed, torn up	2 teaspoons honey
4 tablespoons smooth unsalted peanut butter	1 tablespoon unsalted tomato paste
3 tablespoons reduced-sodium soy sauce	2 3-pound broiling chickens, skin removed
¼ cup fresh lemon juice	¼–½ cup Chicken Stock or water
	¼ teaspoon salt (optional)

1. Quarter ginger, halve garlic, cut onion into 1-inch chunks. Fit workbowl of food processor with steel blade. With machine running, drop ginger, then garlic through feed tube. Stop machine. Scrape down sides of workbowl. Add onion, bread, peanut butter, soy sauce, lemon juice, vinegar, spices, 1 teaspoon honey, and tomato paste; process until very smooth (mixture will be thick).

2. Cut breasts of chicken away from bone, leaving wings attached. Disjoint legs. Cut off backs and reserve for stockpot. Place in a large bowl and cover with pureed mixture, turning several times to coat. Cover and refrigerate for 6 hours or overnight, turning twice. Bring to room temperature before proceeding.

3. Preheat oven to 450°F. Drain chicken until no marinade drips from each piece; arrange in a broiling pan large enough to accommodate all of it in 1 layer. Pour drained marinade into a small heavy-bottomed saucepan (it will contain liquid as well as solids) and set aside. Position oven rack to lower third of oven. Bake chicken for 15 minutes; scoop up with spatula and turn. Bake for 12 minutes. Place pan under broiler at fairly high heat and broil on each side until golden (about 10 minutes on each side; cooking time may vary with intensity of heat, so keep a watchful eye during last cooking stage).

4. Bring marinade to simmering point, adding enough stock or water to thin slightly. Bring to a boil. Reduce heat and simmer, uncovered, for 5 minutes, stirring often. Stir in remaining teaspoon honey. Taste for salt, adding it, if desired. Arrange chicken on warmed serving platter. Serve sauce on the side as a dip.

Yield: 6 servings

Serving suggestion: Holiday Vegetable and Fruit Tzimmes (page 139).

Sweet-and-Tart
Chicken Breasts   *(Meat)*

This delicate-tasting chicken derives its taste from the unusual cooking technique, and the mixture of 4 piquant spices. Not a grain of salt has been added.

*1¼–1½ pounds skinned and
  boned chicken breasts*
2 tablespoons unbleached flour
*¼ teaspoon each ground ginger
  and dried crushed thyme
  leaves*
*½ teaspoon each curry powder
  and ground cardamom*
1½ tablespoons Italian olive oil
*1 tablespoon finely minced
  garlic*
3 tablespoons finely minced

shallot
½ cup kosher dry white wine
*3 tablespoons frozen orange
  juice concentrate*
About ⅓ cup water
*¾ cup fresh cranberries, rinsed
  and picked over*
*3 carrots, peeled, diced into
  ¼-inch pieces*
2 tablespoons honey
2 tablespoons minced parsley

1. Rinse breasts; dry completely with paper toweling. Cut each breast in half vertically. In cup, combine and blend flour with spices. Spread half across a sheet of wax paper. Lay breasts atop mixture. Sprinkle with remaining mixture. Press to adhere.

2. Spread 1 tablespoon oil across a large well-seasoned iron skillet. Over medium heat, sauté garlic and shallots for 1 minute. Lay chicken pieces over herb mixture and cook for 3 minutes on each side, adding remaining oil before turning.

3. Pour wine around the sides of skillet. Cook without stirring for 30 seconds. Add concentrate, ¼ cup water and cranberries. When concentrate liquefies, spoon over chicken. Bring to simmering point; cover and cook over low heat for 25 minutes, turning once, midway.

4. Turn chicken pieces; add carrots and enough water to barely cover them. Bring to simmering point. Re-cover and cook for 20 minutes longer, turning once, midway. Stir in honey and parsley; baste. Simmer, uncovered, for 3 minutes.

Yield: 4 to 5 servings

Serving suggestion: Barley Pilaf (page 151).

Baked Chicken with Sun-Dried Tomatoes   *(Meat)*

The idea for this dish came to me when I received a package of unsalted sun-dried tomatoes from a friend in Israel. I prefer the unsalted variety; it bestows an explicit taste to the chicken, a certain pungency that salted sun-dried tomatoes lack. In the baking, the sun-dried tomatoes impart a burgundy hue to the dish, which is very pretty when served with colorful vegetables. (Of course, American unsalted sun-dried tomatoes taste great and cook beautifully, too.)

*2 ounces unsalted sun-dried
   tomatoes**
*1 3½–4-pound broiling chicken
   or 4 legs and thighs (about
   2½ pounds), skinned, legs
   disjointed*
*⅓ cup unsweetened pineapple
   juice*
3 tablespoons potato starch
¼ teaspoon allspice
*½ teaspoon each ground sage,
   ground coriander and celery
   seed*

1½ tablespoons Italian olive oil
½ cup minced onion
2 teaspoons minced garlic
½ cup kosher dry white wine
*1 teaspoon unsalted prepared
   Dijon mustard*
1 tablespoon minced parsley
*¼ pound snow-white fresh
   mushrooms, ends trimmed*
¼ teaspoon salt
½ teaspoon sugar
Minced fresh basil or parsley

*Available in health food stores and some supermarkets.

1. Rinse tomatoes. Place in small bowl. Pour enough boiling water over them to cover. Let stand for 10 minutes. Drain in colander and cut into small pieces. Set aside.

2. Wash chicken under hot running water; paper-dry. Prick all over with a sharp-pronged fork. Place in a large bowl. Pour pineapple juice over chicken, turning several times to coat. Let stand at room temperature for 30 minutes (or cover and refrigerate for several hours). Preheat oven to 325°F.

3. Combine potato starch, allspice, sage, coriander and celery seed in a cup. Spread half across a sheet of wax paper. Drain chicken, reserving pineapple juice. Drain on paper toweling. Place chicken atop dry mixture; sprinkle remaining mixture over chicken, pressing to adhere.

4. Using a large well-seasoned iron skillet, heat 1 tablespoon oil until hot. Spread onion and garlic across the skillet. Over medium heat, cook for 1 minute without stirring. Arrange coated chicken on onion and garlic and lightly brown on both sides (6 to 7 minutes), adding remaining oil after turning once.

5. Pour wine into a measuring cup; add mustard and blend with a fork. Pour around the sides of skillet. Cook without stirring for 30 seconds. Add reserved pineapple juice, tomatoes and 1 tablespoon parsley. Turn chicken several times to coat. Bring to a boil on top of stove. Reduce heat to simmering, cover tightly and cook for 5 minutes. Place in center section of oven and bake for 30 minutes.

6. Damp-wipe mushrooms. Cut into quarters; then thin-slice. Add to skillet with salt and sugar. Turn chicken and baste several times. Re-cover and bake for 10 minutes. Repeat procedure. If all of the liquid from the sauce has evaporated, stir in ¼ cup of water. Re-cover and bake for 5 minutes longer.

7. Arrange chicken on hot serving platter. Spoon sauce around it. Sprinkle all over with minced basil or parsley.

Yield: 4 servings

Serving suggestion: Yam and Cabbage Tzimmes (page 140).

6
MEAT

Light Chopped Liver   *(Meat)*

Here "light" means the following: Three servings of traditional American Jewish chopped liver (*with* schmaltz and hard-cooked egg) are extended with eggplant to *six* servings, each bursting with flavor, but with only about half the traditional amounts of fat and cholesterol.

*1 medium eggplant (¾ pound),
  peeled
2 tablespoons fresh lemon juice
¾ teaspoon salt
½ pound fresh chicken livers
1 tablespoon each Seasoned
  Olive Oil and Rendered
  Chicken Fat (page 136), or 2
  tablespoons Seasoned Olive
  Oil
1¼ cups coarsely chopped onion*

*2 teaspoons minced garlic
½ teaspoon each ground sage
  and mild curry powder
2 teaspoons balsamic vinegar or
  wine vinegar
2 large hard-cooked eggs (use 1
  yolk and 2 whites)
2 tablespoons minced fresh dill
  or parsley
Coarsely ground black pepper to
  taste*

1. Cut eggplant into ¼-inch slices and then into ½-inch cubes. Place in bowl. Sprinkle with lemon juice and ½ teaspoon salt. Let stand for 40 minutes. Transfer to colander. Rinse under cold running water. Drain well; with a large spoon, gently press out liquid without crushing. Transfer to doubled sheet of paper toweling.

2. Cut away membranes from livers. Cut each liver in half. Broil on a rack under high heat, turning when liver turns light brown. Rinse under cold running water; dry on paper toweling. Cut into ½-inch pieces.

3. Heat 1 tablespoon oil in large well-seasoned iron skillet (see note). Add eggplant. Sauté over medium heat for 1 minute. Stir in ¾ cup onion, and garlic. Sprinkle with seasonings. Sauté until golden, stirring and spreading mixture across skillet every minute to achieve even browning (about 5 minutes). Add liver and sauté for 1 minute. Then stir in vinegar. Cook for 1 minute.

4. Transfer mixture to workbowl of food processor fitted with steel blade (or wooden bowl, if chopping by hand). Add eggs, remaining uncooked onion and dill or parsley. Fine-chop in processor in 2 or 3 on/off turns, taking care not to puree. Scrape into a bowl. Stir in remaining oil and/or chicken fat, balance of salt, and pepper. Serve warm or at room temperature.

Yield: 6 servings as an appetizer

Variation: In step 4, eliminate remaining ¼ teaspoon salt and substitute 1 tablespoon drained and rinsed capers.

Note: *To prepare a well-seasoned iron skillet:* With soapy water, wash the skillet and dry thoroughly. Rub interior bottom and sides with a small amount of oil. Place the utensil over medium heat for three minutes. Let it cool, then use paper toweling to wipe out excess oil. Your skillet has been well seasoned, and it's ready to use. After each use, wash in soapy water (do not use steel wool) and wipe dry. After some time your skillet will begin to look dry. When it does, repeat the entire seasoning process.

Friday Night Pot Roast   *(Meat)*

The leanest of beef cuts, combined with juicy vegetables, herbs and fruit juice, and flavor-enhanced with wine and provocative spices and herbs— that's the formula for a modern pot roast for the nineties. I like to squirrel away two servings, freeze in a boilable plastic bag and serve another day open-faced on my Brown Rye Bread with 3 Seeds (page 167).

3½–4 pounds thick-cut brisket of beef (about 2 inches thick), well-trimmed
1 large onion, coarsely chopped
2 large carrots, peeled and coarsely chopped
1 medium green bell pepper, seeded and coarsely chopped
6 cloves garlic, coarsely chopped
4 large shallots, coarsely chopped
6 sprigs each parsley and dill, 1 bay leaf and ½ teaspoon dried thyme wrapped in rinsed piece of cotton

cheesecloth and tied with white cotton thread
6 whole cloves
½ teaspoon each allspice and mild curry powder
¾ cup unsweetened apple juice
1 cup water
1 cup kosher dry red wine
1½ tablespoons Italian olive oil or Seasoned Olive Oil
1 cup unsalted Italian tomato puree
¼ teaspoon salt
Crisp watercress or parsley for garnish

1. Put meat into large but narrow pot or bowl that will just accommodate it, leaving room for liquid (if necessary cut meat in half to fit). In medium saucepan combine onion, carrots, green pepper, garlic, shallots, herb bundle, cloves, spices, apple juice and water. Bring to a boil. Reduce heat to simmering and cook for 3 minutes. Stir in wine. Pour over meat. Cover and refrigerate overnight.

2. Preheat oven to 300°F. Drain meat, pushing off vegetables. Remove and reserve herb bundle. Strain marinade into a bowl, reserving solids. Heat oil in heavy Dutch oven over medium-high heat. Brown meat all over; add drained vegetables. Stir and cook with meat until they begin to soften.

3. Add reserved marinade, herb bundle and tomato puree, turning meat and spooning several times with sauce. Cover and cook over moderate heat for 5 minutes.

4. Position oven rack to lower third of oven. Bake for 1 hour. Turn meat and baste. Repeat turning and basting procedure 3 more times until meat is tender (3½ to 4 hours). Remove pot from oven and let stand for 30 minutes. Discard herb bundle after pressing out juices.

5. Transfer meat to a bowl with cover. Place pot over medium-high heat and bring sauce to a boil. Cook, uncovered, until reduced by ¼. Let cool; then pour into another container with tight lid. Refrigerate meat and sauce until well chilled.

6. Cut away any congealed fat from sauce. Pour sauce into a wide heavy-bottomed saucepan. Heat until bubbling. Sprinkle in salt. Cut meat against the grain into ¼-inch slices. Immerse in sauce and heat through. Arrange meat on warmed serving platter in a neat pattern. Spoon with some of the gravy; serve remainder in gravy boat. Garnish platter with watercress or parsley.

Yield: 8 servings

Serving suggestions: Potato Latkes (page 117), Smooth-and-Sweet Applesauce (page 199).

Top-of-the-Stove Pot Roast (Meat)

An old favorite with a new taste. Slightly sweet with a hint of tartness. Dried mushrooms add to the full-bodied flavor.

½ ounce dried mushrooms, rinsed and broken up
¾ teaspoon each mild curry powder, ground cumin and allspice
1 tablespoon unbleached flour
2 pounds center-cut chuck or lean brisket of beef, about 1½ inches thick
2 tablespoons Seasoned Olive Oil or Italian olive oil
3 medium carrots, trimmed, peeled and coarsely chopped
4 ribs celery, trimmed, coarse strings removed, and chopped
1 medium turnip, peeled, ends trimmed, and coarsely chopped

4 large cloves garlic, minced
2 tablespoons wine vinegar or balsamic vinegar
1 28-ounce can Italian peeled tomatoes, drained, liquid reserved
1½ tablespoons dark brown sugar
⅓ cup dark seeded raisins
4 large dill sprigs, ½ teaspoon dried thyme and 1 bay leaf wrapped in a rinsed piece of cotton cheesecloth and tied with white cotton thread
1½ tablespoons fresh lemon juice
¼ teaspoon each salt and black pepper
Minced fresh dill

1. Put mushrooms in a cup. Add enough water to barely cover; soak for 15 minutes. In another cup, combine and blend spices with flour.

2. Paper-dry meat. Sprinkle and rub all over with flour mixture, reserving any leftovers. Heat 1 tablespoon oil in a large heavy Dutch oven. Brown meat over medium-high heat on each side. Transfer to a plate. Spread remaining oil across pot. Sauté carrots, celery and turnip until they begin to brown. Stir in garlic and cook for 1 minute. Add any reserved flour mixture. Pour vinegar around sides of pot, scraping up any browned particles. Cook for 1 minute.

3. Puree or mash tomatoes. Add to pot with ½ cup reserved tomato juices, mushrooms and soaking liquid, sugar, raisins and dill bundle. Bring to a boil. Return browned meat to Dutch oven, turning several times to coat. Reduce heat to simmering. Cover and cook until tender (about 3 hours), turning and basting every hour. Remove pot from stove and let stand, covered, for 15 minutes.

4. Transfer meat to a carving board; cover to keep warm. Turn up heat under Dutch oven. Add lemon juice, salt and pepper. Cook sauce until liquid is reduced by ⅓. With very sharp knife, cut meat into ½-inch slices. Arrange on a serving platter. Spoon with some sauce; sprinkle with dill. Serve balance of sauce in sauceboat.

Yield: 6 servings

Note: For easy entertaining, prepare recipe up to 2 days ahead *without* reducing sauce (step 4). Store meat and sauce in refrigerator in separate containers. (Save extra tomato juices for soups, salad dressings or other recipes.) When ready to serve, transfer sauce to a large nonstick skillet and reheat until bubbling. Slice meat and immerse in sauce. Slowly reheat; reduce some liquid from the sauce if necessary.

Roast Stuffed Flank Steak   *(Meat)*

Stuffed foods symbolize abundance; and here's a stuffed food that makes an abundant, albeit calorie-controlled, main course. Any leftovers make excellent sandwiches (particularly when thin-sliced on challah).

FOR THE MEAT AND STUFFING:
1 2-pound flank steak
1½ teaspoons Spice Mix
2 teaspoons finely minced garlic
1 recipe Matzoh Stuffing (page 124), including variation
1½ teaspoons Seasoned Olive Oil or Italian olive oil

FOR THE BASTING SAUCE:
½ cup unsalted tomato puree
½ cup Chicken Stock
½ cup sweet concord grape kosher wine, plus ⅓ cup
1 tablespoon minced dill or parsley

1. Preheat oven to 350°F. Choose a flank steak that is thick enough to slit for a pocket. Along one long end, cut a pocket through center and into meat within 1 inch from 3 edges. Rub Spice Mix inside the pocket and all over meat. Open up cavity and sprinkle in garlic. Flatten meat and roll up. Wrap in plastic film and refrigerate for 3 to 4 hours.

2. Prepare Matzoh Stuffing. Unroll meat. Stuff cavity to within ¾ inch of opening, avoiding overpacking. Sew up or secure with thin skewers and white cotton thread. (Put remaining stuffing into a lightly oiled 1-quart ovenproof casserole, following directions for variation. Cover stuffing tightly with a sheet of aluminum foil; bake during the last half hour of roasting time.) Brush meat all over with oil.

3. To make the basting sauce, pour puree, stock, ½ cup wine and dill or parsley into a small heavy-bottomed saucepan. Over lowest temperature, heat to simmering.

4. Place meat in a baking pan large enough to fit snugly (do not use an oversize cooking vessel or basting sauce will evaporate too rapidly). Roast, uncovered, for 30 minutes. Spoon ⅓ of warmed basting sauce over meat. Loosely cover with a sheet of aluminum foil. Return to oven for 30 minutes. Repeat roasting, basting and covering procedure twice more, basting with pan juices each time. Transfer meat to a carving board. Tent with foil to keep warm. Remove extra stuffing from the oven.

5. Pour remaining ⅓ cup of wine into the roasting pan. Place pan over a medium-high heat on top of stove. When sauce simmers, reduce temperature and cook for 3 minutes, stirring in any stuffing that has exuded from meat.

6. Discard skewers and strings from meat. With a very sharp knife, cut into 1-inch slices. Serve on warmed individual plates, spooned with hot sauce. Serve extra stuffing on the side.

Yield: 4 to 5 servings

Serving suggestion: Fresh Horseradish with Beets (page 180).

Sweet-and-Sour
Stuffed Cabbage *(Meat)*

This is one of the dishes associated with Sukkoth, the autumn harvest festival. It symbolizes abundance (it's a *stuffed* food) and the certainty that gloom can be transformed at once into happiness (it's a food that is at once sour *and* sweet). My version leans to the sweeter side, mainly from fruit juice concentrates, spices and herbs. It's a hearty dish to warm body and soul when the chill of autumn begins to whistle at your windowpanes.

FOR THE CABBAGE AND SAUCE:

1 2½-pound white cabbage
2 teaspoons Italian olive oil
1 tablespoon minced garlic
1 cup finely minced onion
2 teaspoons each cider vinegar and balsamic vinegar
2 tablespoons each frozen apple juice concentrate and pineapple juice concentrate
2 tablespoons firmly packed brown sugar
3 cups unsalted Italian tomato puree
¼ teaspoon each allspice, ground ginger and cinnamon
1 tablespoon minced parsley or fresh coriander
½ cup dark seedless raisins
⅓ cup fresh lemon juice
½ teaspoon salt

FOR THE FILLING:

1 pound extra-lean ground beef, veal or lamb
½ cup uncooked white or brown rice
⅛ teaspoon cayenne pepper
¼ teaspoon salt (optional)
1 tablespoon minced parsley or fresh coriander
1 large egg, lightly beaten

1. To separate outer leaves of cabbage, make deep cuts around core and lift out. Place whole head in large pot of rapidly boiling water. Parboil for 8 to 10 minutes. Drain. Carefully loosen 12 to 16 outer leaves. Make a 1-inch "V" cut into tough ribs nearest core of the larger leaves and discard tough section. Return leaves to boiling water until they're pliable (4 to 5 minutes). Remove with large slotted spoon and set aside. Fine-chop remaining smaller pieces of cabbage.

2. Prepare sauce by heating oil in 3-quart heavy-bottomed saucepan. Over moderate heat, sauté garlic and onion until limp. Spoon half the mixture into medium bowl. To remaining mixture in saucepan, add vinegars. Cook for 30 seconds. Then add concentrates, sugar, tomato puree, spices, parsley or coriander and raisins. Bring to simmering point. Cover and gently simmer for 20 minutes.

3. While sauce cooks, add meat to sautéed mixture in bowl. Combine with rice, cayenne pepper, salt if desired, parsley or coriander and egg. Blend well.

4. Stuff each cabbage leaf, using a tablespoon or less for each leaf, depending upon its size. Roll up each leaf, tucking in ends.

5. Pour ⅓ of the sauce into large Dutch oven (preferably enamel-lined). Arrange half the bundles, seams down, over sauce in one layer. Strew half the chopped cabbage over all. Ladle ⅓ of the sauce over the cabbage. Arrange remaining bundles in sauce. Strew with balance of chopped cabbage; then cover with remaining sauce. Bring to simmering point. Cover and cook over very low heat for 45 minutes.

6. Add lemon juice and salt. Baste, taking care not to tear cabbage leaves. Bring to simmering point. Re-cover and cook for 45 minutes longer, basting once, midway. Remove from heat and let stand for 30 minutes. Reheat briefly before serving.

Yield: 6 servings as a main course; 12 servings as a first course

Note: When serving the next day, re-warm in a large nonstick skillet over a very low heat so that sauce doesn't evaporate. Bundles freeze very well.

Beef and Pepper
Goulash *(Meat)*

Goulash is a popular Hungarian Jewish favorite. I've lightened the usual heavy sauce and given it a slightly tart edge with the addition of cabbage and vinegar.

2 pounds lean chuck or
   shoulder of beef
1½ tablespoons Spice Mix
1½ tablespoons Italian olive oil
1 cup coarsely chopped onion
1 ⅜-inch slice fresh ginger,
   minced
1 tablespoon minced garlic
1 tablespoon wine vinegar
1 tightly packed cup shredded
   cabbage

¼ cup unsalted tomato paste
¾ cup each Chicken Stock or
   water and unsalted tomato
   juice
¼ teaspoon celery seed
10 dill sprigs tied into a bundle
   with white cotton thread
1 large green bell pepper,
   seeded, cut into ¼-inch strips
Minced fresh dill

1. Cut away all visible fat and gristle from meat. Then slice into 1-inch cubes. Sprinkle and rub all over with Spice Mix.

2. Heat oil in a large Dutch oven until very hot. Add onion, ginger and garlic. Sauté over medium-high heat for 2 minutes. Add meat and combine. Continue cooking until meat gives up its raw look and most of liquid in pot evaporates.

3. Add vinegar and cook for 1 minute. Then stir in cabbage; cook for 2 minutes.

4. Combine tomato paste with stock and tomato juice. Pour into pot with celery seed and dill bundle. Bring to a boil; then reduce heat to simmering. Cover and cook for 1 hour, stirring from time to time. Add pepper. Re-cover and simmer until meat is tender (1 to 1½ hours). Discard dill bundle after pressing out juices.

5. Transfer to a warmed tureen; serve with minced dill on the side.

Yield: 6 servings

Serving suggestion: Add 1 cup hot cubed and cooked potatoes just before serving.

Baked Lamb Shanks (Meat)

King Solomon might have savored this dish, for lamb has been a favorite food of the Jewish people since biblical times. This regal entrée, though, benefits from some modern touches. Chicken Stock is added at intervals during baking to enhance juiciness; and suggested side dishes add to the succulence. But the seasonings I use, and the seasonings used in King Solomon's kitchens, do bear a close resemblance. A majestic dish for any festive occasion.

4 koshered lamb shanks, well trimmed, cut into 6 pieces
1 teaspoon each ground sage and curry powder, or 1 tablespoon Spice Mix
1½ tablespoons Italian olive oil
1 tablespoon minced garlic
3 tablespoons minced shallot
⅓ cup each minced onion and green bell pepper

3 tablespoons Worcestershire sauce
¼ cup tomato juice, preferably unsalted
¼ cup dry kosher red wine (optional)
½ to ¾ cup Chicken Stock
¼ teaspoon salt
Minced fresh basil or dill

1. Preheat oven to 375°F. Wash meat under hot running water; dry well with paper toweling. Prick in several places with a sharp-pronged fork. Combine seasonings; rub all over meat.

2. Heat 1 tablespoon oil in large enameled Dutch oven. Add meat and brown over medium heat on one side. Scoop up with spatula and turn. Add remaining oil and minced ingredients. Stir and cook with meat until mixture browns lightly. Pour off any fat.

3. Combine Worcestershire sauce with tomato juice, wine, if desired, and ½ cup of stock. Pour around the sides of pot. Bring to a boil. Cover and bake in center section of oven for 30 minutes. Turn and baste. Re-cover and bake for 1 hour longer, turning and basting every 20 minutes. (Add some of the remaining stock if liquid evaporates before baking is completed.) Stir salt into sauce; then spoon over meat.

4. Serve on warmed individual plates sprinkled with basil or dill.

Yield: 6 servings

Serving suggestions: Yam and Cabbage Tzimmes (page 140) or Carrot/Date Condiment (page 182).

Lamb with Dates   *(Meat)*

This dish is inspired by ancient Hebrew cookery, which mixed ground meat with sweet fruits. Served with just-cooked couscous and steamed peas, and garnished with sliced fresh fruit, it makes a presentation as handsome to look at as it is delicious to taste.

½ cup loosely packed soft bread crumbs (see note)
2 tablespoons frozen orange juice concentrate
¼ cup kosher fruity white or red wine
1¼ pounds extra-lean ground lamb
½ teaspoon each ground cumin, allspice and mild curry powder, combined
½ cup minced red onion
¾ cup peeled and minced green apple

16 pitted dates, coarsely chopped
2 tablespoons minced fresh coriander
2 tablespoons unbleached flour
2 tablespoons Italian olive oil
½ cup Chicken Stock
2–3 tablespoons fresh lemon juice
¼ teaspoon salt
Freshly ground black pepper
Sliced oranges or mangoes
Grapes

1. Put crumbs in medium bowl. Combine concentrate with wine; pour over bread, mashing until smooth. Let stand for a minute or two.

Blend with meat, half the seasonings, half the onion, ¼ cup apple, ¼ cup dates and 1 tablespoon coriander. Using a rounded tablespoon of mixture for each part, shape into 16 firm balls.

2. Sprinkle flour across flat plate. Roll balls in flour, shaking off excess.

3. Heat 1½ tablespoons oil in large nonstick skillet until quite hot. Add meat and sauté over medium-high heat until lightly browned. Carefully turn and brown balls all over (about 7 minutes). Using a slotted spoon, transfer meat to a plate; pour off all liquid from skillet.

4. Add remaining ½ tablespoon oil to skillet. Sauté remaining onion until lightly browned. Stir in remaining apple and cook for 1 minute. Add all the remaining seasonings (except salt), balance of dates and coriander, stock and 2 tablespoons lemon juice. Bring to simmering point and cook for 1 minute. Return meat to skillet, spooning with hot sauce. Cover, regulate heat to a constant simmer and cook for 40 minutes, basting twice at equal intervals. Sprinkle with salt and stir. Remove from heat. Taste sauce; stir in remaining lemon juice, if desired. Re-cover and let stand for 5 minutes. Arrange on warmed platter. Sprinkle with pepper and garnish with fresh fruit.

Yield: 5 servings

Variation: Add ¼ cup ground blanched almonds in step 1.

Note: Your selection of bread will influence the flavor of the finished dish. Sour Rye Bread (page 168) is particularly tasty. For quick crumbs, remove bread crusts, cut into 1-inch cubes and use your food processor fitted with steel blade to process into crumbs.

Kibbeh (Meat)

This is my lighter version of one of Israel's more popular street-stand foods.

FOR THE SHELL:
1 cup bulgur (pre-cooked wheat)
1 cup red or brown lentils
¼ cup each coarsely chopped walnuts and unhulled sesame seeds*
¼ cup each minced onion and shallot
½ teaspoon each cinnamon, allspice, ground coriander, cumin and salt, or 1 tablespoon Spice Mix
¼ teaspoon freshly ground black pepper
⅛ teaspoon cayenne pepper
1 tablespoon minced fresh coriander or parsley
About 3½ tablespoons unsweetened apple juice, chilled
½ cup dark seedless raisins
1 teaspoon sweet pareve margarine, plus 2 tablespoons, melted

FOR THE FILLING:
1 tablespoon Italian olive oil
1 pound extra-lean ground lamb or a mixture of lamb and beef
1 tablespoon minced garlic
½ cup minced onion
1 small carrot, peeled and finely minced or grated
¼ teaspoon each cinnamon, allspice, ground coriander, cumin and salt, or 2 teaspoons Spice Mix
2 tablespoons minced fresh coriander or parsley

*Unhulled sesame seeds are available in health food stores.

1. Prepare shell first. Soak bulgur in water to cover for 2 hours. Pour into strainer, pressing out all liquid. Transfer to a bowl and set aside.

2. Put lentils in a strainer. Pick over and rinse well. Transfer to a 2-quart heavy-bottomed saucepan. Add enough water to cover. Soak for 30 minutes. Drain. Put lentils back into saucepan. Add fresh water to cover and bring to boil. Remove from heat. Cover and let stand for 1 hour. Repeat draining and water-replenishing procedure. Bring to a boil again; reduce heat to simmering. Partially cover and simmer until lentils are tender (about 20 minutes). Drain well. Set aside.

3. Spread nuts and sesame seeds across a heated nonstick skillet. Lightly toast mixture, shaking skillet around every few seconds. Pour into workbowl of food processor that has been fitted with steel blade. Preheat oven to 375°F.

4. To complete shell, measure out 2 cups each firmly packed cooked lentils and bulgur and place in workbowl with seeds and nuts. Add onion, shallot, seasonings and coriander or parsley. With machine running, pour 2 tablespoons apple juice through feed tube, adding enough of remaining juice, if necessary, to make a thick paste-like mixture. Scrape into bowl. Stir in raisins. Set aside.

5. To prepare filling, heat oil over moderate heat in large nonstick skillet. Add meat(s), spreading across skillet. Sprinkle with garlic, onion, carrot, seasonings and coriander or parsley. Combine mixture and sauté until meat gives up its raw look, breaking up chunks with large spoon. Cooking is completed when mixture is moist with no visible liquid remaining in pan.

6. To assemble, grease an 8- or 9-inch square baking pan or ovenproof dish. Spoon half the shell mixture into the pan, spreading out evenly. Arrange meat mixture over shell. Top with remaining shell mixture, smoothing out top.

7. With thin moistened knife, make 2 evenly spaced cuts in mixture; then make 3 perpendicular evenly spaced cuts (there will be 12 squares). Or, after first 2 cuts, cut each section into 12 triangular pieces. Spoon equally with melted margarine. Bake until lightly brown (about 40 minutes). Transfer pan to a wire rack and let stand for 5 minutes before serving.

Yield: 6 servings

Tongue with Juniper Berry Sauce (Meat)

Just the right balance of sweet and sour is achieved with a novel sauce based on slightly sweet juniper berries and raisins, and oven-baking rather than top-of-the-stove simmering. A choice Rosh Hashanah (New Year's) dish, sweet-and-sour tongue is a delicacy you can enjoy any time you feel festive.

2 large fresh veal or lamb tongues
1 large bay leaf
1 tablespoon Italian olive oil
½ cup each minced shallot, green bell pepper and carrot
1 tablespoon Spice Mix
1 cup kosher fruity white wine
1 cup Chicken Stock
1 cup unsalted tomato juice
½ lemon, pitted and cut into thin slices
¼ cup firmly packed dark

brown sugar
1 tablespoon crushed juniper berries
6 sprigs parsley, 1 small bay leaf and ¼ teaspoon dried thyme wrapped in doubled piece of washed cotton cheesecloth and tied with white cotton thread
¼ teaspoon salt
¼ cup dark seedless raisins
1 tablespoon yellow cornmeal
2 tablespoons minced parsley

1. Preheat oven to 350°F. Wash tongues. Place in a large enameled Dutch oven. Cover with water and bring to a boil. Add bay leaf and boil for 3 minutes. Remove tongues and rinse under cold running water. Discard contents of pot; wash out and dry.

2. Heat oil over moderate heat in the pot. Add minced ingredients; sprinkle with Spice Mix. Sauté without browning until mixture begins to soften (about 4 minutes). Stir in wine and stock; bring to a boil. Then add tomato juice, lemon, sugar, juniper berries and parsley bundle. Cook until mixture boils. Immerse tongues in sauce, turning several times to coat. Cover, reduce heat to low and cook for 10 minutes. Baste and turn tongues.

3. Position oven rack to lower third of oven. Place Dutch oven on rack and bake for 1 hour. Turn and baste tongues. Re-cover and bake for 45 minutes longer, or until tender when tip of knife inserts easily into meat. Uncover and let cool for 10 minutes.

4. Skin tongues and cut away gristle and fatty section. Pour sauce into a fine sieve, pressing juices into a saucepan. Place saucepan over medium heat with salt and raisins; slow-boil for 5 minutes.

5. Put cornmeal into a cup. Gradually stir in ¼ cup of the hot sauce. When mixture is smooth, pour it back into the saucepan and stir continually until sauce thickens.

6. Cut tongue into ¼-inch slices and immerse in sauce. Simmer for 10 minutes before serving. Portion out on warmed individual plates sprinkled with parsley.

Yield: 6 servings as a first course; 4 servings as a main course

Serving suggestion: Arrange sliced tongue over a bed of just-cooked Buckwheat Farfel (page 131), noodles or rice.

Moussaka (New Style) *(Meat)*

This eggplant-meat dish comes to contemporary American Jewish cookery via Greece (its country of origin), the Middle East and Israel. Usually casserole-baked, it is served as a hearty one-dish meal. In my version, herbs and spices (including my ever-ready Spice Mix) usurp salt; and another of my Ready Access concoctions, Mushroom-Tomato Sauce, replaces fat-laden béchamel.

1¼ cups Chicken Stock
½ teaspoon whole saffron
2 tablespoons minced parsley
⅔ cup pre-cooked whole-wheat couscous*
2 medium eggplants (about 1½ pounds), ends trimmed, well scrubbed
2 tablespoons Italian olive oil

¼ cup minced shallots
1 teaspoon minced fresh ginger
1 tablespoon Spice Mix
¾ pound extra-lean ground lamb, beef or veal
3 cups Tomato-Mushroom Sauce
1 tablespoon fresh lemon juice

*Available in health food stores and some supermarkets.

1. Put stock into a saucepan. Bring to a boil. Stir in saffron, 1 tablespoon parsley, and couscous. Return to a boil. Remove from heat and stir. Cover and let stand for 20 minutes. Then fluff with a fork.

2. Cut eggplants lengthwise into 4 equal sections. Then cut crosswise into thin slices by hand. Or fit a food processor with slicing blade and thin-slice, using light pressure.

3. Heat 1 tablespoon oil in a large nonstick skillet. Spread shallots and ginger across skillet and cook without stirring over medium-high heat for 1 minute. Add eggplant; stir to combine. Sprinkle in half the Spice Mix and sauté until volume reduces by half, stirring every few seconds. Add remaining parsley. Turn into a bowl. Preheat oven to 350°F.

4. Heat remaining oil in skillet until quite hot. Add meat and sauté over medium-high heat for 3 minutes, breaking up pieces with a large spoon. Sprinkle in remaining seasoning and continue cooking only until meat gives up its raw look (about 3 minutes). Pour off any exuded fat.

5. Put sauce into a saucepan and heat to simmering point. Stir in lemon juice. Lightly grease an ovenproof 2-quart casserole with sweet pareve margarine or olive oil. Using ¼ of each ingredient at a time, arrange ingredients in layers by spooning them into the casserole in the following sequence: eggplant mixture, couscous, meat and sauce, finishing with sauce. Bowl will be filled to the top.

6. Cover tightly with heavy-duty aluminum foil. Bake in center section of oven for 45 minutes. Remove foil and loosely re-cover. Return to oven for 15 minutes. Uncover completely and bake for 30 minutes more. Cooking is complete when top of casserole is nicely browned. Place on a trivet and serve directly from casserole.

Yield: 6 servings

Serving suggestions: Carrot Salad (page 159) and Crusty Italian Bread (page 170).

Veal Hòrs d'Oeuvre   *(Meat)*

Pierce these dainty veal balls with cocktail picks or convert to a majestic stuffing for Breast of Veal (page 89).

4 crisp scallions, tough ends
   removed
2 large cloves garlic
1 rib celery
1 small carrot, ends trimmed,
   peeled
5 teaspoons Italian olive oil
3 tablespoons kasha (whole
   toasted buckwheat groats)
¼ cup Chicken Stock

½ pound extra-lean boneless
   veal
1 teaspoon minced lemon zest
1 tablespoon minced fresh dill
¼ teaspoon each ground ginger
   and cinnamon
⅛ teaspoon salt
1 tablespoon egg white
⅓ cup dry sherry

1. Mince first 4 ingredients by hand, or cut the ingredients for a food processor and mince in workbowl that has been fitted with steel blade, taking care not to puree.

2. Heat 2 teaspoons oil in a small nonstick skillet until hot. Over moderate heat, sauté minced ingredients until they just begin to brown. Add kasha. Stir and sauté for 1 minute. Pour stock around the sides of pan. Bring to a boil. Reduce heat to simmering. Cover and cook for 3 minutes. Transfer to the workbowl of food processor or spoon into a food grinder.

3. Cut meat into 1-inch pieces. Add to food processor or grinder with lemon zest, dill, spices, salt and egg white. If using food processor, process until finely chopped to pâté consistency; if using a grinder, select smallest blade and grind into a bowl; then stir in egg white. Chill mixture for 15 minutes. Shape into 22 or 23 balls.

4. Spread remaining oil across a large nonstick skillet and heat until quite hot. Add balls and cook over medium heat, until lightly brown all over, rolling from time to time to brown evenly.

5. Pour sherry around sides of skillet. When it boils, tilt pan from side to side; then gently combine with meat. Cook until all liquid evaporates (about 2 minutes). Serve hot, pierced with uncolored cocktail picks.

Yield: 6 servings

Serving suggestions: Garnish with low-sodium gherkins; or serve as a first course on a plate with Cucumber and Onion Salad (page 158).

Stuffed Breast of Veal   (Meat)

This is my version of a wonderful dish that once was on virtually every New York Hungarian Jewish restaurant menu. Make the following modifications and it becomes the centerpiece of a festive Passover meal: Replace the veal/kasha stuffing with Matzoh Stuffing (page 124) and substitute potato starch for cornmeal. Bonus: Breast of veal is still one of the most economical cuts of meat.

*1 recipe Veal Hors d'Oeuvre
(page 88)
1 5-pound breast of veal
2/3 cup dry sherry
1 tablespoon frozen orange juice
concentrate
8 cloves, crushed
1/2 teaspoon dried dill weed
2 large cloves garlic, minced
1 large onion, minced
1 tablespoon Italian olive oil
1/2 cup Chicken Stock*

*6 sprigs parsley, 1 bay leaf and
1/4 teaspoon dried thyme
leaves wrapped in doubled
piece of rinsed cotton
cheesecloth and tied with
white cotton thread
1/2 cup unsalted tomato juice
1/4 teaspoon salt
1 tablespoon cornmeal dissolved
in 1 tablespoon water
Minced parsley or dill*

1. Prepare the stuffing by making the hors d'oeuvre recipe through step 3, without shaping into balls. Set aside.

2. When buying the meat, have the butcher cut through the bone to allow 6 servings of meat that can be easily cut through. Also have a pocket cut into the meat, taking care that only one end is left open for stuffing. Trim off any fat from the bone. Then prick all over with a sharp-pronged fork.

3. In a small bowl make a marinade by combining ¼ cup sherry, concentrate, cloves, dill, garlic and half the onion. Lay out a long sheet of heavy-duty aluminum foil. Put meat in the center. Spoon some of the marinade into the pocket; pour the balance over the meat. Turn several times to coat. Fold up sides and ends to make a secure package. Turn upside down several times. Let marinate in refrigerator for 2 hours; then at room temperature for 30 minutes.

4. Drain meat, reserving marinade. Fill pocket with stuffing. Sew up or secure opening with thin skewers and white string. Preheat oven to 325°F.

5. Heat oil in a large enameled Dutch oven. Over medium-high heat, brown meat lightly on both sides (about 5 minutes). Add remaining sherry, remaining onion, stock, reserved marinade and parsley bundle. Bring to a boil. Turn meat so that fleshy side is down. Reduce heat to simmering. Cover and simmer over very low heat for 5 minutes. Position oven rack to lower third of oven. Place pot in center. Bake for 1 hour.

6. Turn meat and baste. Re-cover and bake for 30 minutes. Stir in tomato juice and baste. Re-cover and bake for 20 minutes longer. Ladle 1 cup of the gravy into a heavy-bottomed saucepan and set aside. Return meat, uncovered, to the oven and bake for 30 minutes longer, basting twice at equal intervals. Place meat on a carving board; tent with foil to keep warm.

7. Pour any residue gravy from pot into the saucepan, and bring to a slow-boil. Stir in salt. Dribble in cornmeal mixture. Stir and cook over low heat until lightly thickened.

8. Cut meat into 6 serving pieces. Arrange on individual warmed serving plates. Spoon some gravy over and around each serving. Sprinkle with parsley or dill.

Yield: 6 servings

Serving suggestions: Carrot Salad (page 159) or Salad with 2 Herbs (page 160).

Potted Shoulder of Veal

(Meat)

If there is one dish that's indisputably American Jewish, it's (beef) pot roast. This potted shoulder of veal is a light alternative. Imbued with a braising mixture of seasonings, wine and fruit juice, it has a new and enticing taste. A pot roast with sophistication!

⅓ cup each fresh orange juice and unsweetened pineapple juice
½ teaspoon each cinnamon, chili con carne seasoning and dried rosemary, crushed
2¾–3 pounds boned and rolled veal shoulder (5 inches in diameter)
2 tablespoons, plus 2 teaspoons Seasoned Olive Oil
1 cup combined minced shallot and onion
1 tablespoon minced garlic
2 medium green bell peppers, seeded, cut into ¼-inch strips

1 cup each kosher dry white wine and Chicken Stock
6 sprigs parsley, ¼ teaspoon dried thyme and 1 bay leaf wrapped in doubled piece of cotton cheesecloth and tied with white cotton thread
¾ pound snow-white fresh mushrooms, ends trimmed, damp-wiped, thin-sliced
¼ teaspoon salt
1 tablespoon cornstarch dissolved in 1 tablespoon water
Decoratively cut orange slices for garnish

1. In a large bowl, combine and blend juices with spices and rosemary. Rinse meat under hot running water and paper-dry. Prick all over with a sharp-pronged fork. Add to marinade, turning several times to coat. Cover and refrigerate for 4 hours, turning 2 or 3 times.

2. Preheat oven to 325°F. Drain meat, reserving marinade. Drain on paper toweling, patting lightly with paper. Heat 1 tablespoon oil over moderate heat in a large enamel-lined Dutch oven. Add meat and brown lightly all over (about 8 minutes). Transfer to a plate.

3. Add 1 tablespoon oil to the Dutch oven. Add shallot/onion mixture and garlic. Lightly brown, stirring continually (2 to 3 minutes). Stir in pepper. Sauté for 1 minute.

4. Nestle ingredients to the center of pot. Pour wine around sides. Raise heat. When liquid bubbles vigorously, combine with solids. Reduce heat slightly and cook, uncovered, until juices are reduced by half. Stir in stock, reserved marinade and parsley bundle. Bring to a boil.

5. Return meat to pot, turning several times to coat. Cover tightly and cook on top of stove for 3 minutes. Place in center section of oven and bake for 2 hours, turning and basting 3 times at equal intervals. Remove from oven and let stand, covered, for 20 minutes. Discard parsley bundle after pressing out juices.

6. Heat 2 teaspoons oil in a nonstick skillet until hot. Over medium-high heat, sauté mushrooms until lightly browned and no liquid remains in skillet. Stir into the sauce.

7. Put meat in a covered bowl, and sauce into a jar. Refrigerate overnight. Next day, cut meat into ¼-inch slices. Arrange in wide heavy-bottomed saucepan or nonstick skillet. Cut away any hardened fat from the top of the sauce. Put sauce into a saucepan. Add salt and slowly reheat without covering. Spoon ¼ of the sauce over the meat. Cover meat, and slowly reheat, basting from time to time.

8. Bring remaining sauce to a slow-boil; dribble in cornstarch mixture and cook until lightly thickened. Stir residue sauce from meat into saucepan. Arrange hot slices of meat on warmed serving platter. Garnish with orange slices. Spoon with some of the sauce; serve remainder in a sauceboat.

Yield: 6 servings

Serving suggestions: Potato Latkes (page 117).

VEAL CHOPS

My husband tells me that once when he was about eleven or twelve, he came home for lunch from the neighborhood school and found he had forgotten his key to the family apartment. So he clambered up five stories of a rickety and dangerous exterior fire-escape system to get into the apartment through an open window. My husband says, "I was scared stiff, but my mother had said there would be a fried veal chop waiting for me on the kitchen table, and scared as I was, I just had to get to it."

I, too, remember the appeal of fried veal chops, and recently I visited two Jewish New York restaurants to see whether the tradition had continued. In one restaurant, the veal chop was braised with a thick vegetable sauce. It was succulent and fatty. In another eatery, an Italian Jewish restaurant, the veal was scallopine-thin, deep-fried and topped with a moist salad.

My versions of those current American Jewish veal chops follow. My husband says he'd climb up the sides of buildings to get to *them*, too, even at his age!

Braised Veal Chops
with Cabbage
(Meat)

4 meaty ½-inch-thick shoulder
    veal chops (about 2 pounds),
    trimmed of all visible fat
1 tablespoon Spice Mix
1½ tablespoons Seasoned Olive
    Oil or Italian olive oil
1 cup finely minced onion
2 teaspoons minced garlic
1 teaspoon finely minced fresh
    ginger
2 tablespoons wine vinegar
1 cup fresh cranberries, rinsed
    and drained

2 cups finely minced cabbage
¾ cup each Chicken Stock and
    unsalted tomato juice,
    combined
2 medium yams, peeled, cut
    into ¾-inch cubes
4 sprigs parsley tied into a
    bundle with white cotton
    thread
¼ teaspoon salt
1 tablespoon honey
Minced parsley

1. Wash meat under hot running water; paper-dry. Sprinkle and rub all over with Spice Mix. Cover and refrigerate for 2 hours or longer.

2. Heat a large well-seasoned iron skillet with 1 tablespoon oil. When very hot, lightly brown chops over medium-high heat. Transfer to a plate.

3. Spread remaining oil across the skillet. Add onion, garlic and ginger and sauté until mixture starts to brown (about 3 minutes), stirring often. Nestle mixture to the center of the pan; pour vinegar around the sides. When it bubbles, stir to combine. Cook for 1 minute.

4. Preheat oven to 400°F. Transfer half the sautéed ingredients to a plate; spread the remainder across the skillet. Arrange the chops over it in one layer. Spread balance of sautéed ingredients over the chops. Cover with cranberries, then cabbage. Pour stock and tomato juice over all. Add yams and parsley bundle, pushing into juices. When liquid boils, spoon some over meat. Regulate heat to simmering. Cover and cook on top of stove for 20 minutes.

5. Turn chops and baste. Place in center section of oven; bake for 30 minutes. With paper toweling, blot any visible fat from sauce. Sprinkle with salt and drizzle with honey. Cover and return to oven for 10 minutes longer. Uncover, turn chops and baste. Re-cover and let stand for 10 minutes. Discard parsley bundle after pressing out juices.

6. Arrange meat on a warmed serving plate; cover to keep warm. If sauce is thin, turn up heat under skillet to reduce liquid. If the consistency is to your liking, simply reheat and spoon over and around meat. Sprinkle with parsley and serve at once.

Yield: 4 servings

Crisp Veal Chops
(Italian style)   *(Meat)*

A New York kosher restaurant recently featured crisp, crusty butterflied veal chops (they were deep-fried) topped with a mixed fresh vegetable salad—an unusual presentation.

4 thin-sliced, well-trimmed veal chops, flattened to ⅜ inch
¾ teaspoon dried mint
1 large egg (use ½ yolk and all the white)
1 teaspoon reduced-sodium soy sauce
2 tablespoons Chicken Stock or
dry sherry
½–¾ cup Matzoh Meal Mix
1 recipe Mixed Fresh Vegetable Salad (page 155) or Salad with 2 Herbs (page 160)
2½ tablespoons Italian olive oil
Lemon wedges

1. Wash meat under hot running water. Dry thoroughly with paper toweling. Sprinkle and rub all over with mint. Cover and refrigerate for 2 hours or longer. Preheat oven to 425°F.

2. In wide bowl, combine egg, soy sauce and stock or sherry. Beat with fork to blend. Sprinkle ¼ cup Matzoh Meal Mix across a sheet of wax paper. Dip meat in egg mixture; lift out, draining off excess liquid. Lay atop dry coating, pressing to adhere. Cover with enough of remaining coating to cover evenly, pressing again to adhere. Place in freezer for 20 minutes.

3. Prepare salad and salad dressing. Set both aside.

4. Pour oil into a metal broiling pan large enough to hold chops in one layer. Place pan (without chops) in center section of preheated oven for 10 minutes. Remove from oven and immediately fill with coated chops. Bake for 20 minutes. Turn and bake for 10 to 15 minutes longer (both sides should be nicely browned; baking time may vary with thickness and tenderness of meat). Drain on paper toweling.

5. Add salad dressing to salad and toss. Arrange chops on warmed individual serving plates. Top with portions of salad and garnish with lemon wedges.

Yield: 4 servings

7

FISH

Gefilte Fish

(Pareve)

I remember my grandmother clamping a grinder to a tabletop and laboriously grinding her fish mixture by hand. And there was a lot of it—for her nine children, her many grandchildren, and for her neighbors. She served her gefilte fish ice-cold with beet horseradish. It was wonderful! It was also worth all that grinding, she said.

But use the modern food processor properly and you can grind/chop a perfect mixture for gefilte fish much more rapidly than my grandmother. Follow my recipe—it's simple—and you can get a taste close to the original. I've subtracted Grandma's excessive salt and egg yolks and added spices and wine that make the taste even better than Grandma's—fresher, lighter, zestier. And to me and mine, irresistible.

Hint: If summer carp is unavailable, use 4½ pounds of combined whitefish and pike.

2 pounds each whitefish and pike
½ pound summer carp
4 medium onions (slice 3)
6 large shallots (slice 4)
2 ribs celery, sliced
4 medium carrots, peeled and sliced
1 medium parsnip, peeled and sliced
3 large sprigs parsley
¼ teaspoon each dried thyme and dill
4 2-inch slices lemon zest

1 cup kosher dry white wine
About 7 cups water
½ teaspoon each freshly grated nutmeg, ground ginger and ground white or black pepper
⅛ teaspoon cayenne pepper
1 teaspoon salt
Florets from 2 large sprigs parsley
4 large eggs (use 1 yolk and 4 whites), at room temperature
¼ cup cold fresh seltzer
3 to 4 tablespoons matzoh meal

1. Have fishmonger skin, bone and fillet fish, reserving bones and heads for broth in which fish will be simmered. For best results, the total net weight should be about 2¼ pounds. Rinse bones and heads. Put into a wide enamel-lined heavy Dutch oven. Add 3 sliced onions, 4 sliced shallots, celery, carrots, parsnip, parsley, herbs and lemon zest. Add wine and water. Bring to a boil. Reduce heat to simmering. Cover and cook for 1 hour. Using a fine sieve or a chinois, strain into a large bowl. Pick out some carrot slices and set aside. Then press out juices from solids. Discard solids. Pour broth back into pot and set aside.

2. Cut remaining onion into 1-inch pieces and shallots in half. Place in workbowl of food processor that has been fitted with steel blade. Rinse fish and paper-dry. Run fingers over fish and pull out any thin bones (there will be a few). Cut into 2-inch chunks. Add to workbowl with spices, ½ the salt, and parsley. Process until well chopped (about 30 seconds). Drop 1 whole egg and 1 egg white through feed tube. Let stand until step 3 is completed.

3. Drop remaining 2 egg whites into a mixing machine bowl. Beat until firm peaks form (do not overbeat). Set aside.

4. With processor running, pour seltzer through feed tube. Process for 15 seconds. Scrape mixture into a large bowl. Sprinkle with 3 table-spoons matzoh meal and blend. Fold in egg whites. Cover and chill in freezer for 15 minutes.

5. Bring broth to a boil. Add remaining ½ teaspoon salt. Using moist-ened hands and moistened spoon, shape chilled mixture into 12 ovals, lowering them into the hot broth as they're formed. (If mixture doesn't hold together sufficiently after chilling, fold in remaining ta-blespoon of matzoh meal.) Reduce heat to a steady slow-boil (a little hotter than simmering). Cover and cook for 45 minutes, spooning ovals with broth after they've cooked for 10 minutes. Each piece will puff up and rise to the top. Partially uncover and cool in pot for 30 minutes. Add reserved carrots to broth. Cover and refrigerate over-night; or carefully transfer each piece to container(s), pouring stock over all. Tightly cover and refrigerate. Broth will thicken when chilled. If you prefer jelled broth, add 1 package of pareve unflavored gelatin to boiling stock and dissolve granules before refrigerating.

Yield: 12 large servings

Note: A chinois is a conical sieve with tiny holes that is excellent for catching small bones and skin. If you don't have one, line a large strainer with a doubled piece of washed cotton cheesecloth and strain broth into a bowl, pressing out juices from solids.

Savory Poached Carp
(hot or jelled)
(Pareve)

The recent nutrition revolution has turned the spotlight on fish. But long before there was even a science of nutrition, Jewish families were reaping the health benefits of fish. One fish in particular stands out for its salubrious nutritional content—carp. It has all the right nutritional ingredients and none of the wrong ones.

In my contemporary recipe, carp is prepared with all the right cooking ingredients. Slightly sweet and slightly sour, they ameliorate the fish's authoritative flavor. Caveat: Carefully remove the many wishbone-shaped translucent bones before serving.

*2 medium red onions, minced
(about 1¼ cups)
¼ cup wine vinegar
¾ cup water
1½ cups Vegetable Stock
2 ribs celery, minced
1 large carrot, peeled and
minced
½ large lemon, seeded and*

*thin-sliced
2 tablespoons, plus 2 teaspoons
sugar
4 sprigs parsley tied into a
bundle with white cotton
thread
2½ pounds fresh carp, cut into
1-inch slices
Watercress sprigs*

1. Put onions, vinegar and ¼ cup water into a 3-quart heavy-bottomed saucepan or Dutch oven. Bring to a boil. Cook, uncovered, over medium heat until all liquid evaporates, stirring often.

2. Add remaining water, stock, celery, carrot, lemon, 2 tablespoons sugar, and parsley bundle. Bring to a boil. Reduce heat to slow-boil and cook, uncovered, for 5 minutes. Add fish. Bring liquid to boil and baste fish several times. Reduce heat to simmering. Cover and cook for 30 minutes. Uncover, raise heat slightly and slow-boil for 10 minutes longer.

3. With slotted spatula, transfer slices to plate. Discard skin. Pull out bones, separating large chunks of flesh to make bones visible. Spoon with a little of the hot poaching liquid. Cover to keep warm.

4. Strain contents of pot through a fine sieve. Rinse out pot and fill with strained broth. Stir in remaining sugar. Bring to a boil over high heat; reduce until about ¾ cup remains. Pour exuded liquid from fish into the pot.

5. To serve hot, portion individual servings onto warm plates and spoon with some of the poaching liquid. To serve jelled, arrange fish in a wide casserole in one layer. Pour poaching liquid over it. Cover tightly and chill overnight (poaching liquid will jell). Cut into serving pieces; garnish with watercress.

Yield: 4 servings as a main course; 6 servings as an appetizer

Serving suggestion: Fresh Horseradish with Beets (page 180).

Mock Chopped Herring Hors d'Oeuvre *(Pareve)*

My parents used to play a can-you-guess-what-it-is? game with guests whenever this mixture was served. "Mmmm-mmm—" the first-timers would declare, "such delicious herring salad!" But it wasn't. It was canned skinless and boneless sardines packed in oil—highly salted, of course. This version, with less fat and salt, still carries a distinctive taste. For a charming conversation piece, spread it on bread, roll it up and slice it into pinwheels. Or make it for lunch piled into crisp lettuce cups. A delicious light starter that makes any meal special.

3 large hard-cooked eggs (use 1½ yolks and 3 whites)
1 4¼-ounce water-packed can unsalted skinless and boneless sardines
1½ tablespoons fresh lemon juice
½ teaspoon curry powder
2 tablespoons reduced-calorie mayonnaise, plus 1½ teaspoons

1 teaspoon prepared unsalted Dijon mustard
¼ cup well-drained jarred India relish or sweet relish
3 tablespoons finely minced red onion
11 ⅜-inch slices Challah or good quality white bread
Paprika
Chopped sweet red pepper

1. Place egg yolks and whites in a bowl and mash to fine consistency. Drain sardines, reserving 1 teaspoon of liquid; add both to eggs and mash. In cup combine and blend lemon juice, curry powder, 2 tablespoons mayonnaise, mustard, relish and onion. Stir into sardine mixture.

2. Cut away crusts from bread. Tear 1 slice into small pieces and crumble by hand; or tear into chunks and reduce to fine crumbs in food processor that has been fitted with steel blade. Stir crumbs into mixture.

3. Roll out remaining 10 slices of bread until very thin, taking care not to tear. Overlap the edge of one slice over the edge of another, "sealing" with a dab of remaining mayonnaise and pressing with rolling pin to adhere. Put about 3 tablespoons of filling in center of bread, spreading lengthwise and allowing ½-inch borders on all sides. Roll up, securing ends with another dab of mayonnaise. Repeat procedure with balance of bread. Place roll-ups in one layer on plate and stand in freezer for 15 minutes.

4. With sharp serrated knife and minimum pressure, cut each roll-up into 5 equal slices. Lay slices, cut side up, on serving plate. Lightly sprinkle with paprika. Spoon some red pepper in center of each pinwheel.

Yield: 5 servings; recipe may be doubled

Baked Fish
Mousse Balls *(Pareve)*

Scrod, a young cod, retains its firm consistency when ground with an amalgam of seasonings and egg whites, then baked in a tangy pool of Mushroom-Tomato Sauce.

*2 slices Challah or good quality
   commercial white bread,
   crusts removed
¼ cup tightly packed parsley
   florets
2 pounds fresh scrod fillet
2 large egg whites
3 large shallots, quartered
¼ teaspoon each salt, freshly*

*grated nutmeg and ground
   sage
⅛ teaspoon cayenne pepper
1½ teaspoons white wine
   Worcestershire sauce
2 tablespoons fresh lemon juice
2 cups Mushroom-Tomato
   Sauce*

1. Preheat oven to 325°F. Fit food processor with steel blade. Tear bread into chunks and process with parsley in 3 on/off turns.

2. Rinse and dry fish. Probe for residue curved bones by running fingers horizontally over fillets. Cut into chunks and add to workbowl. Then add remaining ingredients, except sauce, and process for 10 seconds. Pour 3 tablespoons sauce through feed tube and process for 4 seconds. Shape into 12 balls.

3. Spread ¼ cup sauce across bottom of a 2-quart ovenproof casserole. Add a layer of fish balls. Spoon with some sauce. Add remaining balls; then top with balance of sauce. Bake, uncovered, in center section of oven for 45 minutes, basting every 15 minutes. Remove from oven and baste. Cover and let stand for 5 minutes before serving.

Yield: 6 servings

Serving suggestion: 5-Fruit Kugel (page 121).

Layered Fish
(A One-Dish Meal) *(Dairy or Pareve)*

This is a New American Jewish creation that echoes a culinary concept that is virtually as old as the Jewish people. Layered foods are a variant of stuffed foods; and in Jewish gastronomic symbolism, both stand for abundance.

But this edifice of fish, vegetables and tasteful seasonings is abundant in fact as well as symbol. It is, although calorie-restrained, a satisfying whole meal. And, in these busy, busy days, that's a mitzvah (a boon) for the cook.

1½ pounds fillet of brook trout, rainbow trout or red snapper, skinned
3 tablespoons fresh lemon juice
1 pound red-skinned potatoes
¾ cup unsalted Italian tomato puree
¼ cup water
½ cup dry vermouth or dry white wine
¾ teaspoon sugar
3 tablespoons minced fresh coriander, or 2 teaspoons

minced fresh rosemary
1½ tablespoons each Italian olive oil and sweet butter/margarine blend or sweet pareve margarine
2 medium onions, minced
3 large cloves garlic, minced
1 medium green bell pepper, seeded, cut into ¼-inch strips
3 tablespoons cornstarch
¾ teaspoon each ground ginger and dry mustard
¼ teaspoon salt

1. Run fingers over fish in both directions to locate and discard residue small bones. Cut each fillet in half crosswise. Place in a bowl. Sprinkle with lemon juice and let stand for 30 minutes. Preheat oven to 400°F.

2. Half-cook potatoes in rapidly boiling water. Drain, cool and peel. Cut into ⅜-inch slices.

3. In saucepan, combine tomato puree, water, vermouth or wine, sugar and half the coriander or rosemary. Over low heat, simmer, uncovered, for 5 minutes.

4. Heat ½ tablespoon each of the oil and shortening in a nonstick skillet. Over medium-high heat, sauté onions, garlic and green pepper until onions turn light brown. Transfer mixture to a dish.

5. Combine cornstarch with spices and salt in a cup. Then spread across a sheet of wax paper. Drain fillets and coat them with mixture. Put the remaining oil and shortening in a dish. Sauté fillets in batches over medium-high heat for 30 seconds on each side, dividing shortening mixture between batches, reserving about a teaspoon to grease a 2-quart ovenproof casserole.

6. Arrange ingredients in layers in casserole as follows: half the potatoes, half the fish, half the onion mixture. Repeat procedure with remaining ingredients; then lightly compress with spatula. Slowly pour heated sauce around sides of casserole (there should be enough to barely cover solids; if not, add a bit more water). Cover tightly with a sheet of aluminum foil. Bake for 25 minutes. Uncover and bake for 10 minutes longer. Sprinkle with remaining coriander or rosemary. Place on a trivet and serve at the table.

Yield: 4 servings

Variations:

1. Substitute 1 cup Mushroom-Tomato Sauce for tomato puree and eliminate green pepper and sugar.

2. Soak ½ teaspoon whole saffron in 1 tablespoon boiling water for 10 minutes. Add to sauce in step 3.

Serving suggestion: Coleslaw (page 157).

Poached Lemon Sole with Horseradish Sauce   *(Dairy)*

What poupon mustard is to TV-commercial gourmets, horseradish is to the devotees of traditional American Jewish cookery: the ubiquitous seasoning. Here, for example, it pops up in a sauce for poached lemon sole, adding a gourmet *je ne sais quoi* to what otherwise might be a dish *très ordinaire*.

Although the recipe is foolproof, the success of the dish depends on three elementary precautions: Have your side dishes ready before completing the sauce; use the freshest fish you can get; and be sure your container of prepared horseradish has not been opened previously.

FOR THE FISH AND POACHING BROTH:
¾ *cup coarsely chopped onion*
1½ *tablespoons minced fresh ginger*
2 *ribs celery, coarsely chopped*
1¼ *cups kosher dry white wine*
1 *cup water*
4 *sprigs parsley tied into a bundle with white cotton thread*
½ *teaspoon well-crushed coriander seed (not ground)*
½ *large lemon*

1 *teaspoon sugar*
1½ *pounds fillet of lemon sole*
FOR THE SAUCE:
3½ *tablespoons reduced-fat cream cheese (Neufchâtel), at room temperature*
1 *teaspoon prepared horseradish*
1 *teaspoon potato starch dissolved in 2 teaspoons water*
¼ *teaspoon salt*
2 *teaspoons minced parsley*

1. Put first 7 ingredients in wide heavy-bottomed saucepan or skillet. Cut lemon segments with curved serrated grapefruit knife; discard seeds and add to medley. Bring to a boil; reduce heat to simmering. Cover and simmer for 30 minutes (may be prepared several hours ahead, refrigerated and reheated). Stir in sugar.

2. Arrange fish in pot, spooning several times with poaching mixture. Bring to a boil; reduce heat to simmering. Cover and simmer for 8 to 10 minutes (cooking time will vary with thickness of fish). Carefully transfer fish to a warmed plate; cover to keep warm.

3. Discard parsley bundle after pressing out juices. Pour contents of pot into a blender or food processor that has been fitted with steel blade. Add cream cheese and horseradish. Blend to a puree. Pour back into pot and heat until simmering (do not boil). While whisking, dribble in potato starch mixture. Stir in salt, exuded juices from fish and parsley. Whisk and cook until lightly thickened. Remove from heat.

4. Spoon 2 tablespoons sauce onto each of 4 warmed serving plates. Arrange fish over sauce. Serve remaining sauce in sauceboat.

Yield: 4 servings

Serving suggestions: Potato Latkes (page 117), Cucumber and Onion Salad (page 158).

Salmon & Rice Croquettes (or strudel) (Pareve)

Despite the small amount of salmon, its unique flavor still comes through in this "tzimmes" of ingredients. I've used unsalted canned salmon (the standard variety is oversalted) and combined it with seasoned cooked rice (the capers supply a reasonable amount of salt to point up flavor). Matzoh Meal Mix, with its cornucopia of seasonings, gives these croquettes their special taste.

1¼ cups water	*drained capers*
1 tablespoon white wine Worcestershire sauce	*1 tablespoon prepared unsalted Dijon mustard*
⅓ cup raw rice	*1 large egg*
2 3¼-ounce cans unsalted blueback salmon or equivalent large can	*⅛ teaspoon cayenne pepper*
	About 3 tablespoons Matzoh Meal Mix
3 tablespoons fresh lemon juice	*1½ tablespoons peanut oil or Italian olive oil*
¾ cup minced onion	*Lemon wedges*
½ cup finely minced carrot	
3 tablespoons rinsed and	

1. Bring water and Worcestershire sauce to a rolling boil in a heavy-bottomed saucepan; stir in rice. Reduce heat to simmering, cover and cook until all water is absorbed (18 to 20 minutes), stirring once. Fluff with a fork and let cool for 10 minutes. Measure out 1 cup for recipe, refrigerating or freezing the balance for another recipe.

2. Put salmon and juices in a bowl. Discard any skin (there will be very little) and mash. Stir in 1 cup cooked rice and lemon juice. Then add onion, carrot and capers.

3. In cup, combine mustard with egg and cayenne pepper, beating with fork to blend. Stir into salmon mixture. Fold in 2 tablespoons Matzoh Meal Mix; let it stand for 2 to 3 minutes, until it's absorbed. Fold in remainder, if necessary, to make a mixture that holds together and can be shaped into croquettes. Cover and chill for 20 minutes.

4. Shape into 5 croquettes. Spread half the oil across a large nonstick skillet and heat until very hot. Over medium-high heat, cook croquettes until browned on one side (about 4 minutes). Pour remaining oil around the sides of skillet. Turn croquettes and brown on second side. Garnish with lemon wedges.

Yield: 5 servings

Serving suggestions: Mushroom-Tomato Sauce (page 30), Spicy Tomato Sauce (page 186).

Variation: Salmon and Rice Strudel: Preheat oven to 375°F. Make dough wrapper from Chicken/Kasha Strudel (page 114), following instructions through step 2. Cut into 2 pieces, wrap in plastic film and chill for 30 minutes. Sprinkle work surface lightly with flour. Roll out each piece of dough to about a 12- × -16-inch rectangle, flipping it over once and letting it rest when it pulls back. Make a mixture of 1½ tablespoons each peanut oil and melted sweet pareve margarine. Lightly brush dough with some of the mixture, reserving enough to brush over 2 strudels when rolled up. Spoon half the filling along short edge of dough, allowing a ½-inch margin on 3 sides. Press mixture into a smooth compact cylinder. Using spatula, lift up short edge, roll dough over filling and continue rolling over twice more. Tuck in sides; then finish rolling. Transfer to a lightly oiled jelly-roll pan. Brush with oil mixture. Bake in center section of oven until delicately browned (about 40 minutes). Serve with Lemon Sauce (page 185) or alternate serving suggestions.

Sautéed Flounder (Dairy or Pareve)

Two flounder recipes that show off the adaptability of this popular flatfish. The recipe that follows is a quick-to-make update of the simply prepared flounder of my childhood. The next is a New American Jewish version of a Sephardic-style stuffed fish with dates. Both recipes are on the sweet side, broadening your cooking horizons.

1½ pounds flounder fillets, cut into 4 serving pieces
3 tablespoons each fresh lemon juice and pineapple juice
1 large egg yolk
3 tablespoons milk or water
⅔ cup matzoh meal (see note)
¼ teaspoon each sugar, ground cumin and coriander
2 teaspoons each ground ginger

and crushed dried rosemary
2 tablespoons Italian olive oil, sweet butter/margarine blend or pareve margarine
¼ cup minced shallot
¼ cup dry or sweet sherry or kosher sweet white wine
¼ teaspoon salt
Lemon wedges

1. Rinse fish under cold running water; drain on paper toweling and wipe dry. Whisk juices together in wide bowl. Add fish to marinate for 1 hour.

2. In another bowl, whisk egg yolk with milk or water. In a cup, make a mix of matzoh meal, sugar, spices and rosemary. Spread half across a sheet of wax paper. Drain fish and partially dry. Dip into egg mixture, draining off excess; then lay on matzoh medley. Sprinkle fish with remaining dry ingredients, pressing to adhere. Place in freezer for 10 minutes.

3. Use a large nonstick skillet that will accommodate the 4 servings without crowding (or use 2 pans, dividing the oil and shallots). Heat oil until quite hot. Add shallots and sauté over medium-high heat for 30 seconds. Then spread them across the skillet. Arrange fillets atop shallots and cook until browned. Carefully turn and brown on second side.

4. Pour sherry or wine around the sides of pan. When it bubbles, tilt pan from side to side. Cook for 30 seconds; turn fish and cook for 30 seconds longer. Sprinkle with salt; garnish with lemon wedges. Serve hot or cold.

Yield: 4 servings

Serving suggestions: Carrot Salad (page 159), 5-Fruit Kugel (page 121).

Note: Use fine matzoh meal. If the product you have on hand is coarse, pour it into a blender or processor fitted with steel knife and briefly process until fine.

Flounder Paupiettes with Fennel and Dates

(Pareve or Dairy)

FOR THE MOUSSE:
½ teaspoon sugar
4 dried dates, halved
½ small fennel bulb (about 4 inches across), cut into 1-inch pieces
2 large shallots, quartered
½ pound thin flounder or grey sole fillets, cut into 1½-inch pieces
1 teaspoon prepared Dijon mustard, preferably unsalted
1 teaspoon unsalted tomato paste
¼ teaspoon freshly grated nutmeg
Dash cayenne pepper
Florets from 3 sprigs parsley
1 large egg white
FOR THE FISH AND SAUCE:
1½ pounds thin fillets of grey sole or flounder (4 or 5 fillets)
1¼ teaspoons dried rosemary,

crushed
¼ teaspoon freshly grated nutmeg
1 medium onion, cut into 1-inch pieces
Remaining ½ fennel, cut into 1-inch pieces
4 dried pitted dates, cut into thirds, lengthwise, and thin-sliced
¾ cup Israeli chardonnay (Gamla) or kosher dry white wine
1 teaspoon unsalted tomato paste
2 teaspoons cold sweet pareve margarine or sweet butter/margarine blend
¼ teaspoon salt
2 teaspoons cornstarch dissolved in 2 teaspoons water
2 tablespoons fine-chopped blanched almonds, toasted

1. To prepare the mousse, fit workbowl of food processor with steel blade. Add sugar, dates and fennel. Coarse-chop in 3 or 4 on/off turns. Add remaining ingredients and process for about 10 seconds. Mixture should be coarse-chopped (do not puree to a paste). Scrape into a bowl and chill for 30 minutes.

2. Wash fish under cold running water and dry well with paper toweling. In cup, combine rosemary with nutmeg. Sprinkle and rub mixture on both sides of fish. Put 2 rounded tablespoons of mousse in the center of each fillet. Fold over each end and secure firmly with toothpicks. Make 1½-inch balls from any remaining mousse. Preheat oven to 400°F.

3. Grease a 2-quart casserole with sweet pareve margarine. Put onion and fennel in workbowl of food processor and coarse-chop. Strew half the onion mixture and half the dates across casserole. Place paupiettes over mixture (in one layer, if possible). Add mousse balls. Strew remaining onion mixture and dates over all. Whisk wine and tomato paste until smooth and pour into casserole. Cover tightly with sheet of heavy-duty aluminum foil and bake for 40 minutes, if fish is at room temperature, and 45 minutes if it's chilled.

4. Using 2 tablespoons, carefully transfer paupiettes and balls to a warmed bowl and cover. Complete sauce by straining casserole juices and solids into a small heavy-bottomed saucepan. To saucepan add shortening and salt; cook over medium heat until simmering. Whisk in cornstarch mixture, a little at a time, adding enough to make a lightly thickened, smooth sauce. Pour exuded juices from fish into the saucepan and stir. Serve paupiettes and mousse balls on warmed individual plates, spooned with sauce and sprinkled with toasted almonds.

Yield: 4 or 5 servings as a main course; 8 servings as a first course

Halibut with Vegetable Marmalade (Pareve or Dairy)

"**A** meal in Israel would not be complete without vegetables and/or a vegetable salad," a visiting Israeli once revealed to me. She went on to say she often prepared a mélange of seasonal vegetables with onions, leeks or scallions and cooked them down to the consistency of a thick sauce. I remembered our conversation when I fashioned this vegetable sauce to complement the quick-sautéed fish. Saffron is added to unite the flavors.

½ teaspoon whole saffron
4–5 halibut steaks (1½ pounds)
2 tablespoons fresh lemon juice
2½ tablespoons Italian olive oil, sweet pareve margarine or sweet butter/margarine blend
1 teaspoon minced fresh ginger
1½ cups combined coarsely chopped onion and shallot
1 small red bell pepper, seeded, cut into ¼-inch strips

½ pound well-scrubbed zucchini, ends trimmed, coarsely chopped
½ teaspoon each ground marjoram and allspice
2 large ripe tomatoes, skinned, seeded, coarsely chopped
1½ cups Vegetable Stock
½ cup kosher dry white wine
3 tablespoons unbleached flour
¼ teaspoon salt
Lemon wedges

1. Put saffron into a cup. Add 2 tablespoons boiling water and let stand. Lay fish on a large flat plate. Sprinkle with lemon juice, turning to coat. Let stand while sauce is prepared, turning from time to time.

2. Heat 1 tablespoon oil (or alternative) in a large heavy-bottomed saucepan. Over moderate heat, sauté ginger, onion mixture and pepper for 3 minutes, stirring often. Add zucchini. Cook for 2 minutes. Sprinkle in half the seasonings. Combine tomatoes with mixture. Stir and cook for 2 minutes. Pour in stock, wine and saffron. Bring to simmering point. Reduce heat. Cook, uncovered, stirring frequently, until almost all liquid evaporates and mixture is moist. Cover to keep warm.

3. To prepare fish, in cup blend flour with remaining marjoram and allspice. Spread on a sheet of wax paper. Drain fish on paper toweling, patting to dry. Dip in flour mixture, pressing to adhere.

4. Heat 1 tablespoon oil (or alternative) in a large nonstick skillet until hot. Add fish and cook over medium-high heat until lightly browned (3 to 4 minutes). Add remaining ½ tablespoon oil (or alternative), carefully turn and brown lightly on second side. Remove pan from stove.

5. Uncover saucepan. Place over moderate heat and re-warm. If mixture has exuded too much liquid, turn up heat and cook off juices, stirring continually. To serve, ladle about 2 tablespoons of the sauce on individual warmed serving plates. Arrange cooked fish over the sauce. Spoon some of the remainder around fish. (Any extra may be served on the side in a sauceboat.) Sprinkle all over with salt; garnish with lemon wedges.

Yield: 4 or 5 servings

Variation: One cup of water may be substituted for Vegetable Stock; increase wine to 1 cup and increase marjoram and allspice to ¾ teaspoon each.

Serving suggestions: Potato/Spinach Knish (page 131) or just-cooked fine noodles or rice.

Baked Stuffed Fish *(Pareve or Dairy)*

Both Ashkenazic and Sephardic culinary accents add enchantments to the new nutritional syntax of American Jewish cookery in this theatrical presentation: a whole challah-stuffed fish, seasoned with fruit sauce and topped with toasted nuts. Be sure to display the whole fish before portioning.

1 3-pound pike or red snapper or flounder, cleaned, head left on	thin-sliced
	2 teaspoons Spice Mix
2 tablespoons fresh lemon juice	2 tablespoons finely minced parsley
4 ½-inch slices Challah (page 165)	About ⅔ cup each kosher dry white wine and unsweetened apple juice, combined
1½ tablespoons sweet butter margarine or sweet pareve margarine	¼ cup dark seedless raisins
1 rib celery, minced	3 thin lemon slices
3 cloves garlic, 2 minced, 1 thin-sliced	3 tablespoons toasted pine nuts or slivered blanched almonds, toasted
2 medium onions, 1 minced, 1	Watercress sprigs

1. Preheat oven to 400°F. Rinse fish well; dry inside and out with paper toweling. Make 4 diagonal ⅛-inch slices through skin on one side of fish. Sprinkle fish and cavity with lemon juice and let stand while stuffing is prepared.

2. Toast bread. Tear into small pieces and place in a bowl. Heat 1 tablespoon shortening in a nonstick skillet. Over medium-high heat, sauté celery, minced garlic and minced onion until lightly brown. Add to bread. Add 1 teaspoon Spice Mix, 1 tablespoon parsley and enough wine mixture to moisten bread. Stir in half the raisins. Stuff fish, sewing up cavity or securing with thin skewers.

3. Place in a lightly oiled ovenproof dish. Push sliced garlic into slashes; strew sliced onions over and around fish. Top with lemon slices. Heat remaining wine mixture (you'll need ¾ cup) with raisins and remaining teaspoon of seasoning. Spoon over and around fish. Cover tightly with sheet of heavy-duty aluminum foil and bake for 25 minutes; baste. Bake, uncovered, for 10 minutes longer.

4. Discard lemon slices. Skin fish and divide portions between 4 warmed dinner plates. Remove skewers from cavity and distribute stuffing. Spoon raisin-seasoned pan juices over all. Sprinkle with remaining parsley; top with nuts. Garnish each plate with watercress sprigs.

Yield: 4 servings

Serving suggestion: Carrot/Zucchini Puree (page 149).

8
TRADITION

Here are the American Jewish dishes enriched by nostalgia—from matzoh balls to kreplach, from strudels to kugels and latkes—the traditional dishes. These have not been forsaken in the thrust to a New American Jewish cookery, just remodeled with a new charm to start a new tradition.

MATZOH BALLS (A TRIO OF KNAIDLACH)

In my informal poll of matzoh-ball lovers (children included), 50 percent favored the denser variety, and the other half sang the praises of the fluffy kind. Either way, matzoh balls (dumplings made with matzoh meal) are a happy experience for everybody. The first recipe of the following trio is for denser matzoh balls; the two that follow are for the fluffier kind—one with alternate seasonings, and the other a mixture of tasty dumpling ingredients plus chicken and vegetables. All can be cooked in simmering water or chicken soup. The third serves as an appetizer as well as a main course. It's a Passover "must" in chicken soup and a "comfort food" any time of the year.

1. Matzoh Balls (Meat or Pareve)

2 large eggs (use 1 yolk and 2
   whites)
1 tablespoon each melted and
   cooled sweet pareve
   margarine (or chilled
   Rendered Chicken Fat) and
   Italian olive oil; or 2
   tablespoons Seasoned Olive
   Oil
½ teaspoon each ground
   marjoram or sage and curry
   powder
¼ teaspoon each salt and
   coarsely ground black pepper
½ cup Chicken Stock or
   Vegetable Stock, at room
   temperature
About 1 cup matzoh meal
2 tablespoons seltzer
3 to 4 sprigs fresh dill tied into
   a loose bundle with white
   cotton thread

1. In medium bowl, combine eggs with shortening(s) of your choice
and seasonings. Beat with fork to blend. Stir in stock. Add ½ cup
matzoh meal, a tablespoon at a time, stirring gently. Stir in seltzer (a
freshly opened bottle works best). Add enough of remaining matzoh
meal to make a thick batter. Place in freezer for 30 to 45 minutes.
Shape into 14 to 16 walnut-size balls.

2. Bring a wide pot of water (or chicken soup) to a rolling boil. Reduce
heat to slow-boil. Add dill bundle and cook for 2 minutes. Ease matzoh balls into boiling water. When liquid begins to simmer, cover and
cook for 40 minutes; knaidlach will float to the top. If they're cooked
in water, remove with slotted spoon and transfer to hot soup and serve
as soon as possible to preserve pleasing texture and shape. If they're
cooked in chicken soup, remove dill bundle after pressing out juices
and serve as soon as they've finished cooking.

Yield: 14 to 16 matzoh balls; 5 to 6 servings

Serving suggestions: Serve as a side dish sprinkled with minced fresh
herbs. Delicious, too, spooned with Mushroom-Tomato Sauce (page
30) or Spicy Tomato Sauce (page 186).

2. Matzoh Balls (Pareve)

3 large eggs, separated (use 2
   yolks and 3 whites)
1 tablespoon each Seasoned
   Olive Oil and melted and
   cooled sweet pareve
   margarine
½ teaspoon dried dill weed
Dash cayenne pepper
¼ teaspoon each salt, ground
   ginger and allspice
½ cup water
2 tablespoons finely minced
   shallot
About 1 cup matzoh meal

1. Place 2 egg yolks in medium bowl and 3 egg whites in large mixing bowl. To yolks add oil and margarine, beating with fork to blend. Then stir in seasonings, water and shallots. Gradually stir in a scant cup of matzoh meal; let stand until step 2 is completed.

2. Beat egg whites until firm peaks form (do not overbeat). Spoon 4 tablespoons of batter into beaten whites and fold in. Repeat procedure until all batter is incorporated into whites. Then fold in enough of remaining matzoh meal to make a thick batter. Chill for 1 hour. Shape into 14 to 16 walnut-size balls.

3. Bring a wide pot of water to a rolling boil. Reduce heat to slow-boil. Ease matzoh balls into boiling water. When liquid begins to simmer, cover and cook for 40 minutes. Matzoh balls will float to the top. With slotted spoon, transfer to hot soup, and serve at once to preserve pleasing texture and shape.

Yield: 14 to 16 matzoh balls; 5 or 6 servings

Note: If matzoh balls are cooked in chicken soup, remove dill bundle after pressing out juices and serve as soon as they've finished cooking.

3. *Matzoh Balls (Chicken Knaidlach)* (Meat)

½ teaspoon whole saffron
1 small carrot, peeled, ends
   trimmed, cut into ½-inch
   rounds
1 small rib celery, cut into
   1-inch pieces
2 large cloves garlic, peeled,
   each quartered
1 medium onion, peeled, cut
   into 1-inch chunks
1½ pounds skinned and boned
   chicken breast or a mixture
   of equivalent weight of dark

and light meat chicken
4 eggs (use 2 whole eggs and 2
   egg whites)
1 tablespoon seasoned or
   unseasoned Italian olive oil
1 tablespoon fresh lemon juice
¼ teaspoon each salt and
   allspice
⅛ teaspoon cayenne
¼ cup seltzer
1 cup matzoh meal
¼ cup minced dill or parsley

1. Put saffron in a small cup. Add 1 tablespoon of boiling water and let stand for 5 minutes.

2. Mince carrots, celery, garlic and onion by hand; or fit food processor with steel blade and mince. Transfer to a dish. Grind chicken, or cut into 1-inch chunks and fine-chop in food processor; take care not to puree to a paste.

3. In a large bowl, combine 2 whole eggs with oil and lemon juice. Beat with fork to blend. Then stir in seasonings, saffron, minced ingredients and chicken. Add seltzer and stir (a freshly opened bottle works best). Fold in matzoh meal and 2 tablespoons minced dill or parsley.

4. Put 2 egg whites into mixing machine bowl and beat until stiff but not dry. Fold into batter. Place in freezer for 30 minutes. Shape into about 24 walnut-size balls.

5. Bring a wide pot of water to a rolling boil. Reduce heat to slow-boil. Add remaining minced herbs. Ease matzoh balls into pot. When the slow-boil resumes, reduce heat to simmering. Cover and cook for 35 minutes. With slotted spoon, transfer to hot soup or serve as a main course (see serving suggestions for Matzoh Balls 1).

Yield: About 24 matzoh balls; 8 servings in soup and 5 or 6 servings as a main course

Notes:
   1. So as not to inhibit the expansion of matzoh balls as they cook, be sure to use a large pot, or cook them in 2 batches.
   2. If matzoh balls are cooked in chicken soup, remove dill bundle after pressing out juices and serve as soon as they've finished cooking.

STRUDELS

Most of us think of strudels as confections. But for some of my New American Jewish strudel recipes, I've revived a 500-year-old idea: non-confectionery strudels. These are strudel wrappers filled with seasoned poultry, meats, vegetables or grains (the first three recipes in this section). Also in this section are two recipes for more familiar pastry strudels: my version of the classic cheese strudel and an original contribution, my Apple/Cranberry Strudel.

Turkey-Lentil Strudel (Meat)

Here is a filling for today in a wrapping that came into Jewish culinary fashion in the Middle Ages. The filling provides that meaty taste without too much meat. It's a succulent mélange of ground turkey meat fortified with meat-tasting lentils and mushrooms, enlivened by moist herbs and spices. The wrapping is one of the first kinds used for a strudel—fillo dough (also spelled filo or phyllo), which is now available in the frozen-foods section of your supermarket. Filling and wrapping combine to make a delectable first or main course that tastes meatier than it is.

¼ cup dried brown lentils, rinsed and picked over
½ teaspoon dried dill weed
1 tablespoon balsamic vinegar
2 teaspoons Italian olive oil
¼ cup combined minced shallot and garlic
1¼ pounds lean skinned turkey (breast or breast and dark meat), ground
½ teaspoon each mild curry powder, dry mustard and

chili con carne seasoning
⅛ teaspoon cayenne pepper
¼ teaspoon salt
1 tablespoon minced fresh dill
1 large egg, lightly beaten
1 tablespoon fresh lemon juice
3 tablespoons matzoh meal
6 fillo sheets (12×17 inches)
1½ tablespoons each sweet pareve margarine, melted, and Italian olive oil

1. Put lentils in a saucepan. Cover with water; bring to boil. Remove from heat and let stand for 1 hour. Pour into strainer. Drain and rinse under cold running water. Put lentils back into saucepan. Add dill, vinegar and enough water to barely cover. Bring to boil. Cover and cook until tender but not oversoft (about 20 minutes). Pour contents of saucepan into strainer and with a large spoon press out liquid. Set aside. Preheat oven to 375°F.

2. Spread oil across a large nonstick skillet. Sauté shallot and garlic over moderate heat until wilted. Add ground turkey, breaking up pieces, stirring and sautéing until it no longer looks raw. Transfer to large bowl. Stir in seasonings and dill.

3. Combine egg with lemon juice and stir into mixture. Then stir in lentils and matzoh meal.

4. Tear off a long sheet of plastic wrap. Place 1 sheet of fillo over it. Brush sparingly with margarine mixture. Cover with second sheet of fillo, gently smoothing out with fingers. Brush again with margarine mixture. Repeat procedure once more, using a total of 3 fillo sheets. Spoon half the turkey mixture along shorter side of fillo, starting 1½ inches from edge and leaving a 1-inch margin on sides. With hands, compress filling into a firm roll. Using plastic wrap to assist you, lift edge and roll up, jelly-roll fashion, leaving ends unsealed. Using spatula, transfer to lightly margarine-greased cookie sheet. Prepare second roll, using remaining 3 fillo sheets and remaining filling. With a sharp knife, score each strudel into 6 or 10 serving pieces. Brush tops with margarine mixture.

5. Bake in center section of oven for 35 to 40 minutes (top should be golden brown). Cut into serving pieces and serve on warm plates at once.

Yield: 10 or more servings as an appetizer; 6 servings as a main course

Serving suggestion: Hot Red Cabbage with Fennel (page 141).

Chicken/Kasha Strudel (Meat)

This recipe requires *you* to make the wrapper. It's surprisingly easy, and it's an unforgettable experience, much like restoring a lost art form. The filling, on the other hand, is unlike any that has ever graced the interior of a strudel. It's a ground-chicken/kasha combination raised to a new art form with a modernistic miscellany of vegetables, spices and olive oil with perk-up touches of salt and sugar. Like the previous recipe, Turkey-Lentil Strudel, it satisfies the craving for meat, while using less meat than most meat dishes. Serve as a delicious starter or main course.

**FOR THE DOUGH
WRAPPERS:**
*About 2 cups, plus 2
tablespoons unbleached flour*
½ teaspoon baking powder
*¼ teaspoon each salt, ground
ginger and freshly grated
nutmeg*
*¼ cup Seasoned Olive Oil or
Italian olive oil*
1 large egg
*About ½ cup, plus 1 tablespoon
hot tap water*
FOR THE FILLING:
1⅓–1½ cups Chicken Stock
*1 cup whole kasha (roasted
buckwheat groats)*
2 large cloves garlic
1 small green bell pepper
1 large onion

*3 snow-white fresh mushrooms,
ends trimmed, damp-wiped*
*3 tablespoons Seasoned Olive
Oil or Italian olive oil*
*½ teaspoon each allspice and
freshly grated nutmeg*
*2 teaspoons dried oregano,
crushed*
¼ teaspoon salt
1 teaspoon sugar
*½ pound boned and skinned
chicken breast*
*3 tablespoons unsalted tomato
paste*
1 large egg white
*1 whole well-drained unsalted
jarred pimento*
*Florets from 4 large sprigs
parsley*

1. Sift flour into a bowl. Measure out ¼ cup and set aside. Re-sift larger amount of flour with baking powder, salt and spices into a bowl. Transfer to the workbowl of food processor that has been fitted with steel blade (or, if mixing by hand leave mixture in the bowl).

2. Pour oil into a measuring cup. Add egg and beat with fork to blend. With processor running, pour mixture through feed tube; then ½ cup hot water. Stop machine. Dough should form into a mass and feel soft but not dry. If it appears too dry, start processor and drop remaining tablespoon hot water through feed tube. Stop machine and let dough rest for 3 minutes. Scrape onto work surface sprinkled with 1 teaspoon of reserved flour and knead until soft to the touch, adding more flour, if necessary, to make a soft nonsticky dough. (If mixing by hand, make a well in center of bowl. Pour beaten egg/oil mixture into center and combine until all liquid is absorbed. Then stir in water, a tablespoon at a time, and work with hands, adding enough of reserved flour to make a soft, nonsticky dough.) Cut into 2 pieces. Wrap in plastic film and chill while filling is prepared.

3. In a 2-quart heavy-bottomed saucepan, bring stock to a rolling boil. Add kasha, reduce heat to slow-boil and cook, uncovered, for 4 minutes. If liquid boils away before 4 minutes, add remaining stock. (Kasha should be half-cooked and all liquid should be absorbed.) Transfer to a large bowl.

4. Coarse-grind garlic, green pepper, onion and mushrooms. (Or, if using a food processor fitted with steel blade, cut each clove of garlic in half; cut green pepper and onion into uniform chunks; and cut mushrooms into quarters. With processor running, drop garlic through feed tube. Remove cover and add green pepper, onion and mushrooms. Coarse-chop in 2 or 3 on/off turns.)

5. Put oil into a cup. Measure out 1 tablespoon and heat in a nonstick skillet. Sauté chopped mixture until lightly browned. Combine spices, oregano, salt and sugar in a cup. Stir in half the mixture. Combine with kasha.

6. Cut chicken into 1-inch pieces. Place in workbowl. Add remaining seasonings, tomato paste, egg white, pimento and parsley. Process in 4 or 5 on/off turns until chopped (do not process to a paste). Scrape into kasha mixture and stir. Preheat oven to 375°F.

7. Sprinkle work surface lightly with flour. Roll out each piece of dough to about a 12-×-16-inch rectangle, flipping them over once and letting them rest when they pull back. Lightly brush with some of the oil, reserving enough to brush over 2 strudels when rolled up. Spoon half the filling along long edge of dough, allowing a ½-inch margin on 3 sides. Press mixture into a smooth compact cylinder. Using spatula, lift up long edge, roll dough over filling and continue rolling over twice more. Fold in sides; then finish rolling. Transfer to a lightly oiled jelly-roll pan.

8. To serve as an appetizer, with sharp knife partially cut into dough every inch; for main course, make 6 or 7 partial cuts of equal width in each strudel. Brush with oil. Bake in center section of oven until delicately browned (about 40 minutes). Cut through and serve.

Yield: 10 servings as an appetizer; 6 servings as a main course

Lamb Strudel *(Meat)*

The emphasis in this original creation is once again on meat; and technique is similar to that of the preceding two strudels: getting the most meat taste with the least amount of meat. Making the seasoned wrapper is a creative experience (made easy by your food processor). My Lamb Strudel is a fine party server, since it reheats crisply and cuts easily into hors d'oeuvre-size slices.

Dough wrappers from
*   Chicken/Kasha Strudel*
*   recipe (page 114)*
1 small red bell pepper, seeded
1 large onion
3 large cloves garlic
¼ pound snow-white fresh
*   mushrooms, ends trimmed,*
*   damp-wiped*
Florets from 6 sprigs parsley
3 tablespoons Italian olive oil
1¼ pounds extra-lean ground
*   lamb*

½ teaspoon each ground cumin,
*   allspice and ginger*
⅛ teaspoon cayenne pepper
¼ teaspoon each cinnamon and
*   salt*
1 large egg
1 tablespoon honey
2 tablespoons fresh orange juice
1 tablespoon cornstarch
½ cup coarsely chopped
*   blanched almonds*
½ cup dark seedless raisins

1. Prepare dough wrapper, following steps 1 and 2.

2. Cut red pepper and onion into 1-inch chunks; halve garlic cloves and quarter mushrooms. Fit workbowl of food processor with steel blade. Add cut ingredients and parsley. Fine-chop in 3 on/off turns. Heat 1 tablespoon oil in a large nonstick skillet until very hot. Sauté mixture over medium-high heat until softened and all liquid in skillet evaporates. Transfer to a large bowl.

3. Add lamb to skillet, breaking up chunks with a large spoon. Sprinkle with spices and salt. Cook over medium-high heat until it gives up its raw look. Put into a strainer to drain off fat. Add to the bowl.

4. Put egg, honey and orange juice into a cup. Beat with a fork. Gradually stir in cornstarch until dissolved. Pour over mixture and combine. Stir in nuts and raisins. Cover and refrigerate for 1 hour or longer.

5. Follow assembly directions, steps 7 and 8 from Chicken/Kasha Strudel.

Yield: 10 servings as an appetizer; 6 servings as a main course

Serving suggestions: Dipping Sauce (page 186), Lemon Sauce (page 185).

Potato Latkes   *(Pareve)*

A latke (*lot*-kuh) is a pancake. This potato latke, low in salt and fat, flares with other novel flavors. It's the new-taste latke! And for an even more unusual flavor, try the recipe following this one. It's for (did you ever hear of?) asparagus latkes.

4 medium potatoes (about 1¾ pounds), preferably Idaho potatoes, peeled
1 tablespoon fresh lemon juice
2 large eggs (use 1 yolk and 2 whites)
½ teaspoon each freshly grated nutmeg, ground ginger and sugar
¼ teaspoon each salt and coarsely ground black pepper
⅓ cup minced onion
1½ tablespoons minced garlic
1½ tablespoons minced fresh dill or parsley
5–6 tablespoons matzoh meal
About 2½ tablespoons Seasoned Olive Oil or Italian olive oil

1. Fine-grate potatoes by hand or in food processor fitted with grating disk, using light pressure. Squeeze out by handfuls as much liquid from potatoes as possible, then pile into a large bowl. Stir in lemon juice.

2. In a small bowl, beat eggs with spices, sugar, salt and pepper. Pour into potato mixture and stir to blend. Fold in onion, garlic, dill and 5 tablespoons matzoh meal. Let stand for 5 minutes. Add remaining matzoh meal, if necessary, to make a batter that's fairly thick and holds together.

3. Cook pancakes in batches over medium-high heat in 1 or 2 large nonstick skillets (or well-seasoned iron skillets), dividing the oil between skillets and adding a heaping tablespoon of batter for each pancake when a drop of water sprinkled into skillet(s) bounces off.

With spatula, flatten pancakes to 3 inches in diameter. Cook until golden on both sides, adjusting heat when necessary to prevent burning. Serve hot from the skillets.

Yield: About 20 3-inch latkes

Variations:
1. For a more traditional taste, combine 1 tablespoon Seasoned Olive Oil with 1 tablespoon Rendered Chicken Fat (*Meat,* page 136).
2. For puffy pancakes, add 1 egg yolk to batter in step 2. Beat 2 egg whites until firm peaks form (do not overbeat); fold into batter at end of step 2.

Serving suggestions: Smooth-and-Sweet Applesauce (page 199) or reduced-fat sour cream *(Dairy).*

Asparagus Latkes (Dairy)

In most Jewish households, such vegetables as peas, corn and green beans are avoided during Passover. That makes asparagus a much-welcomed vegetable. Combined with this novel batter, asparagus makes a crispy, nutritious, low-calorie and simply delicious latke. I like to make up a double batch so I'll have enough to reheat the next day, when the latkes are just as tasty.

1 pound slender fresh asparagus	1½ teaspoons minced garlic
1 small carrot, peeled, ends trimmed	¼ cup minced onion
2 eggs (use 1 yolk and 2 whites)	¼ cup mashed unsalted dry curd cottage cheese or reduced-fat ricotta cheese
¼ teaspoon each freshly grated nutmeg, allspice, salt, pepper and ground marjoram	About ½ cup matzoh meal
1 teaspoon Italian olive oil	⅛ teaspoon cream of tartar
1 tablespoon minced parsley	About 2 tablespoons Italian olive oil

1. Break off butt ends of asparagus. Fine-chop by hand, or with food processor fitted with steel blade. Scrape into a bowl. Fine-grate carrots by hand, or cut into ½-inch rounds and fine-chop in food processor. Combine with asparagus.

2. In a small bowl, combine 1 egg yolk with seasonings, oil and parsley. Stir in garlic, onion and cottage cheese or ricotta (stir it up first). Combine asparagus mixture with batter. Add matzoh meal, a tablespoon at a time, stirring after each addition.

3. Beat egg whites on high speed of mixing machine until foamy. Add cream of tartar and continue beating until stiff but not dry. Fold into pancakes.

4. Cook the latkes in batches, 4 at a time, or use 2 large nonstick skillets, dividing oil. When oil is hot, over medium-high heat, ladle a heaping tablespoon of batter for each pancake into the skillet, spreading to 3-inch diameter (pancakes should be about ¼ inch thick). Cook until well browned (4 to 5 minutes) before turning. Brown on second side, lifting up with spatula after 3 minutes to check doneness. Keep warm in a preheated 400°F oven-toaster or oven.

Yield: 16 latkes

Kasha Varnishkes *(Meat or Pareve)*

. . . is a much-loved mixture of kasha, onions, seasonings and bow tie-shaped noodles. My version is improved in that each kernel of kasha remains an individual, and doesn't melt into a collective mush. If you prefer your pasta al dente, you'll prefer kasha varnishkes my way.

2 cups Chicken Stock or Vegetable Stock	*Oil*
¾ cup kasha (whole buckwheat groats)	*¾ cup coarsely chopped onion*
1 cup bow tie-shaped noodles	*1 teaspoon minced garlic*
2 tablespoons Seasoned Olive	*1 tablespoon Spice Mix*
	2 tablespoons minced fresh dill, coriander, chives or basil

1. Prepare kasha and noodles shortly before serving. Bring stock to a rolling boil in a 2-quart heavy-bottomed saucepan. Add kasha. Return liquid to a boil and stir several times. Reduce heat to a slow-boil (a little hotter than simmering). Cook, uncovered, for 8 to 9 minutes, stirring often, until kernels are softened but still hold their shape and all liquid is absorbed (add more stock if it evaporates before 9 minutes). Set aside, uncovered.

2. Cook noodles until firm-tender. Drain well in a colander.

3. Heat oil in a large nonstick skillet. Over medium-high heat, sauté onion and garlic until lightly browned. Stir in kasha and noodles; sprinkle with Spice Mix. Using a folding motion so as not to tear the noodles, combine ingredients until heated through (do not overcook or mixture will lose its moistness). Turn into a warmed serving bowl and sprinkle with fresh herb of your choice.

Yield: 6 to 8 servings

Variations: Add ¼ pound snow-white, damp-wiped fresh mushrooms and/or 1 small seeded and skinned red bell pepper cut into narrow strips at the beginning of step 3.

KUGELS

Strictly speaking, kugel means pudding. But every Jewish food lover *knows* kugel means *noodle* pudding (which, strictly speaking, is *lokshen* kugel). Putting verbal niceties aside, kugel means a noodle dish so heavenly that, Jewish folklorists have conjectured, it must have been invented by angels. Of the many kugels my mother and grandmother fussed over, I've selected two for translation into my New American Jewish cuisine. One is a tomato kugel; the other is a side dish or dessert, which I call 5-Fruit Kugel. Two easy-to-make recipes follow.

Tomato Kugel   *(Pareve)*

8 ounces fine noodles (see note)
2 tablespoons sweet pareve
  margarine
3 tablespoons minced fresh dill
  or basil
¼ teaspoon each salt, coarsely
  ground black pepper and
  ground ginger
½ teaspoon freshly grated

nutmeg
2 teaspoons sugar
2 large eggs
2 teaspoons fresh lemon juice
2¾ cups Mushroom-Tomato
  Sauce
3 tablespoons kosher dry white
  wine

1. Preheat oven to 350°F. Cook noodles in a large pot of rapidly boiling water until almost tender. Drain in colander. Turn into a bowl. Add margarine, 2 tablespoons dill or basil, salt, spices and sugar and fold into mixture.

2. In cup, beat eggs and lemon juice with fork until well blended. Stir into kugel. Combine 2¼ cups of sauce with wine and gradually add to mixture.

3. Grease an 8- or 9-inch oven-to-table baking dish with margarine.

Pour kugel into dish. Ladle remaining sauce over all, smoothing out top. Bake in center section of oven until delicately browned (about 45 minutes). Sprinkle with remaining dill or basil. Place on trivet and serve directly from dish.

Yield: 6 or more servings

Variations:

1. For a dairy version, add 3 tablespoons just-grated Parmesan cheese in step 2, and sprinkle with an additional tablespoon of cheese just before placing in oven.

2. For a meat version, add 2 cups of ½-inch diced cooked lamb, chicken or beef at the end of step 2. Generously serves 8 as a main course.

3. If you don't have Mushroom-Tomato Sauce on hand, try this quick-to-make simplified variation: Sauté ½ cup each minced onion and green pepper over moderate heat in nonstick skillet until softened. Add ¼ pound damp-wiped and thin-sliced fresh mushrooms and sauté until onions start to brown. Add 1 tablespoon balsamic vinegar; cook for 1 minute. Then add 2¼ cups unsalted imported tomato puree, 2 teaspoons dried basil leaves. Cover and simmer for 15 minutes.

Note: "No-Yolk Noodles" are now available in supermarkets. Made with egg whites only, they're a good replacement for the whole-egg noodles.

5-Fruit Kugel (Dairy)

8 ounces medium-wide noodles
¼ cup dark seedless raisins
12 pitted dates, cut into small pieces
10 soft pitted prunes, cut into small pieces
1 sweet apple, such as Golden Delicious or Washington State, peeled and coarsely chopped
12 drained unsweetened canned pineapple chunks, cut into small pieces
2 tablespoons fresh lemon juice
1 cup part-skim ricotta cheese
1 cup reduced-fat sour cream
¼ cup honey

¼ teaspoon each salt and freshly grated nutmeg
½ teaspoon each ground coriander, ground cardamom and cinnamon
2 tablespoons granulated or firmly packed light brown sugar
2 tablespoons frozen orange or pineapple juice concentrate
2 tablespoons melted sweet pareve margarine or sweet butter/margarine blend, plus 1½ teaspoons (cold) to grease casserole
3 large eggs (use 2 yolks and 3 whites)

1. Preheat oven to 350°F. Cook noodles in a large pot of boiling water until tender but not oversoft. Pour into a colander and drain well. Transfer to a large bowl.

2. Put raisins, dates, prunes, apple and pineapple into a small bowl. Stir in lemon juice.

3. In a third bowl, combine and blend ricotta cheese (stir it up first), sour cream, honey, salt, spices, sugar and concentrate. Stir in melted shortening. Put eggs into a cup and beat with a fork; combine with mixture. Pour over noodles and fold in. Then fold in fruits.

4. Grease an 8- or 9-×-12-inch Pyrex casserole with shortening. Fill with kugel, distributing fruit evenly. Cover tightly with a sheet of heavy-duty aluminum foil and bake for 40 minutes. Uncover and bake until surface looks set (about 10 minutes). Remove from oven and place on a trivet to cool for 10 minutes before cutting into serving pieces. May be served warm or at room temperature.

Yield: 8 to 10 servings

Cheese Blintzes   *(Dairy)*

Blintzes are thin pancakes wrapped around cottage cheese, apples, blueberries, rhubarb or whatever you can dream up to coddle your sweet tooth. If you guess blintzes look somewhat like French crepes or Russian blinis, you're right. In the two versions that follow—cheese blintzes and apple blintzes—the tastes are classic, but the calorie and cholesterol counts are strictly nouvelle.

FOR THE WRAPPERS:
2 large eggs (use 1 yolk and 2 whites)
½ cup each milk and reduced-fat sour cream
About ⅓ cup water
1 cup unbleached flour
¼ teaspoon ground cardamom or freshly grated nutmeg
1 teaspoon sugar
About 1½ tablespoons melted sweet butter/margarine blend
2 tablespoons brownulated sugar mixed with ½ teaspoon cinnamon

FOR THE FILLING:
2 12-ounce boxes unsalted dry curd cottage cheese, drained
5 tablespoons reduced-fat cream cheese (Neufchâtel)
1 large egg
1½ tablespoons sugar
1 tablespoon honey
¼ teaspoon each cinnamon, freshly grated nutmeg and ground cardamom
1½–2 teaspoons fresh lemon juice
¼ cup dark seedless raisins (optional)

1. To prepare the wrappers, put eggs into a small bowl and whisk until frothy. Whisk in milk, then sour cream and water until smooth.

2. Sift flour with spices onto a sheet of wax paper. Sprinkle with sugar. While whisking, slowly add dry ingredients to liquid mixture. Let stand for 10 minutes. Stir. Batter should be fairly thick (about the consistency of thick buttermilk; if it's too thick, stir in a tablespoon of water).

3. Lightly brush an 8-inch nonstick skillet with shortening. Heat until a drop of water bounces off surface. Ladle in 2½ tablespoons of batter, immediately tilting pan to evenly distribute. (If batter solidifies before the measured amount spreads out, stir in a little more water to the remaining batter.) Cook until set, edges begin to curl and tops of pancakes are dry to the touch. Lift up sides, turn and cook for 10 seconds. Transfer to a plate. Repeat procedure, regulating heat when necessary to assure even cooking. Stack blintzes, second side up, as they're made.

4. To prepare filling, have all ingredients at room temperature. Put cottage cheese, cream cheese, egg, sugar and honey into the workbowl of food processor that has been fitted with steel blade (or beat on high speed with electric mixing machine). Process until cheese curds have broken down and mixture is fairly smooth (don't puree). Drop spices through feed tube; then pour in 1½ teaspoons lemon juice and process for 1 second. Scrape into a bowl. Taste for lemon juice, adding more, if desired. Stir in raisins, if desired. Cover and chill for 30 minutes.

5. To assemble, spoon 1½ tablespoons of filling in center of each blintz. Flip over parallel sides to make a package. Then gently press folds while flipping over remaining open sides.

6. Sauté in 2 batches in a large nonstick skillet (or use 2 skillets, dividing shortening). Add 1 teaspoon shortening to each pan. Arrange half the blintzes, seam down, in skillet(s). Sauté over moderate heat until blintzes begin to brown. Carefully turn and cook for a minute or two. (Blintzes may also be baked in a preheated 375°F oven on a greased cookie sheet until lightly browned, but they're tastier when sautéed.)

7. Slide onto a hot serving plate. Sprinkle with sugar mixture and serve right away.

Yield: 14 or 15 blintzes

Serving suggestions: Side dishes of Smooth-and-Sweet Applesauce (page 199), 3-Fruit Sauce (page 184) or honey.

Apple Blintzes   (Dairy)

Crisp apples are combined with prunes to add sweetness without adding excessive sugar.

Wrappers from Cheese Blintzes
recipe (page 122)
1 teaspoon sweet
butter/margarine blend
1½ tablespoons light or dark
brown sugar
4 crisp sweet apples, such as
Washington State or Golden
Delicious, peeled and
coarsely chopped
¼ teaspoon each cinnamon,

allspice and freshly grated
nutmeg
8 soft prunes, cut into small
pieces
1½ tablespoons fresh lemon
juice
½ teaspoon finely minced
lemon zest
1½ tablespoons coarsely
chopped walnuts or blanched
almonds

1. Prepare wrappers through step 3, page 123.

2. Put shortening into a nonstick skillet. Over medium-high heat, cook until lightly browned but not smoking. Sprinkle in sugar and cook for 30 seconds. Add apples; sprinkle with spices, stirring to combine. Sauté for 1 minute. Turn into a bowl. Combine with remaining ingredients.

3. To assemble and cook, follow instructions for Cheese Blintzes, steps 5 through 7, page 123.

Yield: 14 or 15 blintzes

Matzoh Stuffing   (Pareve)

This exceptionally tasty mixture takes star billing when it's used to stuff poultry, fish or meat. It's just as successful as a filling for peppers, scooped-out zucchini or acorn squash. Leftovers are delicious when reheated in a nonstick skillet.

1 large egg (use ½ the yolk and
all the white)
1½ teaspoons Spice Mix
2 plain matzoh, broken into
small pieces
1 tablespoon Seasoned Olive Oil
or Italian olive oil
2 medium onions, minced
1 teaspoon minced garlic
¼ pound snow-white fresh

mushrooms, ends trimmed,
damp-wiped and minced
¾ cup finely grated potato,
preferably Idaho potato
1 tablespoon minced fresh dill
½ cup peeled and finely
chopped sweet apple
½ teaspoon coarsely ground
black pepper

1. In medium bowl, beat egg and Spice Mix with fork to blend. Add matzoh and stir until all pieces are well coated. Let stand.

2. Heat oil in small nonstick skillet. Over medium heat, sauté half the onion, the garlic and mushrooms, stirring often, until mixture holds together and no liquid remains in pan (5 to 6 minutes). Add to soaking matzoh and combine. Stir in remaining onion.

3. Squeeze out as much liquid as possible from potatoes. Add to stuffing along with dill, apple and pepper. Blend well. Let stand for 5 minutes before using.

Yield: About 2 cups; enough to stuff a 3–4-pound chicken or the pocket of a 5-pound breast of veal. Recipe may be doubled, using 1 egg yolk and 2 egg whites.

Variation: Preheat oven to 350°F. Spoon stuffing into a lightly greased 1¾-quart covered casserole. Cut 2 teaspoons of sweet pareve margarine or sweet butter/margarine blend into small pieces. Strew over stuffing. Cover and bake for 30 minutes. Uncover and return to oven until top begins to brown.

Noodle Dough (Meat or Pareve)

On a visit to a small restaurant in suburban Rome, I was fascinated to see long pasta strips hanging to dry on the backs of chairs. A quaint way to dry pasta; but the idea of drying pasta before cooking is sensible. I find that soft commercial pasta battles for dominance with the sauce, and neither wins. Another high-taste hint: For extremely tasty noodles, try making them with a stock rather than just water.

1⅔ cups unbleached flour
½ teaspoon dried dill weed
¼ teaspoon each salt and
*   freshly grated nutmeg*

1 large egg, lightly beaten
4–5 tablespoons warmed
*   Chicken Stock, Vegetable*
*   Stock or water*

1. Prepare dough in a food processor or by hand. Put 1½ cups flour, dill, salt and nutmeg into workbowl of food processor that has been fitted with steel blade. With machine running, pour egg through feed tube. Immediately pour stock or alternative through tube, 1 tablespoon at a time. Stop machine after 4 tablespoons have been added. Dough should begin to form small balls and congeal without being sticky when pressed with fingers. With machine running, add another tablespoon of stock, if necessary. (If preparing by hand, put 1½ cups flour, dill, salt and nutmeg into a bowl, stirring to combine. Make a well in the center; add egg and combine with flour. Then add enough stock or water to make a dough that's smooth and elastic.)

2. Knead dough briefly by hand. Divide in half. Wrap each piece in plastic film and let rest for 30 minutes. Sprinkle work surface lightly with flour and roll each piece into an 8-×-10-inch rectangle. If dough springs back after rolling, turn and re-roll without adding flour so that dough sticks to work surface and holds its shape. Let it rest for a minute or two before continuing to roll. For kreplach, cut into 2½-inch squares and fill (see recipe below). For noodles, let dough stand until fairly dry to the touch. With sharp knife, cut into strips. Spread strips out to completely dry, or dry them Italian style. Cook in boiling water or soup for 10 minutes.

Yield: Makes about 26 2½-inch squares; about 2 cups noodles

KREPLACH

A kreplach is a triangular-shaped pocket food which, in medieval European Jewish communities, served the same purpose as a fortune cookie. Now, all the good fortune of these delectable tidbits resides in the tastes—the palate-pleasing combinations of pockets and fillings. Following are three new combinations—three new kinds of kreplachs.

Chicken Kreplach   (Meat)

The pocket is made of boiled noodle dough. The filling is seasoned ground cooked chicken.

1 tablespoon Italian olive oil
1 medium onion, minced
2 large cloves garlic, minced
*¼ teaspoon each salt and mild
   curry powder*
1½ cups ground cooked chicken
2 teaspoons egg yolk
1 tablespoon minced dill or

parsley
*1 recipe Noodle Dough (page
   125)*
*Several sprigs dill folded over
   and tied into a bundle with
   white cotton thread, or 1
   teaspoon dried dill weed*

1. Heat oil in small nonstick skillet. Over medium heat, sauté onion and garlic for 2 minutes. Sprinkle with salt and curry powder. Continue sautéing, stirring often, until lightly browned.

2. Put chicken in a medium bowl (or use a food processor to combine all ingredients). Stir in sautéed mixture, egg yolk and minced dill or parsley.

3. Prepare dough, rolling out half at a time, keeping remaining piece wrapped. Cut into 12 or more 2½-inch squares. Put 1½ teaspoons of the filling at one corner of each square, leaving a ⅜-inch border. Lightly moisten all sides with water. With knife, lift dough off work surface at one point and fold over to opposite point, forming a triangle. Pinch edges and flute with fork. Place kreplach on a large plate as they're made. Roll out second piece of dough and repeat procedure.

4. Fill a large wide pot with water or soup. Add dill bundle or alternative and bring to a boil. Add half the kreplach so as not to crowd. Boil for 20 minutes (pieces will rise to the top). With slotted spoon, drain and transfer to a plate. Repeat procedure with remaining kreplach. Serve in soup or sauté and serve as a side dish (Sautéed Kreplach, page 128).

Yield: 24 or more pieces

Note: To freeze, place uncooked kreplach on firm flat surface. Cover with plastic film and freeze. Then transfer to plastic freeze bags and keep frozen until ready to boil. No need to defrost.

Meat Kreplach *(Meat)*

The pocket is made of boiled noodle dough. The filling is seasoned ground beef, lamb or veal mixed with bulgur.

¼ cup bulgur
1½ cups Chicken Stock
1½ tablespoons Seasoned Olive Oil or Italian olive oil
1 cup minced onion
2 teaspoons minced garlic
⅓ cup minced sweet bell pepper
¾ pound extra-lean ground beef, lamb or veal

½ teaspoon each allspice and ground cumin
2 teaspoons dried oregano, crumbled
1 teaspoon balsamic vinegar
2 tablespoons minced parsley
¼ teaspoon salt
2 teaspoons egg yolk (optional)
1 recipe Noodle Dough (page 125)

1. Pour bulgur into a strainer and rinse under cold running water. Transfer to a small saucepan. Add ¾ cup stock. Bring to a boil. Cover and let stand for 30 minutes. All liquid will be absorbed.

2. Heat oil in large nonstick skillet or well-seasoned iron skillet. Add onion, garlic and pepper. Over medium-high heat, sauté until lightly brown. Add meat, breaking up pieces with a large spoon or potato masher. Sprinkle with spices and oregano. Continue sautéing and breaking up meat until half-cooked. Combine with bulgur and continue cooking over medium-high heat for 1 minute.

3. Pour vinegar around sides of pan. Cook for 30 seconds. Then pour remaining stock around sides of pan and stir. Add parsley. Bring to simmering point. Cover and simmer for 10 minutes. Uncover. Sprinkle with salt. Cook over medium-high heat until all liquid evaporates (about 3 minutes). Let cool. Stir in egg yolk, if desired. (Cholesterol watchers: Mixture holds together without the egg, but egg is offered as a flavoring suggestion.)

4. Prepare dough, following rolling, cutting, assembling and cooking directions in steps 3 and 4 for Chicken Kreplach. If egg is not used, compress filling with fingers before placing on each dough square.

Yield: 24 or more pieces

Sautéed Kreplach (Meat)

The pocket is made of boiled noodle dough, which is sautéed—imparting a special taste. The filling can be either a seasoned chicken mixture or a seasoned meat mixture. You'll find this kind of kreplach resembles an Oriental wonton, but it is more tender and succulent.

1½ tablespoons Seasoned Olive Oil, Italian olive oil or sweet pareve margarine
⅓ cup coarsely chopped shallot or onion
1 tablespoon minced garlic

1 recipe Chicken or Meat Kreplach (pages 126 or 127)
2 teaspoons Spice Mix
Minced fresh dill or basil
¼ teaspoon salt
Freshly ground black or white pepper

1. Heat oil or margarine in a large nonstick skillet, or use 2 pans, dividing ingredients. Add shallots or onion, and garlic. Sauté over moderate heat for 1 minute.

2. Arrange kreplach atop mixture without crowding. Sprinkle with Spice Mix. Sauté over medium-high heat on each side until wrappers begin to brown, taking care not to tear when turning. Serve at once, sprinkled with dill or basil, salt and pepper.

Yield: 4 servings as a main course; 6 to 8 servings as a first course

Variations:

1. For an Oriental taste, substitute reduced-sodium soy sauce for fresh herbs, and eliminate salt.

2. Complete recipe and serve with warmed Mushroom-Tomato Sauce (page 30) or Spicy Tomato Sauce on the side (page 186).

Lamb Knishes (Meat)

This is a new and improved knish, or pocket food. The pocket I developed, based on the design of the Spanish empanada, is crispy and retains its crispness while accommodating a moist filling, such as my lamb medley in the Sephardic style. Serve with soup, as an appetizer or as an irresistible nosh. A health plus: This knish is baked, not fried.

FOR THE DOUGH:
*1⅔ cups sifted unbleached
 flour, plus extra for rolling
¼ cup gluten flour*
½ teaspoon baking powder
½ teaspoon ground ginger
¼ teaspoon salt
6 tablespoons Italian olive oil
1 large egg (use ½ yolk and all
 the white)
5–6 tablespoons cold fresh
 orange juice
1 large egg, lightly beaten (for
 glaze)*

FOR THE FILLING:
*1½ tablespoons Seasoned Olive
 Oil or Italian olive oil
1 cup minced onions
¾ pound lean ground lamb
½ teaspoon each cinnamon and
 ground ginger
⅛ teaspoon cayenne pepper
¼ teaspoon each ground cumin
 and salt
½ cup slightly undercooked rice
10 pitted prunes, cut into small
 pieces
1 tablespoon minced parsley*

*Available in health food stores.

1. For the dough, use a food processor fitted with steel blade, or mix by hand. Sift 1⅔ cups flour, gluten flour, baking powder, ginger and salt into workbowl. Process in 3 on/off turns.

2. In measuring cup, beat oil with ½ the egg yolk (reserve the balance of yolk for the filling) and all the egg white. With machine running, pour mixture through feed tube. Then spoon a tablespoon of orange juice at a time through tube. When dough forms a ball, immediately stop machine. Let it rest for 2 minutes. Remove dough from workbowl and shape into a smooth ball. Wrap in plastic film and refrigerate while filling is prepared. (If dough is made by hand, combine first 5 ingredients in a large bowl. In cup, beat ½ the egg yolk and all the egg white with a fork. Make a well in dry mixture. Add to the well and combine with dry ingredients. Using a fork, then hands, gradually work enough orange juice into the dough to make a ball. Knead briefly until smooth.)

3. To prepare the filling, use a large well-seasoned iron skillet. Using a medium-high temperature, heat oil until quite hot but not smoking. Add onions. Immediately reduce heat to low and sauté onions slowly, stirring often, until they begin to turn golden (about 15 minutes), taking care not to dry out. Add meat, breaking up pieces with a large spoon or potato masher. Sprinkle with spices and salt. Cook over low heat until meat gives up its raw look (about 7 minutes). Remove from heat.

4. Stir in rice, prunes, parsley and reserved ½ egg yolk. Cover while dough is rolled out. Preheat oven to 375°F.

5. Cut dough into 2 parts. Sprinkle work surface very lightly with flour. Roll each piece to a 12-×-14-inch rectangle. (Dough should stretch to ⅛-inch thickness.) Spoon ¼ of the filling along long edge of dough, allowing ½-inch margin on 3 sides. Pat filling to the shape of a rope. Using spatula, lift up long edge and flip over dough. Make another turn until filling is completely encased. Repeat procedure on the other long edge of dough, using ¼ of filling and rolling up to meet the other roll. With the aid of 2 spatulas, transfer to a lightly oiled cookie sheet. To facilitate easier cutting when baked, partially cut through dough crosswise into 5 pieces, leaving pieces intact. Repeat procedure with remaining dough. Brush tops with beaten egg (less than half will be used).

6. Bake in center section of oven for 35 to 40 minutes until golden all over. Remove from oven and let stand for 5 minutes before serving.

Yield: About 20 pieces; 4 to 6 servings

Serving suggestions: Lemon Sauce (page 185), colorful Warm Vegetable Salad (page 158).

Potato/Spinach Filling for Knish *(Pareve)*

Far more interesting than the all-potato knish. Prettier, too.

1½ tablespoons Seasoned Olive
  Oil
1 cup minced onion
2 cups warm mashed Idaho
  potatoes (see note)
1 large egg
½ 10-ounce package frozen

chopped spinach, cooked
½ cup fine-grated carrot
1 teaspoon freshly grated
  nutmeg
⅛ teaspoon cayenne pepper
¼ teaspoon salt
1 teaspoon sugar

1. Heat oil in a nonstick skillet until hot. Add onion and sauté over medium-high heat until lightly browned, stirring often. Put potatoes into a bowl. Add onion and combine.

2. Break egg into a cup. Spoon out half the yolk and reserve. With fork, beat remaining half yolk with the white; stir into potatoes.

3. Pour spinach into a strainer or colander and press out as much liquid as possible. Add to mixture, along with remaining ingredients.

4. Put reserved egg yolk and 1 teaspoon water into a cup and blend with fork. Brush over knish before baking.

Yield: About 20 pieces; 4 to 6 servings

Notes:
  1. See Lamb Knishes recipe (page 129) for dough and assembly.
  2. The dry texture of the Idaho potato makes for a crispier crust while baking. To completely dry out cooked potatoes after draining, put them back into the pot and, over medium-high heat, briefly cook off any residue moisture; then mash.

Buckwheat Farfel *(Pareve or Meat)*

Buckwheat farfel, tiny pieces of buckwheat dough, is an American contribution to the New American Jewish cuisine (other farfels are fashioned from other kinds of dough). Use my Buckwheat Farfel in soup; or, combined with onions and fresh herbs, as a side dish (see variation).

1¼ cups unbleached flour
3 tablespoons buckwheat flour*
½ teaspoon each ground ginger
  and ground cardamom
¼ teaspoon salt

2 large eggs (use 1 yolk,
  reserving second yolk, and 2
  whites), combined and lightly
  beaten

*Available in health food stores and some supermarkets.

1. Place first 4 listed ingredients in a bowl. Make a well. Add eggs and gradually incorporate into dry ingredients with fork, and then with fingers. Dough will be dry.

2. Using palms and fingers, shape into a firm ball. (If mixture doesn't hold together sufficiently, add a scant teaspoon more of reserved egg yolk and work into dough.) Divide into 5 or 6 parts. Squeeze and shape each part into a firm cylinder. Arrange on large plate and let stand, uncovered, for 3 hours or longer to dry out.

3. Grate dough by hand with a sharp grater, or fit food processor with grating attachment and grate. Any chunks that resist grating can easily be chopped by refitting the processor with steel blade and chopping in a few on/off turns. Spread the morsels across a large sheet of wax paper or a plate and let dry completely.

4. Bring a large pot of water to a rolling boil. Cook farfel, uncovered, at a steady boil until tender but not oversoft (13 to 14 minutes). Pour contents of pot into a fine-meshed strainer and drain completely. Serve in soup or as a side dish (see variation).

Yield: 2 cups uncooked farfel; 6 servings

Variation: Heat 1 tablespoon Italian olive oil in a large nonstick skillet. Add 1 teaspoon each minced garlic and fresh ginger, ½ cup minced onion, ½ cup slivered red bell pepper and ½ teaspoon mild curry powder. Sauté over moderate heat until mixture begins to brown. Stir in drained farfel and heat through. Serve sprinkled with minced fresh coriander, basil or mint. Yield: 6 servings.

Matzoh Brei Pancakes (Pareve or Dairy)

Do you enjoy a light breakfast? *And* you're a fan of matzoh brei (so-o-o heavy!)? Well, here's a matzoh brei pancake that's light. Fine textured, too, because I soak the matzoh in water, not milk, and I press out the soaking liquid. Cook the pancakes in a hot skillet and serve as soon as you lift them out of the pan. Convert to lunch pancakes by following the variation.

4 plain matzohs
About ¾ cup water
4 large eggs (use 2 yolks and 4 whites)
½ teaspoon each dried tarragon leaves, crumbled, and mild

curry powder
⅛ teaspoon coarsely ground black pepper
¼ teaspoon salt
About 1½ tablespoons peanut oil or Italian olive oil

1. Break matzoh into very small pieces into a medium bowl. Add ⅓ cup of water and stir with fork. Let stand for 2 minutes. Add enough of remaining water to barely cover matzoh. Let stand for 5 minutes. Pour contents of bowl into a strainer and press out as much water as possible.

2. Put 2 whole eggs and 2 egg whites into the emptied bowl. Add seasonings and beat with fork to blend. Stir in drained matzoh. Let stand for 2 minutes.

3. Brush 2 large nonstick skillets with oil. Place over medium-high heat. When a drop of water added to the skillet bounces off, the pan is hot enough to begin cooking. Prepare 4 pancakes at a time, ladling about 2 tablespoons of batter for each 3-inch pancake into the skillet. Cook until set and lightly brown (about 2 minutes). Turn and crisp on second side (about 1 minute). Repeat procedure with remaining batter.

Yield: About 18 pancakes

Variation: Drain ¼ cup unsalted dry curd cottage cheese. Mash, then add to batter in step 2 along with ½ cup finely minced onion, scallion or chives.Yield: About 20 pancakes.

Serving suggestions: Smooth-and-Sweet Applesauce (page 199) or 3-Fruit Sauce (page 184).

Matzoh Crisp   *(Pareve or Dairy)*

The things you can do with matzohs! Like these seductive tidbits of what seems like pure taste.

3 tablespoons Seasoned Olive Oil or Italian olive oil
2 teaspoons Spice Mix
1½ teaspoons minced garlic
2 tablespoons minced shallot or onion

2 whole-wheat matzohs
⅛ teaspoon each salt and coarsely ground black pepper
2 teaspoons minced fresh dill or fresh coriander (or a combination of both)

1. Heat 2 tablespoons oil in small nonstick skillet. Stir in Spice Mix, garlic and shallot or onion. Sauté over very low heat, stirring often, for 5 minutes. Remove from heat. Add remaining oil and combine.

2. Break matzoh into 8 pieces. Place under hot broiler for 30 seconds. Immediately spread with sautéed mixture. Return to broiler for about 1 minute or until matzoh are very hot. Sprinkle with salt, pepper and fresh herbs. Serve at once.

Yield: 4 servings

Variation: For a dairy meal, sprinkle with 1 tablespoon freshly grated Parmesan cheese before final heating.

Cheese Strudel (Dairy)

Fillo (also spelled filo or phyllo) is very thin pastry that produces a featherweight flaky dough when baked. It's a favorite among the Jewish people of Greece, who like to fill it with sweet mixtures of fruits and honey (baklava). It is also adaptable to just about any mixture of meat, poultry, cheese, grain or fish fillings. What most people *don't* know—what every cook who's about to prepare a baked dessert *should* know—is that fillo contains *no fat or cholesterol;* and it's very low in calories and sodium. Labeled by most manufacturers as "pareve," it's a versatile ingredient for Jewish cookery. One more nutritional advantage in this recipe: I've found that by combining melted butter/margarine blend with oil, the reduced amount of shortening that I use goes much farther.

1 large egg
8 ounces unsalted dry curd
  cottage cheese, stirred before
  measuring
8 ounces reduced-fat cream
  cheese (Neufchâtel)
About 3 tablespoons sugar
2 teaspoons fresh lemon juice
½ teaspoon minced lemon zest
½ teaspoon each ground
  cardamom and cinnamon
1 tablespoon plain low-fat

yogurt
1 tablespoon honey
½ teaspoon pure vanilla extract
¼ teaspoon almond extract
⅓ cup seedless dark raisins
6 fillo sheets (12×17 inches)
1½ tablespoons each melted
  sweet butter/margarine
  blend and peanut or corn oil,
  combined
Confectioners' sugar (optional)

1. Preheat oven to 375°F. Put egg, cheeses and 2 tablespoons sugar in mixing machine bowl. Beat on medium speed to blend. Combine lemon juice, lemon zest and spices with mixture and blend. Then beat in yogurt, honey and extracts. Stir in raisins.

2. Unroll fillo sheets. Prepare 2 strudels, using 3 sheets of fillo for each roll. Put a long sheet of plastic wrap on dry work surface. Lift off 1 sheet of fillo and lay it on plastic; smooth out. Using pastry brush, paint fillo lightly with shortening mixture. Sprinkle with ½ teaspoon sugar. Lay another sheet of fillo over it. Repeat brushing and sprinkling procedure twice more, smoothing out sheets as they're layered.

3. Spread half the cheese mixture along the short end of the fillo, leaving a 1½-inch border and a ½-inch margin on 2 sides, and manipulating with hands into a compact cylinder. Using extended plastic to assist you, snugly roll up, jelly-roll fashion. Repeat with remaining fillo and cheese mixture.

4. Grease a cookie sheet with sweet butter/margarine blend. Arrange strudels, seam sides down, on pan. With a sharp knife, score each strudel into 4 serving pieces, cutting through about ¼ inch. Brush with remaining shortening mixture; evenly sprinkle with remaining sugar. Bake in center section of oven until golden (about 40 minutes). Serve warm or at room temperature, dusted with confectioners' sugar, if desired.

Yield: 8 servings

Apple/Cranberry Strudel
(Pareve or Dairy)

Enjoy tart cranberries and sweet apples in a crispy, flaky fillo wrapper—an original pastry in the tradition of Hungarian and Viennese fruit strudels.

6 fillo sheets (12×17 inches)
2 tablespoons each melted sweet butter/margarine blend or pareve margarine, and peanut or corn oil, combined
2 firmly packed tablespoons light brown sugar
1 tablespoon granulated sugar
1 teaspoon cinnamon
½ teaspoon each freshly grated nutmeg and ground cardamom
⅓ cup unseasoned fine dry

bread crumbs, preferably homemade from Crusty Italian Bread or Challah
¼ cup ground blanched almonds
2 large Golden Delicious apples, peeled, cored and coarsely chopped
½ cup fresh cranberries, picked over, rinsed and well drained
½ teaspoon minced lemon zest
¼ cup dark seedless raisins
Confectioners' sugar (optional)

1. Preheat oven to 375°F. Unroll fillo sheets and immediately cover with damp cloth. Grease a cookie sheet with shortening mixture.

2. In a bowl, combine sugars and spices. In another bowl, combine crumbs with almonds. Measure out 3 tablespoons crumb/nut mixture and add to sugar/spice mixture. In a third bowl, combine apples with cranberries, lemon zest and raisins. Set all bowls aside.

3. Prepare 1 large strudel. Place a long sheet of plastic wrap on dry work surface, long edge nearest to you. Lift off 1 sheet of fillo and lay it on plastic; smooth out. Using a pastry brush, paint fillo lightly with shortening mixture. Sprinkle with 1½ tablespoons crumb/nut mixture. Lay another sheet of fillo over it, smoothing out. Repeat painting, sprinkling and smoothing procedure with remaining sheets, reserving some of the shortening mixture to brush over rolled-up strudel.

4. Sprinkle sugar/crumb mixture over fruit and combine. Arrange on long end of layers, leaving a 1½-inch border on 3 sides, manipulating with hands into a compact long loaf. Using extended plastic to assist you, carefully roll up, jelly-roll fashion, tucking in any stray bits of fruit as you roll.

5. Place strudel, seam side down, on prepared cookie sheet. With a sharp knife, score 8 servings, cutting through about ¼ inch. Brush with remaining shortening mixture. Place in center section of oven and bake until delicately browned (35 to 40 minutes). Serve warm or at room temperature, dusted with confectioners' sugar, if desired.

Yield: 8 servings

Variation: Apple Strudel: Use 3 apples and leave out cranberries.

Rendered Chicken Fat (Schmaltz) *(Meat)*

Once in a while, why not? Here's how to prepare it in all its traditional glory. But remember, cutting down on all fats is a health goal. Do not overuse. From time to time, try Seasoned Olive Oil (page 31) instead. It's as tasteful *in its own way,* and its numbers look better on the nutritional scorecard.

About 2 pounds chicken fat and fatty skin, cut into small pieces
1 large onion, cut into 1-inch chunks

3 large cloves garlic, each clove halved
½ crisp sweet apple, cored, peeled and coarsely chopped
½ teaspoon ground sage

1. Put fat in medium nonstick skillet. Over very low heat, cook, uncovered, stirring and turning pieces often, until almost all the fat is melted (about 25 minutes).

2. While fat renders, coarse-chop onion and garlic by hand or in workbowl of food processor that has been fitted with steel blade (2 or 3 on/off turns). Repeat process for apple. Stir mixture into hot fat. Sprinkle with sage. Raise heat until mixture boils. Then reduce heat to moderately low. Cook until solids are lightly browned (20 to 25 minutes).

3. Strain into bowl, pressing out liquid. Let cool. Transfer to freeze-proof container and store in refrigerator (it will stay fresh for several weeks). Or, freeze in tightly closed container and use as needed. Frozen fat will stay fresh for up to 3 months.

Yield: About 1 cup

Note: Although the cracklings (they're called grebenes or grieven) remaining after straining the rendered fat are tasty and are traditionally added to chopped liver and many other dishes, I do not use them; the browned onions from Seasoned Olive Oil are preferred (step 2, page 31).

9
VEGETABLES AND GRAINS

Holiday Vegetable and Fruit Tzimmes *(Meat or Pareve)*

This tzimmes is a stew of mixed vegetables, fruits and spices that serves as an out-of-the-ordinary side dish to a festive main course.

But often making a tzimmes is a "tzimmes"—a mess; making a mountain out of a molehill; making a federal case. That's why I developed my Tzimmes for the food processor. Slice all the sliceable ingredients in it before proceeding to the layering.

My Tzimmes is designed for the winter holidays, when yams and winter squash are fresh, inexpensive and plentiful. But serve it on almost any holiday, and whenever you're in a holiday mood.

1 cup slightly undercooked
  brown rice, well drained
1 medium acorn squash, seeded
  and peeled
2 medium yams, peeled
2 crisp sweet apples, such as
  Washington State, peeled and
  cored
2 tablespoons fresh lemon juice
2 medium onions

2 tablespoons firmly packed
  light brown sugar
10 each dried dates and prunes,
  halved
½ cup Chicken Stock or
  Vegetable Stock
1 tablespoon honey
½ teaspoon cinnamon
¼ teaspoon ground ginger

1. Cook rice first and set aside. Preheat oven to 350°F.

2. Fit workbowl of food processor with slicing blade. Cut squash, yams and apples into pieces to securely fit feed tube. Thin-slice them, transferring to separate bowls. Sprinkle lemon juice over apples and squash, turning to coat.

3. Fit the workbowl of processor with steel blade. Coarsely chop onions in 2 or 3 on/off turns. Scrape into a dish. Put sugar and dates into workbowl and process in 3 or 4 on/off turns. Add prunes and process for 2 seconds; scrape into a dish.

4. Put stock, honey and spices in a saucepan; bring to a boil.

5. Grease an 8- or 9-×-12-inch Pyrex dish with sweet pareve margarine. Arrange layers of ingredients in the following sequence, using ⅓ of each for every layer: rice, yam, onion, squash, apple. Repeat layering twice more. Arrange date mixture in clumps across medley; then spread out as evenly as you can. Drizzle stock mixture over and around all. Cover with sheet of heavy-duty aluminum foil and bake in center of oven for 1¼ hours. Uncover and return to oven for 20 minutes longer. Place on trivet and serve directly from casserole.

Yield: 8 to 10 servings

Yam and Cabbage Tzimmes *(Pareve)*

I define tzimmes as "a marvelous mishmash." The marvel is that fruits and vegetables of such disparate tastes can mix so harmoniously. I've combined the sharp tanginess of cabbage with the soft sweetness of yams, and added prunes, fruit juice concentrate and sweet Passover wine.

2 cups shredded savoy cabbage
   (about 1 small head)
2 large yams (about 1½
   pounds), peeled, halved, then
   thin-sliced
2 sweet medium apples, peeled,
   cored and coarsely chopped
15 pitted prunes, halved
3 tablespoons frozen apple juice
   concentrate
¼ cup firmly packed light or

dark brown sugar
½ cup sweet Passover wine
   (cherry or concord grape)
1 teaspoon ground cinnamon
½ teaspoon each ground ginger
   and cardamom
2 tablespoons honey
1 teaspoon sweet pareve
   margarine, plus 2 teaspoons,
   cut into small pieces

1. Preheat oven to 375°F. Grease a 9×11-inch ovenproof casserole with 1 teaspoon margarine. Arrange cabbage, yams, apples and prunes in layers, using ½ of each ingredient for each layer.

2. In bowl, combine and blend concentrate, sugar, wine, spices and honey. Evenly spoon over mixture. Dot with margarine. Cover with sheet of aluminum foil. Bake for 1 hour. Uncover and gently stir. Loosely cover and return to oven for 15 minutes. (Dish may be prepared well ahead of serving time, covered and reheated.)

Yield: 8 servings

Hot Red Cabbage with Fennel

(Pareve)

Not quite sweet, not quite sour. Sautéed, then steamed to crunchy perfection. Hot red cabbage, a specialty of Eastern European Jewish cookery, never tasted so good.

3 tablespoons Italian olive oil
5 cups thin-sliced red cabbage (about ¾ pound)
1 cup fine-chopped fennel (about ½ medium bulb)
½ cup minced onion
1 teaspoon cinnamon
½ teaspoon each freshly grated nutmeg and ground cardamom
2 teaspoons partially crushed caraway seed
1 tablespoon firmly packed dark brown sugar
1 sweet crisp apple, such as Golden Delicious or Washington State, peeled, cored, coarsely chopped
2 tablespoons fresh lemon juice
1 tablespoon cider vinegar
⅓ cup dark seedless raisins
¼ teaspoon salt

1. Heat oil in a Dutch oven (preferably enamel-lined) until very hot. Add cabbage, fennel and onion. Sprinkle with spices and sauté over medium-high heat, stirring often, until bulk diminishes by ⅓.

2. Add caraway seed, sugar, apple, lemon juice, vinegar and raisins and combine. Continue to sauté for 2 minutes. Reduce heat to lowest setting; cover tightly and cook for 40 minutes, stirring every 10 minutes (cabbage will steam in its own juices). Sprinkle in salt and combine. Re-cover and let stand for 15 minutes. Briefly reheat, if necessary, before serving.

Yield: 6 servings

Falafel (an Israeli fast food)

(Pareve or Meat)

Deep-fried chick-pea croquettes heaped into warm split pita bread and topped with succulent mixed vegetable salad—*that's* falafel as it's sold by street vendors in Israel (and throughout the Middle East). You can find reasonable facsimiles in ethnic eateries in major American cities from New York to San Francisco. In my New American Jewish version, I've retained the street-smart taste with a nutrition-smart recipe that holds salt and fat to a bare minimum (quite the reverse of the soaked-in-fat and heavily salted commercial versions).

*¾ cup dried chick-peas
    (garbanzo beans)*
½ cup coarse bulgur*
*1½ cups Vegetable Stock,
    Chicken Stock or water*
4 large cloves garlic
1 medium onion
*2 tablespoons coarsely chopped
    fresh basil or parsley*
*¾ teaspoon each ground cumin,
    coriander and marjoram*
⅛ teaspoon cayenne pepper

*2 teaspoons dried basil leaves,
    crumbled*
*¼ teaspoon salt, plus ⅛
    teaspoon*
3 tablespoons fresh lemon juice
1 large egg
*½–¾ cup soft bread crumbs (see
    note)*
4 tablespoons Italian olive oil
Pita loaves
Salad (see serving suggestion)

*Available in health food stores and some supermarkets.

1. Put chick-peas in a strainer. Pick over; rinse under cold running water. Transfer to a small bowl; cover with cold water and soak for 1 hour. Drain, add fresh water and repeat procedure. Drain, add fresh water and soak overnight. Next day, pour into a strainer and rinse under cold running water. (This soaking method makes dried beans more digestible.) Transfer chick-peas to a medium heavy-bottomed saucepan. Add water to cover. Bring to a rolling boil. Reduce heat, partially cover and slow-boil for 15 minutes. Drain and let cool.

2. Put bulgur into a strainer; rinse under cold running water. Transfer to a heavy-bottomed saucepan. Add stock or water. Bring to a boil; reduce heat to slow-boil and cook, uncovered, for 5 minutes. Remove from heat. Partially cover and let stand for 30 minutes (all liquid should be absorbed). Set aside.

3. Fine-chop garlic and onion by hand, or halve garlic cloves, cut onion into 1-inch chunks and place in workbowl of food processor that has been fitted with steel blade and fine-chop. Scrape into a large bowl.

4. Transfer cooked chick-peas to workbowl. Add fresh basil or parsley, spices, dried basil, ¼ teaspoon salt and lemon juice. Process in 3 or 4 on/off turns until fine-chopped (do not puree). Add to onion mixture.

5. In cup, beat egg with fork. Add to bowl together with bulgur, stirring to combine. Stir in ½ cup bread crumbs. Mixture should hold together when pressed with fingers. If not, add more crumbs, using just enough to bind the mixture. Cover and refrigerate for 45 minutes.

6. Shape into 1-inch balls, flattening slightly (or use a falafel maker), placing balls on platter as they're formed. Cook in 3 batches. Preheat a large well-seasoned iron skillet over medium-high heat. For each batch, drizzle in 1 tablespoon plus 1 teaspoon oil, tilting pan to coat. Heat oil for 30 seconds. Then arrange ⅓ of the croquettes in the skillet without crowding. Cook until browned on both sides, turning once with a metal spatula (total cooking time about 12 minutes). Repeat procedure with remaining ingredients.

7. To serve, warm single-serving pita loaves (or cut large loaves in half). Split open and fill each pocket with 4 or 5 falafels. Sprinkle with remaining salt. Top with Mixed Fresh Vegetable Salad (page 155).

Yield: About 40 falafels; 8 or more servings

Note: The type of bread crumbs used will affect the flavor of the croquettes. Use Challah (page 165) or Brown Rye Bread with 3 Seeds (page 167) or a good quality commercial bread. To make the crumbs, tear up 3 slices of bread (crusts removed). Process to crumbs in the workbowl of a food processor that has been fitted with steel blade.

Vegetable Loaf
with Leek   (Pareve or Meat)

The leek is a Jewish gastronomic symbol of good luck, which means it is used often; and that *is* good luck for vegetable lovers. Leek, a sophisticated member of the garlic family, adds its refined pungency to any dish, especially when the leeks are orchestrated, as they are here, with harmonious herbs and spices. Serve my Vegetable Loaf as a midday main course, or at lunch or dinner as a side dish with stewed meats or poultry.

½ cup dried apricots, preferably unsulphured
2 tablespoons Italian olive oil
1 cup minced leeks (white part only)
2 teaspoons minced garlic
½ pound snow-white fresh mushrooms, ends trimmed, quartered and thin-sliced
1 cup chopped nuts (not ground)
1 cup each minced cabbage and carrot
1 tablespoon Spice Mix
1 tablespoon honey
2 large eggs (use 1 yolk and 2 whites)
½ cup Vegetable Stock or Chicken Stock
½ cup matzoh meal
2 teaspoons sweet pareve margarine, cut into small pieces
Watercress sprigs

1. Preheat oven to 350°F. Put apricots in a cup; add enough boiling water to barely cover. Set aside.

2. Heat 1½ tablespoons oil in a large nonstick skillet until very hot. Add leeks and, over medium-high heat, sauté until they begin to brown. Stir in garlic and mushrooms. Continue to sauté, stirring often, for 2 minutes. Sprinkle in nuts and combine.

3. Pour in remaining oil; then add cabbage, carrot and Spice Mix, folding over several times. Cook for 10 minutes, folding mixture over often (volume will decrease). Turn into a large bowl.

4. Squeeze out liquid from apricots and cut them into small pieces. Combine with mixture. Put honey and eggs in a cup and beat with a fork. Stir into mixture along with stock. Then fold in matzoh meal.

5. Pile into an 8-inch margarine-greased loaf pan, smoothing out top. Strew with pieces of margarine. Cover tightly with a sheet of heavy-duty aluminum foil. Spread a dishcloth across the bottom of a medium-size broiling pan (with sides about 2 inches high). Place loaf pan on cloth. Pour 2 inches of boiling water around the pan. Bake in center section of oven for 35 minutes. Remove foil and bake for 10 minutes longer. Take out of the oven and stand on a wire rack for 5 minutes. Run a blunt knife around the sides of loaf. Place a serving plate over it and invert; a sharp rap to the bottom of pan should loosen it. With serrated knife, cut into 8 serving pieces. Garnish with watercress and serve.

Yield: 8 servings

Serving suggestions: Lemon Sauce (page 185) or Spicy Tomato Sauce (page 186).

Vegetable Cornbread *(Dairy)*

A beautiful way to serve vegetables: Layer them alternately with spiced cornbread batter, top with an embroidery of paper-thin carrot slices and bake until crusty. Slice to a panorama of colors.

½ pound carrots (about 4 carrots), peeled, sliced paper-thin
1 cup coarsely chopped broccoli florets
7 teaspoons sweet butter/margarine blend, cold
¼ teaspoon salt
2 cups stone-ground yellow cornmeal
1 cup unbleached flour
¾ teaspoon baking soda

3 teaspoons baking powder
1½ tablespoons Spice Mix
3 eggs (use 2 yolks and 3 whites)
3 tablespoons Italian olive oil
Pinch cream of tartar
1 tablespoon sugar
2 cups low-fat buttermilk, preferably unsalted
¼ teaspoon freshly ground black pepper

1. Preheat oven to 400°F. Drop carrots into a pot of rapidly boiling water and cook for 3 minutes. Drain; transfer to a bowl. Drop broccoli into a pot of rapidly boiling water. Cook for 1 minute. Drain; transfer to a separate bowl. To each bowl add 2 teaspoons shortening and ⅛ teaspoon salt. Stir until vegetables are evenly coated. Set both bowls aside.

2. Sift cornmeal, flour, baking soda and baking powder into another large bowl. Stir in Spice Mix.

3. Separate eggs, putting 2 yolks in a cup and 3 whites in a mixing machine bowl. To yolks add oil; beat with fork to blend. To whites add cream of tartar. Using whisk attachment, beat on medium-high speed until foamy. Turn up to highest setting; gradually add sugar while beating until firm and glossy peaks form (do not overbeat).

4. Make a well in the center of cornmeal mixture. With wooden spoon, stir in egg-yolk mixture. Then add 1½ cups buttermilk; stir until all of the dry ingredients have moistened. Let stand for 3 minutes; then stir in remaining ½ cup buttermilk. Fold in beaten egg whites.

5. Grease an 8- or 9-inch springform pan with 1 teaspoon shortening. To assemble, arrange batter and vegetables in layers as follows: Spread ⅓ of batter across pan, smoothing out. Cover with ½ the carrots, arranging evenly over batter. Cover carrots with ⅓ batter, smoothing out with spatula. Arrange all of the broccoli over batter. Cover broccoli with remaining batter (layers will be thin). Evenly top with remaining carrots. Sprinkle with pepper. Cut remaining 2 teaspoons shortening into small pieces and strew over all.

6. Bake in center section of oven for 45 to 50 minutes, testing for doneness after 45 minutes. Bread is done when edges become lightly browned and when toothpick inserted in center comes out almost clean. Stand pan on a wire rack for 10 minutes. Loosen around sides with a blunt knife. With spatula, loosen bread from bottom of pan and slide onto a serving plate. Cut with a sharp serrated knife and serve warm.

Yield: 8 to 10 servings

Variation: Substitute coarsely chopped fresh green beans for broccoli, increasing cooking time to 3 minutes.

Stuffed Peppers   (Dairy or Pareve)

Ashkenazic or Sephardic *meat*-stuffed vegetables are economy dishes with exorbitant flavors. *Vegetable*-stuffed, they are even more appealing to the dollar-watcher, and likely to be more nutritious. This is the case with my Stuffed Peppers. Meat is replaced by whole grains and chestnuts, a combination that implies a taste of meat. And pampered by my Tomato Sauce, the dish is every bit as delicious.

6 large sweet bell peppers
1½ cups slightly undercooked rice
1 cup slightly undercooked kasha (roasted whole buckwheat groats; see note)
1½ tablespoons sweet butter/margarine blend or sweet pareve margarine
2 tablespoons minced garlic
¾ cup each minced red onion and celery
1 tablespoon Spice Mix
½ teaspoon ground marjoram
2 tablespoons fresh lemon juice
2 tablespoons minced fresh

basil or mint
1 cup soft bread crumbs
1 large egg, lightly beaten
1 cup whole-cooked fresh chestnuts, or unsweetened drained canned chestnuts packed in water, coarsely chopped
About 2½ cups Spicy Tomato Sauce (page 186) prepared with Vegetable Stock or water, heated
½ teaspoon salt
¼ teaspoon coarsely ground black pepper

1. Cut away stem ends from peppers; remove seeds and membranes. Rinse well inside and out. Stand upright in a pot of boiling water and cook for 5 minutes. Drain and set aside. Preheat oven to 350°F.

2. Put rice and kasha into a large bowl. Heat shortening in a nonstick skillet until hot. Sauté garlic, onion and celery for 1 minute. Sprinkle with Spice Mix and marjoram. Sauté until mixture begins to soften. Add to rice mixture.

3. Stir in lemon juice, fresh basil or mint, crumbs, egg, chestnuts, ½ cup sauce, salt and pepper. Pile into peppers. (May be prepared in advance up to this point and refrigerated; bring to room temperature before baking.)

4. Choose an ovenproof casserole that will snugly accommodate all of the peppers. Spread 1 cup of sauce across bottom of casserole. Add peppers. Top each pepper with 1 tablespoon of sauce. Cover tightly with aluminum foil and bake for 45 minutes, basting once, midway.

5. Arrange peppers on warm platter, surrounded with sauce from the casserole. Reheat remaining sauce and serve on the side.

Yield: 6 servings

Note: To cook kasha to firm consistency, in a small heavy-bottomed saucepan, bring 1½ cups water or stock to a boil. Add ½ cup whole-kernel kasha (roasted buckwheat groats). Reduce heat to slow-boil and cook, uncovered, stirring often, until all liquid evaporates. Remove from heat and cover for 5 minutes before using.

Spinach and Carrot Pie
(Dairy)

This recipe spins off from the classic Sephardic spinach pie. The crust is traditional fillo dough, but the filling is new-textured: softer than a mousse (because I've cut down on egg yolks). To heighten flavor, I've introduced sour cream (reduced-fat, of course). Adorned with sliced carrots, it's a colorful main course and side dish (particularly with fish).

2 medium carrots, peeled, trimmed and thin-sliced
3 10-ounce boxes frozen leaf spinach (see note)
¼ cup reduced-fat sour cream
4 tablespoons Italian olive oil
1 tablespoon minced garlic
1 cup combined minced shallot and onion
4 large eggs (use 2 yolks and 4 whites)

2 tablespoons fresh lemon juice
1 teaspoon each freshly grated nutmeg and dried crumbled oregano
¾ teaspoon cinnamon
½ teaspoon salt
1 cup drained part-skim ricotta cheese
¼ cup freshly grated Parmesan cheese
5 fillo sheets (12×17 inches)

1. Steam carrots until crisp-tender. Set aside.

2. Cook spinach, following directions on box. Transfer to a strainer and, using a large spoon, press out as much liquid as possible. (Carrots and spinach may be cooked a day ahead and refrigerated separately.) Transfer spinach to workbowl of food processor that has been fitted with steel blade. Add sour cream and process until smooth. Turn into a large bowl.

3. Heat a nonstick skillet with 1½ tablespoons oil. Add garlic, shallot and onion. Over moderate heat, sauté until wilted but not brown. Combine with spinach.

4. Break one whole egg into a large bowl. Separate remaining 3 eggs, adding 1 yolk to the bowl and 3 whites into a large mixing machine bowl. To yolk mixture add lemon juice, nutmeg, oregano, cinnamon and ¼ teaspoon salt. Fold into spinach medley. Then fold in ricotta and Parmesan cheeses. (Recipe may be prepared ahead up to this point and refrigerated until ready to complete.) Preheat oven to 350°F.

5. Beat egg whites until firm but no dry peaks form. Fold into spinach medley.

6. To prepare crust, tear off a long sheet of plastic wrap. Place 1 sheet of fillo over it. Pour remaining oil into custard cup. Very lightly brush fillo with oil. Cover with second sheet, smoothing out with fingers. Brush again lightly with oil. Repeat procedure three more times.

7. Sparsely brush a 10-inch pie pan with oil. Lift short ends of fillo and place in pan, letting long edges reach to rim. Press bottom and sides to fit. Spoon in filling, spreading to edges and mounding slightly in center. Cut away hanging edges of dough to within 2 inches from edges. Fold over and press remaining pieces to rim. Moisten edges with oiled pastry brush. Arrange carrots in one layer across top of pie, pressing gently into mixture. Sprinkle with remaining ¼ teaspoon salt.

8. Bake until crust browns (40 to 45 minutes). Place on a wire rack for 10 minutes before cutting. Delicious served hot or warm.

Yield: 6 servings as a main course; 8 servings as a side dish.

Variation: Prepare a crustless variation (mousse) that's suitable for Passover. Reduce oil measurement to 2 tablespoons. Follow steps 1 through 5. Rub remaining ½ tablespoon oil on bottom and sides of a 1¾–2-quart casserole. Put casserole into a preheated 350°F oven for 10 minutes; quickly pour mousse into it. Arrange carrots on top in one layer; sprinkle with remaining salt and bake for 40 to 45 minutes (toothpick inserted in center should come out clean).

Note: For the sake of taste, I prefer to use leaf spinach rather than the chopped variety, and then puree until smooth.

Carrot/Zucchini Puree (Pareve)

Crisp carrots and crunchy zucchini, slightly undercooked, then pureed to smoothest consistency, supply contrasting texture when served with roast meats, chicken or strudels. The taste of this dish helps you remember that carrots symbolize golden days ahead.

1 pound fresh carrots, peeled, ends trimmed, thin-sliced
½ pound zucchini, ends trimmed, well scrubbed, cut into ¼-inch cubes
1 tablespoon Italian olive oil
1 tablespoon minced fresh ginger
2 tablespoons finely minced
shallot
1 tablespoon sweet pareve margarine
½ teaspoon each freshly grated nutmeg and cinnamon
⅛–¼ teaspoon salt
2 tablespoons minced parsley or fresh coriander
1 tablespoon honey

1. Drop carrots into a large saucepan of boiling water and cook for 5 minutes, maintaining a rolling boil. Add zucchini and cook for 5 minutes more. Pour into a colander and let drain.

2. Heat oil in a small nonstick skillet. Add ginger and shallot. Sauté, stirring continually, until softened without browning (about 3 minutes). Transfer to a dish.

3. Put margarine into the skillet (no need to clean it) and cook over moderate heat until it turns golden. Remove from heat.

4. To workbowl of food processor that has been fitted with steel blade add drained vegetables, sautéed mixture, spices, ⅛ teaspoon salt, parsley or coriander, golden margarine and honey. Puree until smooth. Taste for salt, adding remainder if desired. Reheat briefly in the nonstick skillet.

Yield: 6 servings

Variation: For a dairy meal, stir in ¼ cup reduced-fat sour cream before pureeing.

Creamy Spinach *(Dairy or Pareve)*

Yes, Jewish mothers *may* have been responsible for that infamous phrase: "Eat your spinach!" Don't be too hard on them; they only wanted the best nutrition for their children. Attempting to disguise the taste, some mothers creamed the vegetable by adding cream. Kids loved it. But then mothers learned that cream carried a cargo of no-no fats and cholesterol. Cream was out. And the problem of how to get kids to stop hating spinach went on. Until now. With the aid of the food processor, I've solved the problem: You can make creamy spinach with reduced-fat sour cream or no cream at all (see variation). It puffs up ("creams") to delectable goodness. Kids I know like it. Including kids over twenty-one.

2 10-ounce boxes frozen leaf spinach
⅓ cup reduced-fat sour cream
½ teaspoon freshly grated nutmeg

2 teaspoons dried basil or oregano, crumbled
Dash cayenne pepper
¼ teaspoon salt (optional)

1. Cook spinach according to directions on box. Place in strainer and press out most of liquid.

2. Transfer to workbowl of food processor that has been fitted with steel blade. Add sour cream, nutmeg, dried herb and pepper. Process until pureed and fluffy. (May be prepared up to 1 hour before serving.) Taste for salt, adding it if desired. Reheat in a small nonstick or enameled saucepan.

Yield: 5 or 6 servings

Variation: For the pareve version, omit sour cream; add 2 tablespoons good quality Italian olive oil, ½ teaspoon onion powder and remaining ingredients before processing.

Baked Spiced Yam Slices *(Pareve)*

The yam is a favorite during the New Year season, when sweetness is a symbol of optimism for the coming year. This preparation will remind you of Potatoes Anna (without the butter), but on second taste you'll recognize that you've never tasted anything like it before. Reasons are: the spice selection and my novel cooking technique.

1½ pounds yams, peeled
1 teaspoon each cinnamon and dry mustard
½ teaspoon ground ginger

2 tablespoons Italian olive oil
¼ teaspoon salt
Freshly ground black pepper

1. Cut yams by hand into ¼-inch slices. Or fit workbowl of food processor with slicing disk; using light pressure, slice potatoes ¼-inch thick. Transfer to a colander and rinse under cold running water, separating slices. Turn into a large bowl. Cover with cold water; chill for 30 minutes. Drain and dry slices with paper toweling.

2. In a cup, combine cinnamon, mustard and ginger.

3. Position oven rack in lower section of oven. Preheat oven to 450°F. Spread oil across rectangular metal pan (10 × 13 inches). Place pan in oven for 10 minutes. Quickly place potatoes in hot oiled pan, shuffling with spatula to coat. Spread slices across the pan in 1 layer. Sprinkle with half the mixed seasonings. Bake for 8 minutes. Sprinkle with remaining seasonings; shuffle slices, then spread them across the pan in 1 layer; return pan to the oven for 8 minutes longer. Repeat shuffling, spreading and baking procedure twice more.

4. Remove pan from oven. Sprinkle potatoes with salt and pepper, turning several times with spatula. Arrange on a hot plate and serve at once.

Yield: 4 or 5 servings

Barley Pilaf   (Pareve or Meat)

Barley, an especially popular grain in biblical times, is welcomed back to an esteemed role in Jewish cookery as a stand-in for rice in this exciting new high-fiber pilaf, which also features a bright array of fruits and vegetables.

6 cups water
¾ cup barley
1 tablespoon white wine Worcestershire sauce
½ cup frozen baby lima beans
1½ tablespoons Italian olive oil
1 cup minced shallot, or a combination of onion and shallot
1 tablespoon minced garlic
1 small red bell pepper, seeded, cut into narrow 1-inch strips
½ pound snow-white fresh

mushrooms, ends trimmed, quartered and thin-sliced
1½ tablespoons Spice Mix
1 small tart apple, peeled, cored, coarsely chopped
⅔ cup Vegetable Stock, Chicken Stock or low-sodium tomato juice
2 tablespoons minced fresh coriander or parsley
¼ teaspoon each freshly ground black pepper and salt

1. Pour water into a 2- or 3-quart heavy-bottomed saucepan and bring to a rolling boil. Add barley and Worcestershire sauce. When liquid returns to a boil, reduce heat to slow-boil, cover and cook for 50 minutes, stirring twice at equal intervals. Pour into a strainer and drain. Cook lima beans, following directions on the box. Combine barley and lima beans in a large bowl. Preheat oven to 350°F.

2. Heat oil in a large nonstick skillet until hot. Over medium-high heat, sauté shallot or shallot/onion mixture and garlic until it begins to brown. Add red pepper and sauté for 2 minutes. Then stir in mushrooms; sprinkle with Spice Mix. Sauté until all liquid accumulating from mushrooms evaporates. Mix with barley medley.

3. Stir in apple, stock or tomato juice, coriander or parsley, pepper and salt. Turn into a 2-quart ovenproof casserole that has been greased with sweet pareve margarine, smoothing out top. Bake, uncovered, in center section of oven for 40 minutes. Place on a trivet and serve directly from the casserole.

Yield: 6 servings

Variation: To serve with a dairy meal, use ½ cup unsalted tomato puree mixed with ⅓ cup Vegetable Stock or water. Sprinkle ¼ cup Parmesan cheese over top just before baking. (Parmigiano Reggiano is a superior Italian low-fat Parmesan cheese which will impart a delightful taste to all recipes calling for Parmesan cheese).

Rice Omelette   (Dairy or Pareve)

I always keep extra rice frozen so that I can prepare this delicious and easy-to-make omelette.

> 2½ teaspoons sweet
>   butter/margarine blend,
>   pareve margarine or
>   Seasoned Olive Oil
> ¼ cup minced onion or scallion
> ½ cup cooked brown or white
>   rice
>
> 2 large eggs (use 1 yolk and 2
>   whites)
> 1½–2 teaspoons Spice Mix
> 2 teaspoons reduced-sodium soy
>   sauce
> 2 teaspoons minced parsley
> ⅛ teaspoon salt

1. Heat shortening in an 8-inch nonstick skillet until hot. Add onion or scallion and sauté over moderate heat until it begins to brown. Stir in rice and cook over medium heat for 2 minutes. Then spread mixture evenly across pan.

2. In a small bowl, combine eggs, Spice Mix, soy sauce and parsley, beating with fork to blend. Pour evenly over rice mixture, tilting pan from side to side after omelette starts to congeal. Cook until bottom of omelette is browned and top is almost firm. Slide onto a luncheon plate. Flip over and cut in half. Sprinkle with salt and serve immediately.

Yield: 2 servings; recipe may be doubled and cooked in 2 batches (or in 2 pans)

10
9 SPECIAL SALADS

The salad is a culinary concept: creating a dish by anointing an edible, or any combination of edibles, with a dressing composed of oil; a foil for the oil such as vinegar; and salt, plenty of salt (as a matter of fact, the word "salad" is derived from *sal*, which is Latin for salt).

But the recent nutrition revolution has refined the concept of salad. The oil must be a "good" oil; the edibles must be nutritious; and the use of salt must be sparse.

The New American Jewish salads meet these specifications. Plus one more specification that's stood the test of time in Jewish cookery: The salads must have taste—a lot of taste.

Chicken Salad   (Meat)

In my mother's kosher kitchen, chicken from the chicken soup of the day before was always used for a cold salad. It tasted like mayo, celery and salt. Here's a more interesting way of using the boiled chicken—without added fat from mayo or any other source. To bring out its best flavor, serve the chicken salad warm, or at room temperature, in a thicket of crisp lettuce leaves.

1 red bell pepper
¾ cup canned chick-peas or
   white beans, rinsed under
   cold running water, well
   drained
½ cup each coarsely chopped
   scallion or red onion, and
   celery
½ cup firmly packed chopped
   watercress leaves
2½–3 cups cooked chicken, cut

   into 1-inch chunks
⅛ teaspoon cayenne pepper
1 recipe Dipping Sauce (page
   186)
1 cup canned mandarin
   oranges, drained
   Crisp lettuce leaves
1 small ripe avocado, cut into
   ½-inch crescents
¼ cup coarsely chopped
   blanched almonds

1. Preheat broiler. Remove skin from pepper by placing it on a rack in broiling pan 3 inches from heat and blacken all over. Transfer to a plastic bag and seal. Let stand for 15 minutes to steam. Peel off skin (it will slip right off). Seed and cut into ¼-inch strips, then cut crosswise into 1-inch pieces.

2. Put pepper strips, chick-peas, scallion or red onion, celery and watercress into a large bowl. Fold in chicken.

3. Stir cayenne pepper into the Dipping Sauce. Pour ½ cup sauce over all and stir until salad is moistened. Add half the oranges and combine. Let stand for 10 minutes. Fold over ingredients. Measure out 3 tablespoons of remaining sauce and reserve for last step. Taste for more dressing, adding remaining sauce, if desired.

4. Line a salad bowl or a plate with lettuce leaves. Spoon with salad. Garnish with remaining oranges and avocado in a decorative pattern. Drizzle reserved sauce over avocado and orange garnish; sprinkle with nuts.

Yield: 6 servings

Serving suggestion: Sour Rye Bread (page 168).

Mixed Fresh Vegetable Salad (an Israeli favorite)

(Pareve)

Israelis love salads. All kinds of salads. They enjoy them as first courses, main courses, piled into pita bread and even over crisply cooked meats. "For the best results," some Israeli cooks told me, "peel, cut, slice, grate and tear vegetables just before serving." Added bulgur contributes to the chewiness. Use just enough dressing to lightly coat; serve right away.

1/3 cup bulgur (pre-cooked wheat)

2 medium cucumbers, peeled and diced

1 medium red onion, coarsely chopped

1 sweet red bell pepper, seeded (skinned, if desired), cut into 1/4-inch strips

1 small head romaine lettuce, tough center sections of leaves removed, torn into bite-size pieces

1/4 cup Italian olive oil

2 tablespoons fresh lime or lemon juice

1 tablespoon balsamic vinegar

1/2 teaspoon dry mustard

2 teaspoons dried sweet basil leaves or several fresh basil leaves, chopped

2 firm ripe tomatoes, cored, seeded (skinned, if desired), cut into small pieces

1/4 teaspoon salt

Freshly ground black pepper

Minced parsley

1. Pour bulgur into a strainer and rinse under cold running water. Transfer to a small bowl. Add just enough water to cover and let stand for 30 minutes. Transfer to a strainer and press out as much liquid as possible. Place in a large salad bowl.

2. To bowl, add cucumbers, onion, red pepper and lettuce; toss.

3. In a cup, whisk together oil, juice, vinegar, mustard and dried basil (if you use fresh basil, stir it in after coating with salad dressing). Let mixture stand for 3 minutes. Add tomatoes to salad bowl. Pour dressing over all and gently toss.

4. Arrange on individual salad plates. Using fingers, sprinkle each serving with salt, pepper and parsley. Serve at once.

Yield: 4 or more servings

Serving suggestion: Over Falafel (page 142).

Eggplant Salad   (Meat or Pareve)

Eggplant soaks up liquids like a sponge. When the liquid is oil, as it is among many Sephardic cooks, that creates a problem. I solve the problem by feeding the eggplant only a limited amount of oil (and a "good" oil at that), plus liquids that in excess are nutritionally beneficial, not potentially harmful. This New American Jewish salad is as flavorsome as it is wholesome. Serve it as a compliment-garnering appetizer or as a spread on Brown Rye Bread with 3 Seeds (page 167) or Two-Grain Herb Loaf (page 174).

½ cup bulgur
Scant cup Chicken Stock or
    Vegetable Stock
½ teaspoon each ground cumin
    and chili con carne
    seasoning
2 teaspoons dried oregano
1 pound eggplant, peeled, cut
    into ⅜-inch slices
3 tablespoons Italian olive oil
1 tablespoon minced garlic
1 cup coarsely chopped onion
⅓ cup coarsely chopped celery

1 large green bell pepper,
    seeded, coarsely chopped
1 tablespoon balsamic vinegar
¼ cup unsalted tomato juice
1½ tablespoons wine vinegar
2 whole unsalted jarred
    pimentos, drained, coarsely
    chopped
¼ teaspoon each salt and
    freshly ground black pepper
Crisp lettuce leaves
Tomato wedges

1. Put bulgur in a strainer and rinse under cold running water. Bring stock to a boil in a saucepan. Stir in half the spices, half the oregano, and bulgur. Bring to a boil again. Reduce heat to slow-boil and cook for 1 minute. Cover and remove from heat. Set aside.

2. Arrange eggplant slices across a doubled sheet of paper toweling. Cover with another doubled sheet and press out as much liquid as possible. Stack slices and cut into ½-inch cubes.

3. Heat 2 tablespoons oil in a large well-seasoned iron skillet. Add eggplant; sprinkle with remaining seasonings. Sauté over medium heat, stirring often, until eggplant begins to soften (about 4 minutes). Add half each the garlic and onion, all of the celery and green pepper. Cook for 2 minutes.

4. Pour balsamic vinegar around sides of skillet. Combine with mixture and cook for 30 seconds. Then add tomato juice. Reduce heat to simmering. Cover and simmer for 7 to 8 minutes, stirring often, until all liquid is absorbed. Transfer to large bowl. Fold in remaining garlic and onion. Cool for 5 minutes.

5. Transfer soaked bulgur to strainer and press out any residual liquid. Carefully stir into salad along with wine vinegar. Let stand for 5 minutes. Then stir in remaining tablespoon of oil. Fold in pimentos and combine mixture with salt and pepper.

6. Spoon into a lettuce-lined salad bowl. Arrange tomato wedges around salad. Serve at room temperature or slightly chilled.

Yield: 1 quart; 6 servings

Note: To any chilled leftovers, stir in ½ tablespoon balsamic or wine vinegar before serving.

Coleslaw (Dairy)

A delightful tempered version of this traditional American Jewish staple—the original of which relies upon egg-laden mayonnaise, salt and sugar. Fast-chop the vegetables in your food processor; add the dressing and let the flavors develop for at least 2 hours in the refrigerator before serving.

1 medium head green cabbage
1 carrot, trimmed and peeled
1 medium green bell pepper, seeded, membranes removed
1 rib celery, strings discarded
1 medium onion
Florets from 6 large sprigs crisp parsley
¼ cup cider vinegar
1 tablespoon fresh lemon juice
1 tablespoon prepared Dijon

mustard, preferably unsalted
⅓ cup reduced-calorie mayonnaise
¾ cup low-fat buttermilk, preferably unsalted
1 tablespoon sugar
¼ teaspoon each salt and freshly ground black pepper
2 teaspoons partially crushed caraway seeds

1. Hand-cut vegetables. Or, fit workbowl of food processor with shredding disk. Cut away core of cabbage and slice into wedges that snugly fit the feed tube; shred, using medium pressure; measure out 4 lightly packed cups and turn into a large bowl. Grate carrot and add to bowl. Re-fit workbowl with steel blade. Cut pepper, celery and onion into 1-inch chunks, add parsley and coarse-chop in 2 or 3 on/off turns. Scrape into bowl.

2. Add vinegar and lemon juice and toss. In a cup, combine mustard and mayonnaise; fold into mixture. Then add balance of ingredients and combine.

3. Cover and refrigerate for at least 2 hours before serving, stirring several times. Salad will stay refrigerator-fresh for 4 days in a tightly closed container.

Yield: About 4½ cups

Warm Vegetable Salad   *(Dairy)*

The idea for a warm vegetable salad comes from Sephardic cookery. For peak crunchiness and flavor, cook it in a hot wok for just 4 minutes. An appealing starter for, or accessory to, a dairy meal. Option: You can enjoy it chilled as a side dish.

FOR THE SALAD:
½ pound crisp green beans
1 crunchy medium bok choy (about ¾ pound)
1 sweet red bell pepper
1 large sweet onion, such as Vidalia
2 large cloves garlic
1 ½-inch slice ginger
¼ pound snow-white fresh mushrooms
1½ tablespoons Italian olive oil

½ teaspoon each dry mustard, mild curry powder and crumbled dried tarragon or basil
¼ teaspoon each salt and coarsely ground black pepper

FOR THE DRESSING:
1 tablespoon each fresh lemon juice and orange juice
1 tablespoon balsamic vinegar
½ teaspoon sugar
¼ cup reduced-fat sour cream

1. Trim beans; drop into a pot of rapidly boiling water and cook for 2 minutes. Pour into colander and immediately rinse under cold running water. Cut into ½-inch pieces and set aside.

2. Cut away root end of bok choy and rinse. Seed pepper and cut away membranes. Peel onion, garlic and ginger (if skin is crinkled). Trim ends of mushrooms and damp-wipe. Using a food processor fitted with slicing disk (or a very sharp knife), thin-slice these ingredients.

3. Heat oil in a wok. Add vegetable mixture from step 2. Over very high heat, stir-fry (stirring continuously) until volume decreases by half (about 4 minutes). Transfer to a large bowl. Add green beans. Toss with spices, tarragon or basil, salt and pepper.

4. Whisk juices, vinegar and sugar together in a small bowl. Then whisk in sour cream. Pour over salad and combine. Let stand for 5 minutes before serving.

Yield: 1 quart; 6 to 8 servings

Cucumber and Onion Salad   *(Pareve)*

A popular Hungarian Jewish salad, which goes with virtually *any* food. Its taste varies with the thinness of the cucumbers and onions. The thin-slicing blade of the food processor gets the thinness just right within seconds. Health bonus: no fat or cholesterol!

3 medium cucumbers, peeled
   and thin-sliced
1 red onion, peeled and
   thin-sliced
1/3 cup white vinegar
2 tablespoons fresh lemon juice
2 tablespoons minced dill, plus

sprigs for garnish
1/2 teaspoon sugar
1/8 teaspoon crushed cloves
   (optional)
1/4 teaspoon salt
Paprika
Freshly ground black pepper

1. Spread sliced cucumbers across tripled sheets of paper toweling. Cover with additional paper and press to remove excess liquid. Repeat procedure if necessary. Transfer to a medium bowl. Add onions.

2. In a measuring cup, combine and blend vinegar with lemon juice, minced dill, sugar, and cloves if desired. Pour over salad and stir. Let stand for at least 30 minutes before serving; or cover and chill several hours, stirring from time to time.

3. To serve, with slotted spoon transfer to a medium serving bowl. Sprinkle all over with salt; stir to combine. Then top with sprinklings of paprika and pepper. Garnish with dill sprigs.

Yield: 5 servings

Carrot Salad *(Pareve)*

This is a theme salad: sweetness. According to Jewish gastronomic tradition, sweetness in foods reaffirms the sweetness of life (even when times are bad). The sweetness comes from carrots and a cornucopia of dulcifying companions.

6 large carrots, shredded
2 medium onions, chopped
2 large cloves garlic, minced
3 crisp ribs celery, strings
   removed, chopped
1 tart apple, peeled, cored and
   coarsely chopped
1/2 cup dark seedless raisins
1 1/2 tablespoons sugar
1 tablespoon balsamic vinegar
1/3 cup frozen orange juice

concentrate
1 tablespoon unsalted prepared
   Dijon mustard
1/4 cup reduced-calorie
   mayonnaise
1 tablespoon dried oregano or
   basil, crushed
2 tablespoons honey
1/4 teaspoon each salt and
   freshly ground pepper

1. Combine first 6 ingredients in large bowl. Sprinkle with 1 tablespoon sugar and vinegar and toss.

2. In small bowl, mix remaining ingredients. Stir into salad. Cover and refrigerate for at least 1 hour before serving. Taste for sugar, adding remainder if desired.

Yield: 1 quart

Farfel and Egg Salad   *(Pareve or Meat)*

A tasty spin-off of the Passover chopped egg staple.

¾ cup matzoh farfel
¾ cup hot Vegetable Stock or
   Chicken Stock
4 large hard-cooked eggs (use 2
   yolks and 4 whites)
2 tablespoons Seasoned Olive
   Oil
¼ pound snow-white fresh
   mushrooms, damp-wiped,
   ends trimmed, minced
½ cup each minced onion and

green bell pepper
2 teaspoons Spice Mix
1 medium Golden Delicious
   apple, peeled and minced
1 teaspoon honey
2 tablespoons minced dill or
   coriander, or a combination
   of both
¼ teaspoon salt
Freshly ground black pepper

1. Put farfel in a small bowl. Add stock and stir. Let stand until completely cooled.

2. Place eggs in a medium bowl and mash. Stir in softened farfel.

3. Heat oil in a nonstick skillet. Add mushrooms, onion and pepper. Sprinkle with Spice Mix and sauté over medium heat until mixture starts to soften (about 3 minutes). Stir in half the apple; sauté for 1 minute. Add to the bowl along with remaining apple.

4. Drizzle honey over salad, then combine with mixture. Add herb(s), salt and pepper and combine. Serve at room temperature.

Yield: About 2½ cups; 5 servings as an appetizer; 8 to 10 servings as a spread

Salad with 2 Herbs   *(Dairy)*

Slightly bitter watercress and fennel, which is redolent of licorice, are combined with a mélange of salad staples, then topped with Parmesan cheese and moistened with a 2-vinegar salad dressing. Serve it as a first course, as a side dish or go Italian Jewish and use this salad to top crisp Sautéed Flounder (page 104).

½ cup fine-chopped fennel
1 4-ounce jar marinated
mushrooms, drained
1 tablespoon each balsamic
vinegar, red wine vinegar
and tomato juice, preferably
unsalted
4 tablespoons Italian olive oil
1 crisp bunch watercress
4 crisp romaine lettuce leaves,
tough centers discarded, torn
into small pieces
1 medium cucumber, peeled,
seeded, cut into ¼-inch
pieces
3 scallions, tough ends
discarded, thin-sliced
2 tablespoons minced parsley or
coriander
1 large ripe tomato, cored,
seeded, cut into ½-inch
chunks
3 tablespoons freshly shredded
Parmesan cheese
¼ teaspoon salt
Freshly ground black pepper

1. Put fennel into a salad bowl. Put mushrooms in a strainer and rinse under tepid water. Drain, thin-slice and add to the bowl.

2. In a cup, combine the 2 vinegars with tomato juice; blend with a fork. Stir 2 teaspoons into the bowl. Then add 2 teaspoons oil to the mixture and combine.

3. Break off watercress leaves. Rinse and dry with paper toweling. Add to the salad, along with lettuce, cucumber, scallions and parsley or coriander and toss. Divide between 4 salad plates. Top each portion with tomatoes; then sprinkle with cheese. Drizzle each serving with equal amounts of remaining vinegar mixture; spoon with remaining oil. Using fingers, distribute salt evenly over all; sprinkle with pepper. Serve at once.

Yield: 4 large servings

11
BREADS AND MUFFINS

Challah Rolls (Pareve)

Waiters in the now legendary Jewish dairy restaurants on the Lower East Side of New York City used to greet diners with large baskets of crusty soft rolls and "How about some borscht?" The combination was heaven. The borscht is still featured, but the basketful of breads has been replaced by a single roll, and the quality is just not the same. These crusty rolls (the centers have that special challah texture) are reminiscent of those restaurant rolls of bygone years. Mixed in your food processor, they rise majestically and complement *any* food. Although they can be made with 2 rises, I suggest an extra rise for the authentic texture and aroma of old-fashioned challah.

About 2²/₃ cups unbleached
    flour
½ teaspoon sugar
1 package dry yeast
¼ cup warm water (105–115°F)
¾ cup fresh orange juice
3 tablespoons honey (see note)
2 large eggs
3 tablespoons corn oil or Italian
    olive oil
1 teaspoon finely minced orange
    zest from navel orange

¾ cup stone-ground
    whole-wheat flour
½ teaspoon salt
½ teaspoon baking powder
¼ teaspoon each cinnamon,
    ground cardamom and
    ground ginger
About 2 teaspoons stone-ground
    cornmeal
2 teaspoons each honey and
    warm tap water
Poppy and/or sesame seeds

1. In tall water glass, combine and blend with fork 2 tablespoons flour, sugar, yeast and water (a chopstick does a fine job here). Let stand until mixture foams and rises to the top of glass (7 to 8 minutes).

2. In a saucepan, combine juice with honey. Over very low heat, stir and warm until honey is dissolved. Remove from heat. Break eggs into a cup and beat with fork; measure out 2½ tablespoons and reserve for egg wash. Add oil and zest to remaining eggs; beat with fork to blend. Set 3 mixtures aside.

3. In workbowl of food processor fitted with steel blade, put 2⅓ cups unbleached flour, the whole-wheat flour, salt, baking powder and spices. Process for 10 seconds. With machine running, pour yeast mixture through feed tube, scraping out glass; then pour orange juice mixture through tube, followed by egg mixture. Process for 15 seconds. Stop machine and let batter rest for 2 minutes. Uncover workbowl. If dough has formed into cohesive ball(s), re-cover and process until ball(s) rotate around the bowl 20 times. If dough feels sticky to the touch (the humidity in the air and the temperature of the liquids when added will affect dough texture), sprinkle with 2 tablespoons of remaining flour; re-cover and process until ball(s) rotate around the bowl 20 to 25 times. Stop machine and let dough rest for 2 minutes. Shape into a ball.

4. If dough appears slightly sticky, sprinkle work surface lightly with flour and knead dough by hand, adding more flour, if necessary, to make a smooth and pliable dough. If dough is *not* sticky after removing from workbowl, do not add any additional flour. Shape into a ball, and drop into a lightly oiled, large and fairly straight-sided bowl, turning to coat. Cover tightly with plastic wrap. Let stand at room temperature (70–80°F) until double in bulk (1½ to 2 hours). Punch down and knead on work surface, squeezing out any air bubbles. Repeat rising procedure for a fine-textured crumb. For a coarser crumb, proceed to cutting dough into 12 pieces, and then cover with plastic wrap to rest for 5 minutes.

5. Shape pieces into smooth balls, pinching seams where necessary. Grease a cookie sheet with sweet pareve margarine. Sprinkle with cornmeal, shaking out excess. Arrange balls in 4 rows of 3, seams down. Cover with greased sheets of wax paper and let rise until almost double in bulk (about 1¼ hours). Preheat oven to 350°F after dough has risen for 1 hour.

6. Prepare egg wash by putting reserved egg, honey and water in a cup and blending with fork. Gently brush all over rolls. Sprinkle with poppy or sesame seeds (or a combination of both). Bake until puffed up and golden, with bottoms firm to the touch (about 25 minutes), shifting pan midway to assure even baking. Cool bread on wire rack.

Yield: 12 large rolls

Serving suggestion: Second-day rolls (or frozen ones) are delicious when sliced, lightly toasted and spread with Bagel Cheese Spread (page 187).

Note: The quality of the honey will significantly affect the taste of the rolls.

Challah *(Pareve)*

One of my apartment neighbors, a gourmet and bread aficionado, tells me that he stands at my door and breathes in deeply when I'm baking bread. He sampled this challah, smiled and said, "Francine . . . one hasn't *lived* until one's tasted this challah!" It's my number-one bread choice, too, eaten as is, or as a superlative soaker-upper for gravies and my Onion Soup (page 46).

*About 6¼ cups unbleached
    flour*
*1½ tablespoons dry yeast (1½
    packages)*
1 teaspoon baking powder
*¾ cup each unsweetened apple
    juice and water*
*⅓ cup honey, plus 2 teaspoons
    (see note)*
¼ teaspoon whole saffron

*3 large eggs (use 2 yolks and 3
    whites)*
*⅓ cup Italian olive oil or corn
    oil*
*1 teaspoon finely minced lemon
    zest*
1½ teaspoons salt
*½ teaspoon ground ginger and
    freshly grated nutmeg*
Poppy seeds

1. Put 2 cups of flour, yeast and baking powder in a large mixing machine bowl. Combine apple juice, water, ⅓ cup honey and saffron in a saucepan and heat to 105–115°F. Let stand for 2 minutes. Then pour over flour mixture. Beat with wooden spoon until dry ingredients are absorbed; then beat with paddle attachment of mixing machine on medium-high speed for 2 minutes. Stop machine. Scrape off the batter from the paddle into the bowl. Cover the bowl with plastic film and let stand for 30 minutes. Batter will puff up.

2. Break 1 whole egg into a small bowl. Break second egg into bowl, using ½ the yolk and all of the white. Add oil and lemon zest, beating with fork to blend.

3. Stir down batter. Pour egg mixture over batter and beat with mixing machine for 2 minutes. Scrape off all the batter from paddle attachment. Using wooden spoon, beat in salt, spices and all but ½ cup of remaining flour, a ½ cup at a time, beating well after each addition. When dough becomes too difficult to handle with spoon, set bowl on base of mixing machine and, using dough hook, knead at low setting, adding flour a little at a time, until dough cleans the sides of bowl. (If you're kneading by hand, when dough becomes too difficult to handle with wooden spoon, scoop up and turn onto a lightly floured board and knead in remaining flour to make a smooth elastic dough. Do not add more than total flour measurement, but continue kneading until dough becomes silky, soft to the touch and extremely pliable.)

4. Shape into a ball. Drop into a lightly oiled, fairly straight-sided large bowl, turning to coat. Cover tightly with plastic wrap. Let stand at room temperature (70–80°F) until double in bulk (about 1½ hours). Punch down. Knead briefly on board, squeezing out bubbles (you'll hear them pop). Shape into a ball and return to bowl, covered, to rise again until doubled (about 1½ hours).

5. Lightly grease 2 jelly-roll pans with sweet pareve margarine. Punch dough down. Transfer to board. Knead out air bubbles. Divide dough into 2 pieces. Cover loosely with plastic wrap and let rest for 10 minutes. For 2 round loaves, lightly flour board. For each loaf, take one piece of dough and cut away ⅓. Shape the larger and smaller pieces into smooth balls. Place the larger ball in the center of one of the greased pans, flattening slightly. Put the smaller ball atop the larger one, gently pressing to hold. Repeat procedure for second round loaf.

6. For 2 braided loaves, cut each piece of dough into 3 equal pieces. Roll each piece into a 14-inch rope, letting dough briefly rest between rolling action. When ropes hold the 14-inch length without springing back, they're ready to braid. Using 3 ropes for each loaf, lay ropes alongside each other. Start to braid from the center down to ends without pulling, tucking ends under and pinching to hold. With hands at ends of loaves, press gently, diminishing length. Carefully transfer to a greased pan. Repeat procedure for second braided loaf. Cover breads with greased sheets of wax paper. Let rise at room temperature (70–80°F) until almost doubled in bulk (about 1 hour).

7. Preheat oven to 350°F. Break remaining egg into a cup using half the yolk. Stir in 2 teaspoons honey until dissolved. Brush gently over challah. Sprinkle with poppy seeds. Bake in center section of oven for 40 minutes, covering loosely with a sheet of aluminum foil after 25 minutes. Test for doneness by inserting a toothpick between braids at center of loaves. If it comes out dry, bread is fully baked. Carefully transfer with 2 spatulas to wire racks (they're very fragile) and let cool completely before slicing.

Yield: 2 large loaves

Note: The quality of the honey will significantly affect the taste of the challah.

Brown Rye Bread
with 3 Seeds *(Pareve or Dairy)*

The precursor of this brown and chewy loaf is the Ashkenazic pumpernickel. But, thanks to gluten flour, which helps leaven the rye flour, the texture of this pumpernickel-type rye is lighter. Carob powder, natural sweeteners and three seeds will surprise and delight your palate.

About 4½ cups unbleached
   flour
2½ cups light or medium rye
   flour*
½ cup gluten flour*
2 packages dry yeast
3 tablespoons unsweetened
   carob powder*
1 tablespoon finely grated
   orange zest from navel
   orange
1 tablespoon each caraway
   seed, poppy seed and

well-crushed coriander seed
1½ teaspoons salt
1 cup unsweetened apple juice
1¼ cups water
2 tablespoons unsulphured
   molasses
1 tablespoon honey
3 tablespoons corn oil
1½ teaspoons softened sweet
   pareve margarine or sweet
   butter/margarine blend
1 tablespoon stone-ground
   cornmeal

*Available in health food stores.

1. In a large mixing machine bowl, combine 1 cup unbleached flour, 1 cup rye flour, all of the gluten flour, yeast, carob, orange zest, seeds and salt.

2. In saucepan, combine and slowly heat apple juice, water, molasses, honey and oil to 115°F. (Finger test: Liquid should be hot to the touch but not too hot to immerse finger.) Pour over dry ingredients and beat with wooden spoon until well blended. Cover with a sheet of wax paper and let stand for 30 minutes (mixture will puff up).

3. Stir down. By hand, beat in remaining rye flour, and all but ½ cup unbleached flour. When mixture becomes too difficult to handle with wooden spoon, set bowl on base of mixing machine and, using dough hook, knead at low setting, adding some of remaining flour, a little at a time, until dough cleans sides of bowl. Continue to knead for 5 minutes. (If you're kneading by hand, when dough becomes too difficult to handle with wooden spoon, scoop up and turn onto a lightly floured board and knead, adding enough of remaining flour to make a smooth elastic dough. Bulk diminishes as kneading continues.) Whether you're kneading by machine or by hand, add only enough flour to make a dough that's smooth and elastic. Cover tightly with a sheet of plastic wrap and let rise at room temperature (70–80°F) until double in bulk (about 1½ hours).

4. Punch down. Divide dough in half. Shape each piece into 9-inch oval loaf. Grease a jelly-roll pan with margarine; sprinkle with cornmeal, shaking out excess. Place loaves in pan, ends perpendicular to long sides of pan, leaving a 4-inch margin from short sides of pan. Rub bread with remaining margarine. With sharp serrated knife, cut 2 shallow diagonal slashes across each loaf. Cover with oiled sheet of wax paper. Let rise at room temperature until almost doubled (about 1 hour). Preheat oven to 400°F.

5. Place bread in center section of oven. Bake for 20 minutes. Reduce heat to 375°F. Bake for 25 minutes longer, covering loosely with a sheet of aluminum foil if tops of loaves brown too rapidly. Transfer bread to wire rack. Dip a pastry brush into cold water and brush over loaves. Let them cool completely. Tightly wrap each bread in plastic film for several hours (or overnight), and let stand at room temperature (this procedure improves taste).

Yield: 2 large loaves

Variation: In step 4, roll out each half of dough into an 8-×-12-inch rectangle. Sprinkle each piece evenly with ½ cup dark seedless raisins, leaving a 1-inch border on all sides. Tightly roll up, tucking in ends. Pinch ends and seams to hold.

Sour Rye Bread *(Pareve)*

The man seated next to me at a dinner party told me he was a promotion executive for a food-distribution company. He tasted a slice of the restaurant's bread and said that when he was a child in Chicago, his mother sent him to the store every day to buy bread. It was always a crisp Jewish rye *with* seeds. "Its shape," he said, "was crucial to the taste. It was a hand-shaped oval loaf with tapered ends, all slightly different in shape. When it was machine-sliced, I would devour both ends (the heels) long before my walk home." He asked wistfully, "Why can't I find that bread anymore?" My reply was: "Bakers prepare breads in huge batches now, and don't have the time or labor to individually hand-shape the dough, which gives it that memorable texture and taste."

The recipe that follows is for the kind of bread that my dinner companion remembered. It *does* take time to make, and your home oven will never duplicate a bread from a baker's brick oven, but try this Sour Rye Bread once, and the chances are you'll hoard your starter to make the bread again and again. And again.

FOR THE RYE STARTER:
1 cup each light rye flour and
    unbleached flour
1 package dry yeast
2 cups warm water (105–115°F)
1 tablespoon partially crushed
    caraway seed
1 medium onion, peeled
FOR THE SPONGE:
1½ cups starter
2 cups unbleached flour
1 cup warm unsweetened apple
    juice
1 tablespoon partially crushed
    caraway seed
FOR THE BREAD:
1 package dry yeast

¾ cup warm water (105–115°F)
1 teaspoon sugar
5–5½ cups unbleached flour
2 tablespoons unsulphured
    molasses
1 teaspoon ground cardamom
2 teaspoons salt
2 tablespoons Italian olive oil
1 tablespoon finely grated
    orange zest from navel
    orange (optional)
Stone-ground cornmeal
1 egg (use ½ teaspoon yolk and
    all the white), beaten with 1
    tablespoon water
Caraway seeds

1. Prepare the starter 4 days before bake day. In a large bowl, combine flours, yeast, water and caraway seed. Beat with wooden spoon until blended. Prick onion all over with a sharp-pronged fork. Bury it in the starter. Cover tightly with plastic wrap and set in a warm place (70–80°F). Mixture will bubble up, rise and fall, and develop a slightly sour but not unpleasant aroma. On the third day, discard the onion and re-cover.

2. To prepare the sponge, stir starter on fourth day. Measure out 1½ cups and pour into a large mixing machine bowl. Add unbleached flour, apple juice and caraway seed. Stir and re-cover with plastic wrap. Let stand overnight.

3. On bake day, combine yeast, water and sugar in a small bowl. When foamy (about 8 minutes), pour into the sponge and stir with wooden spoon. Add 2 cups flour, molasses, cardamom, salt, oil and orange zest, if desired. Beat by hand until smooth. With wooden spoon, beat in remaining flour, a ½ cup at a time, combining well after each addition. When mixture becomes too difficult to handle with wooden spoon, set bowl on base of mixing machine and, using a dough hook, knead at low setting, adding some of the remaining flour, a little at a time, until dough cleans the sides of bowl. Continue to knead for 5 minutes. (If you're kneading by hand, when dough becomes too difficult to handle with a wooden spoon, scoop up and turn onto a lightly floured board and knead, adding enough of remaining flour to make a smooth and elastic dough. Bulk diminishes as kneading continues.) Whether you're kneading by machine or by hand, add only enough flour to make a dough that's smooth, elastic and only slightly sticky. Kneading is complete when dough is barely sticky and doesn't adhere to hands. (Take care not to add too much flour or the bread's texture and taste will be impaired; most of the stickiness will disappear after the multiple rises.)

4. Shape dough into a ball. Drop into an oiled and fairly straight-sided warmed large bowl. Cover tightly with plastic wrap. Let rise at room temperature (70–80°F) until double in bulk (about 1½ hours). Punch down, squeezing out air bubbles. If dough remains sticky, transfer to a board, sprinkle with up to 1 tablespoon flour and knead until smooth. Place in bowl, re-cover and let rise again until doubled.

5. Preheat oven to 375°F. Punch dough down. Sprinkle board lightly with flour. Transfer dough to board and briefly knead. Divide in half. Press or roll each piece into an 8-inch square. Roll up tightly, tucking in and tapering ends. Place, seams down, in a lightly greased jelly-roll pan that has been sprinkled with cornmeal. Cover with oiled sheet of wax paper and let rise until almost doubled (about 45 minutes).

6. Brush loaves with egg wash; sprinkle with seeds. Bake in center section of oven for 30 minutes. If bread browns too rapidly, cover loosely with a sheet of aluminum foil and bake for 10 minutes longer. Remove bread from pan. Place loaves directly on oven rack and bake for 5 minutes. Tap them on the bottom with knuckles. A hollow sound indicates that they're done. Cool completely on wire rack before slicing.

Yield: 2 large loaves

Note: To keep starter alive, replenish with equal amounts of warm water and flour (½ rye and ½ unbleached) and ½ teaspoon partially crushed caraway seeds. Cover and let stand for 6 to 8 hours (it will bubble up). Then pour into a 1-quart glass jar and refrigerate. Use or replenish at least once a week.

Crusty Italian Bread (Pareve)

A popular bread of Italian Jewish people is—Italian bread. And with reason. Those crunchy, golden-crusted loaves are objects for any food lover's affections. Made from flour, water, yeast, salt, sugar and sometimes a sour starter, it's one of the easiest breads to make. It deserves a place in the New American Jewish cuisine, which draws its inspirations from Jewish cooking and baking favorites around the world.

My version is flavored with fruit juices, aromatic spices, a hint of salt and just a suggestion of sugar. Mixed flours, with a minimum amount of yeast, account for its excellent crumb. This crusty Italian bread is my frequent dinner-party gift as a visiting chef, as well as the bread I serve most often when *I* am the cook.

1 package yeast
½ teaspoon sugar
1½ cups unsweetened apple
    juice
1 cup water
1 tablespoon honey
1 cup stone-ground
    whole-wheat or rye flour
About 6 cups unbleached flour

1 teaspoon salt
2 tablespoons well-crushed
    coriander seed (not ground
    coriander)
1 teaspoon ground cardamom
1 egg white beaten with 1
    tablespoon water
Unhulled sesame seeds*

*Available in health food stores.

1. Put yeast and sugar into a large mixing bowl. Combine apple juice, water and honey in a heavy-bottomed saucepan. Slowly warm to 105–115°F. Pour into the bowl and stir with a wooden spoon until yeast dissolves.

2. Add whole-wheat or rye flour, 3 cups unbleached flour, salt, coriander and cardamom. Beat with wooden spoon to blend. Cover and let stand for 30 minutes. Mixture will puff up.

3. Beat in all but ½ cup of remaining flour, a ½ cup at a time, blending well after each addition. When mixture becomes too difficult to handle with wooden spoon, set bowl on base of mixing machine and, using a dough hook, knead at low setting, adding some of the remaining flour until dough cleans the sides of the bowl. If more flour is needed to accomplish this, add a tablespoon at a time, kneading after each addition, until dough is smooth and no longer sticky (about 7 minutes). (If you're kneading by hand, when dough becomes too difficult to handle with a wooden spoon, scoop up and turn onto a lightly floured board and knead, adding enough flour to make a smooth and elastic dough.) Whether you're kneading by machine or by hand, add only enough flour to remove any stickiness (too much flour makes for a heavy bread).

4. Shape dough into a ball. Drop into an ungreased fairly straight-sided large bowl. Cover tightly with plastic wrap and let rise at room temperature (70–80°F) until doubled.

5. Punch dough down. Scrape out of bowl onto a lightly floured board and knead for 2 minutes, squeezing out air bubbles. Cut into 4 equal pieces. Cover with a piece of plastic wrap and let dough rest for 5 minutes. Then shape each piece into a 5-×-10-inch rectangle. Fold over lengthwise, pinching seam. Roll back and forth until each piece is rounded and stretched to a smooth 14-inch-long rope (you may have to let the dough rest intermittently if it springs back after rolling).

6. Lightly grease four 14-inch French-bread pans with sweet pareve margarine or butter blend. Lay loaves in pans. With sharp serrated knife, slash loaves diagonally in four places. Brush with egg wash.

Arrange pans alongside each other. Lightly oil long sheets of wax paper and cover pans, loosely tucking in ends. Let rise at room temperature until double in bulk (50 to 60 minutes).

7. Preheat oven to 450°F. To simulate the effect of a brick oven, half-fill a roasting pan with boiling water and slide onto the bottom shelf of the oven. Position oven rack to the center section of the oven. When loaves have fully risen, gently brush again with egg wash and sprinkle with sesame seeds.

8. Bake bread for 15 minutes. Reduce oven heat to 375°F. Shift position of pans to assure even baking and bake until well browned (about 25 minutes longer). Run a blunt knife around and under loaves (egg wash may cause sticking). Slide bread out of pans and check bottoms for doneness by lightly pressing with thumb. Baking is completed when bread resists pressure. If not done, place breads directly onto oven rack and bake for a few minutes longer. Cool completely on wire racks before slicing.

Yield: 4 loaves

Note: Bread stays fresh for just one day. For single servings, I like to cut remaining breads into 5-inch pieces, wrap them in aluminum foil and freeze. Reheat while still frozen in a preheated 375°F oven for about 15 minutes. Tastes wonderful.

Sponge Bread   *(Dairy)*

Sponge *cake* is a deep-rooted habit of traditional American Jewish cooks. So why not a sponge *bread?* Here it is—moist, with a suggestion of sweetness, and, oh, that sponge-like texture! It makes wondrous French toast and dairy sandwiches, and is scrumptious thick-sliced and unadorned.

2 packages dry yeast
About 7 cups unbleached flour
1 cup buckwheat flour*
2 tablespoons nonfat dry milk solids
1 teaspoon salt
1 teaspoon each ground cardamom and coriander
1 cup each unsweetened apple

juice and water
2 tablespoons corn oil
2 tablespoons honey
½ cup plain low-fat or nonfat yogurt
1 large egg white mixed with 1 tablespoon water
Poppy seeds or unhulled sesame seeds*

*Available in health food stores.

1. Put yeast, 2 cups unbleached flour, buckwheat flour, dry milk, salt and spices in large bowl of mixing machine. Stir to combine.

2. In a saucepan, combine apple juice, water, oil and honey. Heat to the temperature of hot tap water (120–130°F). While stirring with wooden spoon, pour over dry ingredients. Beat briskly to blend. Cover bowl with plastic wrap and let stand for 30 minutes (mixture will puff up).

3. Stir down batter. Beat in yogurt. Add 4½ cups of unbleached flour, a ½ cup at a time, beating well after each addition. When dough becomes too difficult to handle with wooden spoon, set bowl on base of mixing machine and, using dough hook, knead at low speed until dough forms a ball and cleans the sides of the bowl (add some of the remaining flour, if necessary, to accomplish this). Continue kneading for 5 minutes as bulk decreases. Shape into a ball. (If you're kneading by hand, when dough becomes too difficult to handle with a wooden spoon, scoop up and turn it onto a lightly floured board and knead, adding enough flour to make a smooth elastic dough. Fully kneaded dough will remain slightly sticky but will work into a pliant ball.) Drop ball in a lightly oiled fairly straight-sided large bowl. Cover with a sheet of lightly oiled plastic wrap and let stand at room temperature (70–80°F) until more than doubled in bulk (about 1½ hours).

4. Punch down. Transfer to a work surface and knead out air bubbles (you'll hear them pop). Sprinkle with some of the remaining flour, if necessary, to reduce stickiness. Then cut into 2 pieces. Cover loosely with wax paper and let rest for 5 minutes. Flatten each piece, then roll out to a 7-×-10-inch rectangle. Roll up tightly, tucking in ends and pinching seams. Place in 2 lightly greased 8- or 9-inch loaf pans. Lightly oil a large sheet of wax paper and cover breads. Let rise at room temperature until dough rises above the sides of pans (about 1¼ hours). Preheat oven to 375°F.

5. Brush with egg wash; sprinkle with poppy or sesame seeds. Bake in center section of oven for 35 minutes. Remove from pans and place loaves back in oven directly on rack; bake for 5 minutes longer to evenly crisp the crusts. Cool breads completely on wire rack before slicing.

Yield: 2 large loaves

Variation: Substitute stone-ground whole-wheat flour or light rye flour for buckwheat flour.

Two-Grain Herb Loaf *(Dairy)*

Elsewhere in this book, I sing the praises of traditional—that is to say, old-fashioned—Jewish rye bread. Here is a new provocative variant: an herb-infused loaf of rye and wheat. It was created to break the Yom Kippur fast—with zest. It also heightens the enjoyment of dairy soups, cheese and fish.

About 2⅓ cups unbleached
   flour
1 teaspoon sugar
1 package dry yeast
½ cup warm water (105–115°F)
½ cup unsweetened apple juice,
   warmed
2 tablespoons Italian olive oil
¼ cup light rye flour*
½ teaspoon salt
¼ teaspoon baking soda

1 tablespoon crushed dried
   rosemary
½ teaspoon crushed dried
   oregano
¼ cup freshly shredded
   Parmesan cheese
Stone-ground cornmeal
1 egg white mixed with 1
   tablespoon water
Caraway seeds

*Available in health food stores and some supermarkets.

1. Put 1 tablespoon flour, sugar, yeast and ¼ cup water in a tall water glass, stirring well to combine. Let stand until mixture foams and rises to the top of the glass (7 to 8 minutes).

2. In a saucepan, combine remaining water with apple juice and oil. Heat until tepid; set aside.

3. In workbowl of food processor fitted with steel blade, put 2 cups unbleached flour, rye flour, salt, baking soda, dried herbs and cheese. Process for 10 seconds. With machine running, pour yeast mixture through feed tube, scraping out glass; then immediately pour tepid juice mixture through tube. Process for 10 seconds. Stop machine and let batter rest for 2 minutes. Remove cover of workbowl, add 2 table-spoons flour. Process until dough forms a mass and rotates around the bowl about 20 times. Stop machine and let dough rest for 2 minutes.

4. Transfer to a lightly floured work surface and briefly knead by hand. If dough remains sticky, sprinkle in 1–2 teaspoons of remaining flour at a time and knead until stickiness disappears and dough is smooth to the touch (about 2 minutes). Shape into a ball. Drop into a lightly oiled, fairly straight-sided large bowl, turning to coat. Cover tightly with plastic wrap. Let stand at room temperature (70–80°F), until more than double in bulk (about 1½ hours).

5. Punch down and knead on a board, squeezing out air bubbles. Shape into a ball, cover with inverted bowl and let stand for 5 minutes. Shape into a smooth loaf, tucking in, then pinching ends.

6. Lightly grease an 8- or 9-inch loaf pan with sweet butter/margarine blend; sprinkle with cornmeal, shaking out excess. Place bread in pan. Cover with a lightly oiled sheet of wax paper and let rise until doubled (about 1¼ hours). Preheat oven to 400°F.

7. Brush bread with egg wash; sprinkle with seeds. Bake in center section of oven for 10 minutes. Reduce oven heat to 350°F and bake for 15 minutes. If bread is brown at this point, cover loosely with a sheet of aluminum foil while bread bakes 15 minutes longer. Test for doneness by removing bread from pan and tapping the bottom with knuckles. A hollow sound indicates that it's done. If not done, put it back in the oven directly on the rack for 3 minutes longer. Cool completely on a wire rack before slicing.

Yield: 1 loaf

MUFFINS

During my growing-up years, it seemed to me that my mother and all the mothers of my friends were never without three staples: kasha (for side dishes), grapenuts (for a breakfast cereal) and bran cereal (for breakfast muffins). In my kitchen, I use all three ingredients to make two kinds of muffins: Kasha/Grapenut Muffins and Bran Muffins with Fruit.

Kasha/Grapenut Muffins (Dairy)

Kasha muffins are a standard of traditional American Jewish cookery, but kasha/grapenut muffins are new. Let's compare the new with the old. The new uses evaporated skim milk, which is sweeter than the whole milk in the old-style kasha muffins. Additional sweetness in the new muffins comes from frozen fruit concentrates so the amount of sugar needed is reduced to only 3 tablespoons—at least 50 percent less than in the old muffins. The result is a gentle sweetness in the new muffins, as contrasted with a cloying sweetness in the old. Kasha/grapenut muffins are crunchy breakfast treats that keep you "up" all morning without weighing you down.

¾ cup kasha (whole roasted
   buckwheat groats)
¼ cup grapenuts cereal
3 tablespoons firmly packed
   dark brown sugar
1⅓ cups undiluted evaporated
   skim milk
2 tablespoons each frozen
   pineapple juice concentrate
   and honey

¼ cup peanut oil or corn oil
1 large egg
2 tablespoons cornstarch
1¼ cups unbleached flour
2 teaspoons baking powder
½ teaspoon baking soda
1 teaspoon cinnamon
½ teaspoon ground cardamom
   or coriander
½ cup raisins

1. Preheat oven to 375°F. Put kasha and grapenuts into the workbowl of food processor that has been fitted with steel blade (or use a blender). Process until pulverized. Transfer to a large bowl. Stir in sugar, 1 cup milk, and concentrate. Let stand for 5 minutes.

2. In small bowl, combine honey, oil and egg, beating with a fork to blend. Stir into kasha mixture with remaining milk.

3. Sift together cornstarch, flour, baking powder, baking soda and spices. Stir into batter. Then fold in raisins.

4. Grease 12 3-inch muffin cups lightly with sweet butter/margarine blend or sweet pareve margarine (for the sake of crunchiness, I prefer *not* to use cupcake liners). Divide batter equally between cups. Bake until browned (about 20 minutes). Stand pan on wire rack for 5 minutes before loosening around sides of cups with blunt knife. Remove muffins and serve warm.

Yield: 12 muffins

Variation: Substitute ¾ cup rinsed and picked-over fresh blueberries for ½ cup raisins. Bake until surface is lightly browned (about 25 minutes). After removing muffins from pan, let them cool on wire rack for 5 minutes before serving.

Bran Muffins
with Fruit
(Dairy)

Compared to the bran muffins of my memory, my new version goes lighter on the bran; uses low-fat buttermilk instead of whole milk; cuts down on sugar (from ½ cup to 2 tablespoons); and creates a novel kind of sweetness with a mixture of frozen fruit concentrates, honey, fresh fruits and raisins. More delicately textured than the old-fashioned bran muffins, these new creations satisfy today's gustatory demand for lightness while meeting the nutritional preference for bran.

1 cup bran cereal
1⅓ cups unsalted low-fat
   buttermilk
2 tablespoons each sugar, frozen
   apple juice concentrate and
   honey
About 1½ cups unbleached
   flour
2½ teaspoons baking powder
½ teaspoon baking soda
½ teaspoon each cinnamon and

allspice
¼ teaspoon freshly grated
   nutmeg
1 large egg
¼ cup corn oil or peanut oil
1 small crisp apple or bosc
   pear, peeled, cored and
   coarsely chopped
⅓ cup dark seedless raisins
   (optional)
¼ teaspoon pure vanilla extract

1. Preheat oven to 400°F. Put bran in a bowl with buttermilk and sugar. Stir and let stand for 4 to 5 minutes. Then stir in concentrate and honey.

2. Put 1¼ cups flour, baking powder, baking soda and spices in a large mixing bowl. In cup, beat egg and oil with fork. Stir into dry ingredients with wooden spoon. Then pour in bran mixture and combine. Add fresh fruit, raisins if desired, and vanilla. Let batter rest for 2 minutes; it should be fairly thick but not dry. If it doesn't appear thick enough, stir in some of the remaining flour to improve the consistency.

3. Grease 12 3-inch muffin cups with sweet butter/margarine blend or sweet pareve margarine. Divide batter equally between cups. Bake in center section of oven until browned (about 25 minutes). Stand pan on wire rack for 10 minutes before loosening around sides of cups with blunt knife. Remove muffins and let them cool on rack for 5 minutes before serving.

Yield: 12 muffins

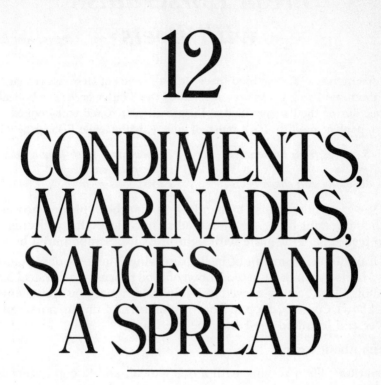

12

CONDIMENTS, MARINADES, SAUCES AND A SPREAD

CONDIMENTS

Any edible added to a food on the table to enhance taste is a condiment (salt, for example). The condiments that follow deserve a place in the New American Jewish cuisine since they resemble tzimmes (that's traditional American Jewish) and are designed to have you reach for them instead of the salt shaker (and that's *New* American Jewish).

Following are my version of the traditional horseradish condiment, two new condiments created around the cranberry and, just as new, a carrot/date condiment that can also be served as a side dish in place of a vegetable.

Fresh Horseradish with Beets   *(Pareve and Dairy)*

Horseradish, a "Jewish food" ever since the ancient Hebrews reached the Promised Land, is my taste favorite of the 5 bitter herbs symbolically served during the Passover Seder. I use it all year round with cooked meat, poultry and fish. It's a must, of course, with Gefilte Fish (page 95).

4–5 ounces fresh horseradish, peeled
1 8¼-ounce can sliced beets

2 tablespoons fresh lemon juice
¼ teaspoon salt
2 teaspoons sugar

1. Fine-grate horseradish by hand. Or fit workbowl of food processor with fine-grating blade. Cut horseradish into pieces that will snugly fit into feed tube. Fine-grate with light pressure. Scrape into a bowl.

2. Drain liquid from can of beets, reserving 3 tablespoons. Coarsely chop beets by hand. Or fit workbowl of food processor with steel blade to chop. Place beets, reserved beet juice and remaining ingredients in workbowl. Coarsely chop in 2 or 3 on/off turns. Stir into horseradish. Cover and let stand for 1 hour before using.

Yield: About 1 cup

Variation: When serving with a dairy meal, add ¼ cup reduced-fat sour cream in step 2.

1. Cranberry Condiment   *(Pareve)*

Cranberries are virtually calorie-, sugar- and fat-free, and contain a significant amount of fiber. Buy several bags while they're in season and freeze. They'll stay fresh for many months.

1½ cups fresh cranberries, rinsed and picked over
12 dried pitted dates
¼ cup sugar
2 sweet apples, such as Washington State, cored and coarsely chopped
2 navel oranges, peeled and cut into small pieces

½ cup raisins
2 ribs celery, coarsely chopped
1 ¼-inch slice lemon, pitted and cut up
½ teaspoon cinnamon
5 whole cloves
½ cup unsweetened apple juice
¼ cup cider vinegar
1–2 tablespoons honey

1. Fit food processor with steel blade. Add cranberries, dates and sugar to workbowl and process in several on/off turns until coarsely chopped. Scrape into a 2- or 3-quart heavy-bottomed saucepan. Add remaining ingredients, except honey, and bring to a boil. Reduce heat to simmering. Cover and simmer for 1½ hours, stirring from time to time (finished chutney will be thick).

2. Remove from heat. Uncover and let cool for 20 minutes. Stir in 1 tablespoon honey. Spoon into a large jar and chill. Taste for sweetness, adding remaining honey, if desired, before serving.

Yield: 1 quart

2. Cranberry Condiment   *(Pareve)*

1½ cups cranberries, rinsed and
   picked over
16 dried pitted dates
¼ cup sugar
1½ cups coarsely chopped onion
1 cup coarsely chopped green
   bell pepper
1½ cups unsweetened pineapple

   juice
2 ¼-inch slices lemon, pitted
   and cut up
½ teaspoon each allspice and
   ground coriander
¼ teaspoon salt
1–2 tablespoons honey

1. Fit food processor with steel blade. Add cranberries, dates and sugar to workbowl and process in several on/off turns until coarsely chopped. Scrape into a 2- or 3-quart heavy-bottomed saucepan. Add remaining ingredients, except salt and honey. Bring to a boil. Reduce heat to simmering. Cover and cook for 45 minutes.

2. Remove from heat. Uncover and let cool for 20 minutes. Stir in salt and 1 tablespoon honey. Spoon into a large jar and let cool for 10 minutes longer. Taste for honey, adding remaining tablespoon if desired. Serve warm or at room temperature.

Yield: About 5 cups

Carrot/Date
Condiment   *(Pareve)*

Mildly spicy—temptingly sweet.

*¾ cup each minced carrot,
  celery and onion
1 cup each unsweetened
  pineapple juice and water
½ cup dark seedless raisins
20 pitted dates, cut up*

*Scant cup cider vinegar
½ teaspoon each cinnamon and
  allspice
¼ teaspoon salt
2 tablespoons minced parsley
3 tablespoons honey*

1. Put all ingredients, except honey, in a 2-quart heavy-bottomed saucepan. Bring to a boil. Reduce heat to simmering and cook, uncovered, for 15 minutes.

2. Stir mixture; cover and continue cooking until chutney becomes thick (10 to 15 minutes), stirring from time to time. Stir in honey. Cover and let stand for 10 minutes before serving.

Yield: About 1 quart

MARINADES

These are liquids in which foods are soaked before cooking. In antiquity, the liquids were mainly salt solutions (the word "marinade" derives from the Latin *marinus,* which translates into "pertaining to the briny deep"). In my New American Jewish cuisine, marinades fulfill their millennia-old purpose, but with a constraint on salt. That purpose is to tenderize (meat and poultry) and to infuse (virtually any food) with flavor.

Dried Fruit Marinade   *(Pareve)*

Israelis are fond of cooking with fruits, as are the Jewish people of most Mediterranean countries.

10 dried dates or dried apricots,
  preferably unsulphured*
1 teaspoon sugar
1 ¾-inch slice fresh ginger
  (about 1-inch diameter)
3 large shallots
3 medium cloves garlic
¼ cup frozen pineapple/orange

juice concentrate
2½ tablespoons cider vinegar
½ teaspoon each ground cumin,
  allspice and curry powder
1 tablespoon dried rosemary,
  crushed
¼ teaspoon salt

*Available in health food stores and some supermarkets.

1. Fit workbowl of food processor with steel blade. Halve the fruit and put into the bowl with sugar. Process for 30 seconds. Leave in workbowl.

2. Cut ginger and shallots into quarters; cut garlic cloves in half. With machine running, drop the cut ingredients through feed tube and process for 10 seconds. Scrape mixture into a bowl.

3. Stir in remaining ingredients; mixture will be thick. Let stand for 15 minutes. Stir again before using.

Yield: 1 cup (enough to marinate a large roasting chicken, 6 to 8 chicken legs with thighs, 8 chops or up to a 5-pound roast)

ORIENTAL MARINADES

Chinese Jewish cooking, and the affection with which so many American Jewish people regard Chinese food, prompted my invention of the following pair of marinades. I've used this marinade in my Chicken with Caramelized Sugar (page 62).

1. Oriental Marinade   *(Pareve)*

1 tablespoon reduced-sodium
  soy sauce
1 tablespoon Worcestershire
  sauce
¼ cup unsweetened apple juice
1 teaspoon rice wine vinegar

2 tablespoons dry sherry
1 teaspoon dry mustard
1 tablespoon light or dark
  brown sugar
½ teaspoon dried cilantro
Dash cayenne pepper

1. In a small bowl, whisk together first 6 ingredients until well blended.

2. Stir in remaining ingredients. Let stand for 10 minutes. Stir again before using.

Yield: About ⅔ cup (enough to marinate a 4–5-pound chicken, 4-pound boned roast, 6 chops or 2 pounds of fish fillets)

2. Oriental Marinade *(Pareve)*

Differing from the preceding marinade in that it contains no sugar but does include Oriental sesame oil, this marinade exudes an unmistakable east-of-Suez flavor.

⅓ cup fresh orange juice
2 teaspoons Oriental sesame oil
1 tablespoon reduced-sodium
  soy sauce
1 tablespoon Spice Mix

2 teaspoons minced fresh ginger
1 teaspoon minced garlic
1½ tablespoons minced fresh
  coriander, or ½ teaspoon
  dried cilantro, crumbled

1. In a small bowl, whisk together first 4 ingredients.

2. Stir in ginger, garlic and coriander or cilantro. Let stand for 15 minutes. Stir again before using.

Yield: About ⅔ cup (enough to marinate a 3½-pound boned roast, 6 chops or a 4-pound chicken)

Note: Oriental sesame oil is available in most supermarkets (look for it on the shelf displaying sodium-reduced soy sauce).

SAUCES

There are sauces that are custom-made for specific foods, and there are sauces that are generic—suitable for a whole class of foods (such as fish) or for many classes of foods (such as fish, meat and poultry). This section is composed of *generic* sauces.

3-Fruit Sauce *(Pareve)*

For this fat-free dessert sauce, strawberries, pears and canned pineapples in their own juices are pureed to appetizing goodness. Wonderful with pancakes and blintzes.

*1 dry pint ripe strawberries,
rinsed, hulled, cut into small
pieces
2 ripe bosc pears, peeled, cored,
cut into small pieces
¼ teaspoon each ground
cardamom and freshly*

*grated nutmeg
½ teaspoon cinnamon
2 tablespoons sugar
1 cup well-drained unsweetened
pineapple chunks
2 tablespoons honey
¼ teaspoon almond extract*

1. Put berries, pears, spices and sugar in a 2-quart heavy-bottomed saucepan. Cover and cook over very low heat for 10 minutes, stirring often (pears should just begin to soften and still hold their shape).

2. Fit food processor with steel blade (or use a blender). Add mixture together with pineapple, honey and extract. Puree until very smooth. Serve at room temperature or chilled.

Yield: About 2 cups

Lemon Sauce (Meat or Pareve)

Sephardic cooks often use lemon sauce with hot fish, chicken, crisp meat and strudels. For best results, always use fresh lemon juice and plan on serving as soon as the recipe is completed.

*1 cup Chicken Stock or
Vegetable Stock
5 tablespoons fresh lemon juice
2–2½ teaspoons sugar
2 teaspoons egg yolk
1½ tablespoons Italian olive oil
or corn oil*

*2½ tablespoons unbleached
flour
½ teaspoon each curry powder
and dried mint leaves
Dash cayenne pepper
¼ teaspoon salt*

1. In small bowl, whisk together stock, lemon juice, 2 teaspoons sugar, and egg yolk. Set aside.

2. Heat oil in small heavy-bottomed saucepan (preferably enameled). Stir in flour. Sprinkle with curry powder, mint and cayenne. Stir and cook over low heat until smooth (about 1 minute). While whisking, dribble in ⅓ of liquid medley until well blended. Cook until sauce begins to thicken. Dribble in remaining medley and continue to whisk until sauce lightly coats a spoon (do not boil). Stir in salt. Taste for sugar, adding remainder, if desired. Finished sauce should be the consistency of heavy cream. Serve immediately or keep warm by setting saucepan in a tub of hot water.

Yield: About 1¼ cups

Spicy Tomato Sauce (Meat and Pareve)

When moderately seasoned tomato sauce won't satisfy, and super-hot salsa is too feisty, try this assertive, but not overwhelming, sauce. It's a palate-pleaser with fish, pasta, ground meat, strudel and kreplach.

1½ tablespoons Italian olive oil
1 cup minced red onion
3 tablespoons minced shallot
1 cup minced green or red bell
  pepper
1 teaspoon each curry powder,
  ground cumin, ground
  coriander and chili con
  carne seasoning (see note)
¼ teaspoon crushed cloves

2 tablespoons wine vinegar
1 6-ounce can unsalted tomato
  paste
2½ cups Chicken Stock,
  Vegetable Stock or water
1 teaspoon sugar
6 sprigs parsley or dill, folded
  over and tied with white
  cotton thread
¼ teaspoon salt

1. Heat oil in a 2-quart heavy-bottomed saucepan. Add onion, shallot and pepper; sprinkle with spices. Sauté until wilted but not brown, stirring often. Pour vinegar around sides of saucepan; cook for 1 minute. Combine with sautéed mixture.

2. In a bowl, whisk tomato paste with stock or water. Stir into saucepan with sugar. Add herb bundle. Bring to a boil. Reduce heat to simmering. Cover and cook for 30 minutes. Discard herb bundle after pressing out juices. Stir in salt.

Yield: 1 quart

Note: Chili con carne seasoning manufactured by Spice Islands is available in most supermarkets. If you can't find it, substitute ½ teaspoon chili powder.

Dipping Sauce (Meat)

A savory uncooked accompaniment to simply cooked meat, fish and poultry. Use it, too, in place of mayonnaise in Chicken Salad (page 154).

2½ tablespoons prepared Dijon
  mustard, preferably unsalted
3 tablespoons fresh lemon juice
1 tablespoon reduced-sodium
  soy sauce

4 tablespoons honey
3 tablespoons Chicken Stock
1 tablespoon minced fresh
  coriander or ½ teaspoon
  dried cilantro, crumbled

1. Put mustard in a small bowl. While whisking, add lemon juice; then whisk in soy sauce.

2. Dribble in honey and stir (do not whisk) until dissolved. Stir in stock and coriander or cilantro. Let stand for 10 minutes. Stir and serve.

Yield: Scant cup

Bagel Cheese Spread *(Dairy)*

Say "bagel" and what comes to mind? Cream cheese—a schmeer. No two Jewish foods have been so closely wedded for so long. But now the schmeer is different. It's about 90 percent lower in fat because the cream cheese is replaced largely by cottage cheese plus tofu. Schmeer it on bagels, of course, for that taste-alike sensation; and it is equally delicious schmeered on dark bread, honey cake or muffins. And why not convert this spread to a creamy-textured dip? The variation will tell you how.

1 8-ounce box plain low-fat or nonfat yogurt
½ pound firm tofu
2 tablespoons reduced-fat cream cheese (Neufchâtel)
⅓ cup unsalted dry curd
cottage cheese, well drained
¼ teaspoon salt
½ teaspoon onion powder
2 teaspoons prepared Dijon mustard, preferably unsalted
1–2 dashes cayenne pepper

1. Lay out a large doubled piece of cotton cheesecloth. Drain off any liquid from the container of yogurt; spoon solids onto cheesecloth. Fold up ends, twisting then tying them together with a long string. Wind string around jutting kitchen faucet and let whey drain for 2 hours. Gently squeeze out any residue liquid. Transfer to workbowl of food processor that has been fitted with steel blade.

2. Break up tofu. Place on absorbent doubled sheets of paper toweling and press out liquid. Transfer pieces to workbowl. Add remaining ingredients, using 1 dash of cayenne. Puree until very smooth. Taste for additional cayenne.

3. Spoon into a glass jar. Tightly cover and refrigerate for several hours before using. Mixture will firm up when well chilled.

Yield: 1 cup

Variation: Prepare a dip by adding, in step 2, ¼ cup chopped onion, ¼ cup unsalted tomato juice, 1 teaspoon reduced-sodium soy sauce and 1 tablespoon minced parsley. Puree until smooth. Yield will be about 1½ cups.

13
SWEETS

Luxurious Strawberry Cheesecake   *(Dairy)*

"No jumping around in the kitchen," my mother would call out to us, "or my cheesecake will fall down." Actually, her cheesecake *always* fell down. Made with pot cheese, cream cheese, cream and lots of eggs, it was a heavy concoction—much too heavy to serve after a full meal. The following version, which uses 50 percent less egg yolk, sugar and fat, won't fall down and will evoke oohs and aahs at the table. A fine finale for a dairy meal.

FOR THE COOKIE CRUST:
14–16 honey graham crackers
2 tablespoons regular wheat germ
¼ cup stone-ground whole-wheat flour
½ teaspoon each cinnamon and ground cardamom
2 tablespoons each sweet butter/margarine blend, melted, and peanut or corn oil, combined
4–5 tablespoons ice-cold unsweetened apple juice
FOR THE CAKE:
¾ pound tofu, cut and drained on paper toweling
1 12-ounce box unsalted dry curd cottage cheese, drained of any visible liquid
8 ounces reduced-fat cream cheese (Neufchâtel)
½ cup reduced-fat sour cream

½ cup super-fine sugar
½ teaspoon ground cardamom
5 eggs (use 3 yolks and 5 whites)
1½ tablespoons finely minced orange zest from navel orange
2 tablespoons fresh lemon juice
3 tablespoons flavorful honey
½ teaspoon pure vanilla extract
¼ teaspoon cream of tartar
¼ cup cornstarch
FOR THE TOPPING:
1 10-ounce box frozen strawberries in syrup
¼ teaspoon each ground coriander and cardamom
2 tablespoons each fresh orange juice and lemon juice
¾ teaspoon finely minced lemon zest
4 teaspoons cornstarch
½ teaspoon almond extract

1. Preheat oven to 450°F. Break up crackers and put in workbowl of food processor that has been fitted with steel blade. Process to fine crumbs. Measure out 1¼ cups, and return to workbowl. Add wheat germ, flour and spices. With machine running, pour shortening mixture through feed tube. When mixture appears evenly moistened, pour 4 tablespoons apple juice through feed tube and blend. Stop machine. Crumbs should hold together when pressed with fingers. If mixture appears too dry, with machine running, add remaining apple juice and briefly process.

2. Gather up and press into a 9-inch springform pan, pressing ¾-inch up the sides, and then to bottom of pan. (The crust will be thin.) Bake for 6 minutes. Cool pan on rack. Reduce oven heat to 350°F.

3. Put tofu in food processor and blend to the consistency of sour cream. Scrape into a measuring cup. You will need a full cup.

4. Put cheeses into large mixing machine bowl. Beat on high speed until very smooth. Add tofu and sour cream and combine. Beat in half the sugar and the cardamom. Stop machine.

5. Separate eggs, dropping 3 yolks into batter and 5 whites into another mixing machine bowl. To the batter add orange zest, lemon juice, honey and vanilla. Beat on medium speed for 30 seconds. Set aside.

6. Beat egg whites with whisk attachment on medium-high speed until foamy. Sprinkle in cream of tartar. Increase to highest speed. Add remaining sugar, a little at a time, and beat until stiff but no dry peaks form. Stir about a cup into the batter. Fold in half of the remainder; then pour folded mixture into balance of beaten egg whites. Sift cornstarch over all and fold in.

7. Pour into prepared crust, smoothing out top. Bake in center section of oven for 50 minutes. Turn off oven. Open oven door a crack and wedge. Let cake cool in oven for 1 hour. Place pan on wire rack and remove rim (crust will hug the filling and cake may slightly crack). Refrigerate until cooled.

8. To prepare topping, put berries into a small heavy-bottomed saucepan. Cook, uncovered, over low heat until defrosted. Stir in spices, juices and lemon zest. Continue to cook for 1 minute. Pour 1½ tablespoons of berry liquid into a cup. Gradually stir in cornstarch until dissolved and smooth. Drizzle mixture back into the saucepan. Cook and stir over low heat until thickened. Combine with extract. Pour into a bowl and refrigerate until completely cooled (about 1 hour). Spread evenly over cake. Return to the refrigerator for at least 2 hours before serving.

Yield: 10 servings

Note: When refrigerated, cake keeps fresh for up to 3 days. It also freezes well.

Fig and Date Cake   *(Pareve)*

Dried fruits have always been a delicious and healthful staple in Jewish households. I remember my mother's typical "company" offering of raisins and almonds as well as dried figs, strung like beads and pulled off and savored. Homemade date cake, too, was served with tea or coffee. With these fond memories, I've developed this sweet 2-loaf confection with the healthful addition of high-fiber oat bran. The invention of the food processor has made the meticulous chopping of sticky dried fruits and hard nuts quick and efficient.

10 ounces dried figs (about 22 small figs), preferably unsulphured, stems cut away, each fig halved
8 ounces dried pitted dates (about 35 standard-size California dates), each date halved
½ cup whole shelled almonds
¼ cup granulated sugar
2 large eggs (use 1 yolk and 2 whites)
½ cup corn oil or safflower oil
1½ teaspoons pure vanilla extract

1¼ cups unsweetened apple juice
½ cup firmly packed dark brown sugar
2 tablespoons dark honey, such as buckwheat (see note)
2¼ cups unbleached flour
6 tablespoons oat bran
½ teaspoon salt
1 tablespoon baking soda
½ teaspoon each ground ginger and cardamom
1½ teaspoons cinnamon
½ cup dark seedless raisins

1. Preheat oven to 350°F. Fit large food processor with steel blade. Put figs, dates, almonds and granulated sugar into workbowl. Process in 6 on/off turns.

2. In cup combine and fork-blend eggs, oil and vanilla. In small saucepan, combine apple juice, brown sugar and honey; stir and barely warm until sugar and honey dissolve. With processor running, pour egg mixture through feed tube; then immediately pour apple juice mixture through tube. Stop machine.

3. In a bowl, combine flour with bran, salt, baking soda and spices. Remove workbowl cover and add half the mixture. Process for 4 seconds. Repeat procedure with remaining dry ingredients. Remove workbowl from base of food processor. By hand, stir in raisins. Pull out blade, scraping off clinging batter.

4. Grease two 8-inch loaf pans with sweet pareve margarine. Divide dough between pans, smoothing out tops. Bake in center section of oven for 50 to 55 minutes. Loaves are fully baked when cake moves away from the sides of pans, and when a toothpick inserted into centers comes out almost dry. Place pans on wire rack for 15 minutes before running a blunt knife around the sides and inverting. Turn loaves to upright position and let cool completely. Wrap cakes in plastic film for several hours (or overnight) before slicing. Cake will stay fresh at room temperature when wrapped in plastic film for up to 3 days, and freezes extremely well when wrapped in plastic film, then in aluminum foil.

Yield: 2 loaves

Variation: Fruitcake: Stir in 4 ounces fruit and peel mixture (candied fruit) at the end of step 3. Cake will have a chewier texture.

Note: If you don't have dark honey on hand, use 1½ tablespoons good quality light honey and ½ tablespoon unsulphured molasses.

Honey Cake (Pareve)

Rosh Hashanah is honey cake time. My version is a Jewish-style fruitcake—but somewhat different. Toasted sesame seeds give it an unexpected crunch. Fruit juice concentrate and wheat germ coax extra sweetness. Folded-in beaten egg whites lighten the chewy texture. Recipe is for 2 loaves; one to eat as soon as it cools, and one for holiday giving.

3¼ cups unbleached flour
2½ teaspoons baking powder
1 teaspoon baking soda
½ teaspoon each ground ginger, allspice and freshly grated nutmeg
1 teaspoon cinnamon
1 cup honey (see note)
3 tablespoons unsulphured molasses
¼ cup frozen apple juice concentrate
¾ cup strong brewed coffee (may be decaffeinated)
4 large eggs (use 2 yolks and 4 whites)
2 teaspoons finely minced

orange zest from navel orange
¾ cup firmly packed dark brown sugar
½ cup Italian olive oil or peanut oil
¼ cup regular wheat germ
¾ cup dark seedless raisins
½ cup coarsely chopped almonds or walnuts
¼ cup toasted sesame seeds (preferably unhulled)
2 tablespoons brandy or cognac, or 1 teaspoon pure vanilla extract
Confectioners' sugar (optional)

1. Preheat oven to 325°F. Sift first 5 listed ingredients into a bowl. In another bowl, combine honey with molasses, concentrate and coffee.

2. Drop 2 whole eggs into a mixing machine bowl. Combine with orange zest and sugar until well blended. On low speed, beat in oil. Add sifted ingredients and wheat germ alternately with coffee mixture. Add raisins, nuts, seeds and liquor or vanilla to batter and blend.

3. Put remaining 2 egg whites into a mixing bowl and beat until firm peaks form (do not overbeat). Fold into batter.

4. Grease two 8-inch loaf pans with sweet butter/margarine blend. Divide batter between the pans. Bake in center section of oven for 50 minutes. Cover loosely with a sheet of aluminum foil to prevent tops from overbrowning. Return to oven for 10 minutes. Fully baked cake will begin to come away from sides of pan, and when metal tester is inserted in center, it should come out clean. Place pans on rack for 10 minutes. Loosen around sides with blunt knife and carefully invert; then set loaves upright on rack and cool completely. Sprinkle, if desired, with confectioners' sugar before slicing.

Yield: 2 loaves

Note: The quality of the honey will affect the taste of the cake.

Haroset (Pareve)

My version of this staple of the ritual Passover meal (the Seder) draws on the harosets of both Ashkenazic and Sephardic origin. Serve this delicious sweet in many ways to brighten any day. Enjoy it as is (a dessert) or spread it on a matzoh. Topped with reduced-fat cream cheese (Neufchâtel), it's an appetizing breakfast treat; and, with cottage cheese, it is a surprising delight for lunch.

½ pound dried pitted dates
½ cup dark seeded raisins
4 ounces dried apricots, preferably unsulphured,* well rinsed
1 large navel orange, peeled, segments separated
2 Red Delicious apples, peeled, cored and cut into eighths
Zest from ½ lemon
1 teaspoon cinnamon

¼ teaspoon each allspice and ground ginger
½ teaspoon ground cardamom
½ cup unsweetened apple juice
2 tablespoons each dark brown sugar and honey
1 tablespoon fresh lemon juice
½ cup each shelled walnuts and whole blanched almonds
Sweet red Passover wine (optional)

*Available in health food stores and some supermarkets.

1. Put all ingredients except honey, lemon juice, nuts and wine in a 3-quart heavy-bottomed saucepan. Bring to a boil. Reduce heat to simmering. Cover and cook for 10 minutes, stirring often. Mixture will remain thick but moist as fruit exudes liquid as it cooks. Let cool.

2. Fit workbowl of food processor with steel blade. Transfer mixture to workbowl together with honey, lemon juice and nuts. Coarsely chop in 4 or 5 on/off turns (do not overchop). Scrape thick mixture into a bowl. If desired, stir in wine to taste. Store in refrigerator in a tightly closed jar.

Yield: About 3 cups

Peach Cake and
Plum Cake *(Pareve or Dairy)*

The old New York coffee shops and cafeterias that catered to the large Jewish population seasonally featured super-sweet, succulent, fresh peach cakes and plum cakes. The confections were baked in huge shallow pans, and my favorite treat was to have a corner section with lots of browned crust. With only 4 corners to the pan, this preference was hard to come by. The following fine-tasting replicas of those memorable cakes (using less sugar and fat, of course) have four easy-to-get-to corners, with centers that are just as tempting as I remember them.

FOR CAKE BASE:
2 cups unbleached flour
1½ teaspoons baking powder
1 teaspoon baking soda
½ teaspoon each ground ginger and cinnamon
¼ cup sweet butter/margarine blend or sweet pareve margarine
3 tablespoons each granulated sugar and firmly packed light brown sugar
2 tablespoons flavorful honey
2 tablespoons frozen apple juice concentrate
1 large egg
¾ cup unsweetened apple juice or undiluted evaporated skim milk
½ teaspoon pure vanilla extract
¼ teaspoon almond extract

FOR PEACH STREUSEL TOPPING:
1½ pounds firm ripe unpeeled peaches, rinsed, cut into ½-inch crescents
½ teaspoon finely minced lemon zest
2 tablespoons sugar
2 tablespoons unbleached flour
¼ teaspoon each cinnamon, ground ginger and freshly grated nutmeg
1 tablespoon cold sweet butter/margarine blend or sweet pareve margarine, cut into small pieces
1 tablespoon flavorful honey dissolved in 1 tablespoon water

FOR PLUM STREUSEL TOPPING:
1 pound small purple plums (18–20), pitted and quartered
½ teaspoon finely minced lemon zest
2 tablespoons unbleached flour
2 tablespoons firmly packed light brown sugar
½ teaspoon each cinnamon and ground cardamom
1 tablespoon cold sweet butter/margarine blend
1 tablespoon flavorful honey dissolved in 1 tablespoon water

1. Preheat oven to 350°F. To prepare cake base, sift first 4 listed ingredients into a bowl. Set aside.

2. Combine shortening, sugars, honey and concentrate in mixing machine bowl. Beat on medium-high speed until well blended, scraping down sides of bowl twice. Add egg and beat until absorbed. On low speed, beat in dry ingredients alternately with apple juice or milk. When blended, add extracts and beat on medium-high speed for 10 seconds.

3. Grease an 8- or 9-inch square pan with sweet butter/margarine blend. Add batter, spreading into corners and smoothing out evenly.

To complete peach cake:

Place peaches in a bowl. Sprinkle with lemon zest and 1 tablespoon sugar, gently stirring to coat. Arrange in 4 rows atop batter, cut edges down, in a neat pattern. Place remaining sugar, flour, spices and shortening in small bowl. Using 2 knives, cut shortening into dry ingredients until crumbly. Sprinkle over peaches, pressing lightly into batter. Bake in center of oven for 55 to 60 minutes. Cake is done when edges recede slightly from sides of pan and are lightly browned. (Moisture of cake may vary with ripeness of fruit.) Place pan on rack. Drizzle honey/water mixture over cake. Let cool for 45 minutes.

To complete plum cake:

Arrange plums in 4 rows, cut edges down atop batter, in a neat pattern. Combine remaining ingredients, except honey/water mixture, in a small bowl. Using 2 knives, cut shortening into dry ingredients until crumbly. Sprinkle over plums. Press topping gently into batter. Bake until edges recede slightly from sides of pan (55 to 60 minutes; moisture of cake may vary with ripeness of fruit). Set pan on rack. Drizzle all over with honey/water mixture. Let cool for 30 minutes.

Cut peach or plum cake into 9 large or 12 small servings. Serve warm or at room temperature. Cover and refrigerate any leftovers and reheat briefly just before serving.

Yield: 9 to 12 servings

Variation: Pear Cake. Substitute 1½ pounds almost-ripe, peeled, cored and sliced Anjou pears for peaches; add ¼ teaspoon ground cardamom to the topping spice mixture and continue with recipe for Peach Cake. Baking time: 55 minutes.

Note: Cakes freeze very well if wrapped in aluminum foil and reheated in 350°F oven for about 20 minutes; or defrosted at room temperature and briefly re-warmed.

Pineapple/Nut
Passover Sponge Cake *(Pareve)*

"No one makes Pesach sponge cake like Jane Moss," my mother's friends used to say. So spoiled were her admirers, that they *expected* to get their sampling each year. She sometimes baked it in large oblong pans to accommodate the 12 eggs (all the yolks were used). When it was baked in layer pans, she'd split each layer, spread with sweetened mashed strawberries and top with whipped cream and whole, perfect berries. It was luscious. Try it my way as is, or serve it with reduced-sugar jelly or top it with my Banana/Carob Fluff (the variation, page 207).

¾ cup potato starch
¼ cup cake meal
½ teaspoon each ground ginger
  and freshly grated nutmeg
¼ teaspoon salt
10 large eggs (use 4 yolks and
  10 whites), at room
  temperature
⅔ cup super-fine sugar

1½ teaspoons each finely
  minced lemon and orange
  zest from navel orange
3 tablespoons frozen pineapple
  juice concentrate
½ cup blanched almonds,
  ground (see note 1)
1 tablespoon confectioners'
  sugar

1. Preheat oven to 325°F. Line the bottom of a 9-inch tube pan with a doughnut-shaped piece of wax paper, notching around the cut center circle every inch. Do not grease pan. Sift first 4 listed ingredients into a bowl. Set aside.

2. Separate eggs, dropping 4 yolks into one mixing machine bowl and 10 whites into another mixing bowl. Using whisk attachment, beat egg whites on medium-high speed until foamy. Turn speed up to high. Sprinkle in half the sugar and beat until stiff and glossy.

3. Set bowl with yolks on machine stand. Beat until light. Sprinkle in remaining sugar, zests and concentrate. Beat on high speed until well blended. Using a wooden spoon, stir about a ½ cup of beaten whites into yolks. Then pour all of yolk mixture over beaten egg whites. Fold in by hand in 12 sweeping strokes. Sift dry ingredients again over all and continue folding for another 12 strokes. Sprinkle and fold in nuts (another 12 strokes should suffice).

4. Spoon into prepared pan, smoothing out top. Run a blunt knife around sides to dispel any air bubbles. Bake in center section of oven for 55 minutes. Top should be lightly browned and toothpick, when inserted, should come out clean.

5. Remove from oven and invert tube onto a 3-cup mason jar with a 1½-inch neck, or any convenient holder that will fit the tube. Cool for

1½ hours. Gently unmold. Peel off wax paper. When completely cooled, sift confectioners' sugar over cake. Cut with sharp serrated knife or pull apart servings with two forks.

Yield: 10 to 12 servings

Notes:

1. For optimum flavor, buy whole almonds. Drop in boiling water for 1 minute and drain. When cool enough to handle, pinch each almond (the skin will slip right off). Let dry. Then grind in food processor.

2. Cake freezes extremely well. Store in plastic, then cover with aluminum foil. Slices can be cut while frozen and thawed within 1 hour.

Molly's Marble Cake   (Dairy)

How do you cut down on a full cup of sugar (that's the amount my favorite aunt used in her marble cake) and still retain that sweet, sweet taste? I use sweet spices, fruit juice concentrates and a soupçon of honey. I also use evaporated skim milk, which is naturally sweet-tasting, instead of whole milk (so I cut down on fat, too). Instead of 1 cup sugar, I need ⅓ cup to get sweetness. (To compensate for the loss of bulk resulting from reduced sugar, I add cottage cheese.)

Would this New American Jewish baking style raise Aunt Molly's eyebrows? Not after she tasted her first piece.

2 cups unbleached flour
2½ teaspoons baking powder
½ teaspoon each ground coriander and ground ginger
1 teaspoon cinnamon
¼ teaspoon salt
¼ cup sweet butter/margarine blend, plus 1 teaspoon for pan
⅓ cup sugar, plus 2 teaspoons
¼ cup firmly packed unsalted dry curd cottage cheese, skim milk added, stirred before

measuring (see note)
2 large eggs
2 tablespoons each flavorful honey and frozen apple juice concentrate
¾ cup undiluted evaporated skim milk
1½ teaspoons pure vanilla extract
½ cup coarsely chopped walnuts
4 tablespoons Hershey's chocolate syrup

1. Preheat oven to 350°F. Sift flour, baking powder, coriander, ginger, half the cinnamon, and salt into medium bowl.

2. Put ¼ cup shortening, ⅓ cup sugar, and cheese in mixing machine bowl. Beat on medium speed until creamy and smooth, scraping down sides of bowl once or twice. Beat in eggs, one at a time, until well blended. Combine honey and concentrate and add to batter.

3. Add milk alternately with dry ingredients, blending on medium speed. Beat in vanilla and half the nuts.

4. Spoon and spread half the batter into a lightly greased 8- or 9-inch loaf pan. Beat chocolate syrup into remaining batter. Pour evenly over cake. Using knife or spoon, fold bottom layer over top layer in a down and then upward motion in 4 or 5 places (do not mix), smoothing out top.

5. Combine remaining nuts, remaining cinnamon and 2 teaspoons sugar in a cup. Sprinkle over cake, pressing lightly into batter. Bake in center section of oven for 55 to 60 minutes. Cake is done when toothpick inserted into center comes out clean. Stand pan on wire rack for 5 minutes. Run a blunt knife around sides. Carefully remove cake from pan and let cool completely on rack before slicing.

Yield: 8 servings

Note: The dry curd cottage cheese used in developing this recipe is very moist. If the cheese that you buy doesn't have skim milk added, stir in 2 tablespoons of skim milk before measuring.

Smooth-and-Sweet Applesauce <small>*(Pareve)*</small>

What would a Jewish household be without a steady flow of freshly made applesauce? A must with latkes, hot and cold cooked meats or poultry, and as a light sweet dessert following any meal.

3 pounds Cortland apples, scrubbed, quartered, cored and thick-sliced	*allspice*
	2 tablespoons firmly packed dark brown sugar or honey
¾ cup unsweetened apple juice	*Kosher sweet red wine (optional)*
6 whole cloves	
½ teaspoon each cinnamon and	

1. Combine all ingredients except wine in a 3-quart heavy-bottomed saucepan. Bring to a boil. Reduce heat to simmering. Partially cover and cook for 20 minutes, stirring twice at equal intervals. Remove from heat; cover tightly and let stand for 15 minutes. Uncover and let stand for 5 minutes.

2. Turn into a food mill and puree into a bowl. Serve warm or chilled, with small glasses of wine on the side to sip and pour into the applesauce, if desired.

Yield: About 1 quart

Applesauce-Glazed Poppy-Seed Cake   *(Dairy)*

This cake and the one that follows use two favorite baking ingredients of the American Jewish kitchen: buttermilk and poppy seed. Applesauce, another favorite, incorporated in the batter and smoothed atop the cake creates an uncommonly delicious flavor when glazed under the broiler for a few minutes.

1½ cups low-fat buttermilk, preferably unsalted
½ cup poppy seeds
2 tablespoons unsweetened carob powder
2 tablespoons flavorful honey
2½ cups unbleached flour
2 teaspoons baking powder
1 teaspoon baking soda
1 teaspoon ground cinnamon
½ teaspoon allspice
5 tablespoons sweet

butter/margarine blend
½ cup plus 2 tablespoons firmly packed dark brown sugar
3 tablespoons granulated sugar
1 cup Smooth-and-Sweet Applesauce (page 199)
1 teaspoon pure vanilla extract
3 eggs (use 2 yolks and 3 whites)
⅛ teaspoon cream of tartar
¼ cup coarsely chopped walnuts

1. Preheat oven to 350°F. Lightly grease an 8-inch springform pan with sweet butter/margarine blend. Put buttermilk, seeds, carob and honey in a small heavy-bottomed saucepan. Heat until warmed, stirring several times. Remove from stove and let stand.

2. Sift flour, baking powder, baking soda and spices into a bowl.

3. Beat shortening with sugars on high speed, scraping down sides of bowl once. On medium speed combine ⅓ cup applesauce, and vanilla with batter. Separate eggs, dropping 2 yolks into batter and 3 whites into another mixing machine bowl. Blend yolk with batter. On low speed, add dry ingredients alternately with buttermilk mixture.

4. Beat egg whites on medium speed until foamy. Sprinkle in cream of tartar and beat on high speed until soft but cohesive peaks form. Fold into batter. Pour into prepared pan. Bake in center section of oven for 55 minutes. (Cake may crack in several spots.)

5. Spread remaining applesauce over cake. Sprinkle with nuts, pressing gently into cake. Place under high heat of broiler for 4 to 5 minutes to glaze. Remove from oven and cool on rack for 10 minutes before removing the rim of pan. Let cool for 30 minutes before transferring cake to serving plate. Serve warm or at room temperature.

Yield: 10 servings

Honey-Frosted
Poppy-Seed Cake *(Dairy)*

In this variation on the theme of poppy-seed cake, dates replace applesauce in the batter, and a honey/egg white frosting creates an entirely different look and taste.

FOR THE CAKE:
17 dates (about 5 ounces), halved
1/3 cup sugar
1½ cups unsalted low-fat buttermilk
¼ cup poppy seeds
1 tablespoon sweet butter/margarine blend, plus 1½ teaspoons
2 cups unbleached flour
½ teaspoon baking soda
2 teaspoons baking powder
½ teaspoon each ground ginger and ground cardamom
¼ teaspoon salt

5 tablespoons peanut oil or corn oil
¼ cup light brown sugar
3 large eggs (use 2 yolks and 3 whites)
1½ teaspoons pure vanilla extract
⅛ teaspoon cream of tartar
FOR THE FROSTING:
2 large egg whites
2/3 cup flavorful honey
1½ teaspoons finely minced orange zest from navel orange
¼ teaspoon orange liqueur or vanilla extract

1. Preheat oven to 350°F. Put dates and sugar into the workbowl of a food processor that has been fitted with a steel blade, and process until fine-chopped. Set aside.

2. Pour buttermilk into a small heavy-bottomed saucepan (preferably enamel-lined). Add poppy seeds and heat just under simmering point. Stir in 1 tablespoon shortening. Remove from heat. Stir and let stand for 10 minutes.

3. Sift flour, baking soda, baking powder, spices and salt into a bowl.

4. Put oil and brown sugar into large bowl of mixing machine. Beat until smooth. Add 2 egg yolks and vanilla and beat on medium-high speed for 1 minute. Stop machine. Pour in buttermilk mixture and beat on low speed for 30 seconds. Beat in date mixture. Add sifted ingredients, a ½ cup at a time. When all of it is absorbed, beat on medium-high speed for 30 seconds. Batter will be thick.

5. Put 3 egg whites in another mixing machine bowl. Beat on medium speed until foamy. Sprinkle in cream of tartar, raise speed to high and beat until stiff but not dry. Stir ¼ into batter. Fold in remainder. Grease an 8- or 9-inch loose-bottomed springform or tube pan with remaining shortening. Spoon batter into pan, smoothing out top.

6. Bake in center section of oven for 40 to 45 minutes (toothpick inserted in center should come out clean). Stand pan on rack for 10 minutes before loosening around sides with a blunt knife. Place bottom of pan or tube on a wire rack; let stand for 30 minutes before removing cake. Let cool completely before frosting.

7. To prepare the frosting, put egg whites into mixing machine bowl. Pour honey into a Pyrex measuring cup. Add 1 teaspoon orange zest. Set cup in a small saucepan of water. Slowly bring water to a boil. Reduce heat to simmering. Stir mixture, keeping water at simmering temperature for 5 minutes. (This prepares the honey for mixing with beaten egg whites in next step.)

8. Beat egg whites on medium speed until frothy. Turn speed up to high (vigorous beating is necessary for the success of the frosting), and beat until soft peaks form. Dribble in warmed honey mixture. Add extract and continue beating until thick and spreadable (5 to 7 minutes).

9. Slash cake into 2 layers. Spread bottom layer with some frosting. Cover with remaining layer, pressing gently. Frost top and sides of cake. Sprinkle with remaining orange zest. Place in freezer for 30 minutes before serving.

Yield: 10 servings

Variation: Frost cake without slashing into layers, which will leave about 1 cup of frosting. Put it in a freeze-proof container. Place in freezer for 1 hour or longer to serve as a creamy-textured sweet topping over stewed fruit, ice cream, Chocolate/Carob Brownies (page 206) and most other confections in this section (pages 190 to 217).

Apple/Pear Pie   *(Pareve)*

Crunchy, cookie-like, thin-crusted pastry encases this moist mixture of fruits. Compatible spices are the flavor enhancers, with sugar and flour kept to a minimum.

FOR THE PASTRY:
2 tablespoons oat bran
1 1/3 cups unbleached flour
1/4 teaspoon each baking soda and baking powder
1 tablespoon sugar
1/4 teaspoon each salt and ground cardamom
1 large egg
3 tablespoons melted and cooled sweet pareve margarine
2 tablespoons ice water

FOR THE FILLING:
1 tablespoon fresh lemon juice
1 teaspoon minced lemon zest
2 tablespoons frozen apple juice concentrate or sweet sherry
1 pound firm bosc pears, peeled,
cored, quartered and thin-sliced
1 1/2 pounds green apples, peeled, cored, quartered and thin-sliced
1 teaspoon each cinnamon and ground cardamom
1/2 teaspoon freshly grated nutmeg
1/4 teaspoon crushed cloves
3 tablespoons firmly packed light brown sugar
2 tablespoons quick tapioca
1/4 cup dark seedless raisins (optional)
2 teaspoons sweet pareve margarine, cut into small pieces
2 teaspoons confectioners' sugar

1. To prepare pastry, fit food processor with steel blade. Put bran, 1¼ cups flour, baking soda, baking powder, sugar, salt and cardamom in workbowl. Process to blend.

2. Break egg into a measuring cup and beat with fork. You will need ¼ cup; discard any excess. Stir in melted margarine. With machine running, pour mixture through feed tube; immediately dribble in ice water. Process until dough starts to hold together (about 10 seconds). Stop machine. Let dough rest for 3 minutes before removing from workbowl (it will be moist and soft). Shape into a ball. Cut into 2 pieces. Lay each piece on a sheet of plastic film and flatten to an 8-inch circle. Cover with another sheet of plastic and wrap. Lay both wrapped circles on a flat dinner plate. Chill for 2 hours. (Dough may be made a day ahead and chilled in the lower section of your refrigerator.)

3. To roll out, lightly sprinkle work surface with some of the remaining flour. Unwrap 1 piece of dough and roll out to a 12-inch circle, turning dough once or twice, pleating and re-rolling over any torn areas. Ease into an 8-inch pie pan, pressing to sides, letting ends hang over. Preheat oven to 450°F.

4. Put lemon juice, zest and concentrate or sherry in a large bowl. Drop pears and apples into mixture as they're cut, turning often to coat. Combine spices with sugar and tapioca. Stir into the fruits with raisins, if desired. Fill crust with mixture, mounding in the center. Drop margarine pieces evenly over fruit.

5. Remove remaining pastry from the refrigerator and roll out. Dust the rolling pin with flour and roll dough onto it. Unroll dough over pie. Press both crusts together. Trim to ½-inch beyond edge of pan and turn under. Crimp edges with a fork. Re-roll any surplus dough and cut into decorative pieces freehand or with a small cookie cutter. Gently press into crust symmetrically. Pierce crust with sharp-pronged fork in several places.

6. Position rack in lower third section of oven. Bake pie for 10 minutes. Reduce heat to 375°F and bake for 15 minutes longer. Cover loosely with a sheet of aluminum foil and bake for an additional 10 minutes. Put confectioners' sugar in a strainer and shake over crust. Loosely cover with foil and return to oven for 5 minutes. Stand pan on rack. Serve slightly warm.

Yield: 6 to 8 servings

Variations:
1. For a sweeter pie without using more sugar, substitute Golden Delicious apples for green apples.
2. For a dairy meal, add 3 tablespoon reduced-fat sour cream to filling mixture in step 4.

CAROB DESSERTS

In Jewish schoolrooms, for thousands of years beginning in biblical times, carob was a reward for achievement; and the best and brightest youngsters vied for it. This prized Jewish sweet is the pod of the carob tree. Dried, the pods are about as long and as wide as a big man's index finger. The pods are chewed to extract their exquisite sweetness—which is fun when you're young.

Today, you can reach out to a supermarket or health food store shelf and come away with carob packaged as a finely ground powder, which is the way I use it. Its rich brown hue suggests chocolate (but it's caffeine- and sugar-free), and it has a taste all its own. Yes, you can make carob taste chocolate-like with the proper mixture of fruit juice and spices, and I've worked out the recipe; but I prefer to use carob for its own taste. Following are three carob desserts in which carob plays its own role as a superlative sweetener—in cookies, brownies and a one-of-a-kind fluff.

Carob-Sesame
Cookies
(Dairy or Pareve)

1/3 cup unhulled sesame seeds
2 cups plus 2 tablespoons
   unbleached flour
1/3 cup unsweetened carob
   powder
1/2 teaspoon each baking powder
   and baking soda
1/2 teaspoon each ground ginger,
   allspice and cinnamon
1/4 teaspoon salt
5 tablespoons sweet
   butter/margarine blend or

sweet pareve margarine
3 tablespoons corn oil
1/2 cup firmly packed dark
   brown sugar
2 tablespoons frozen pineapple
   juice concentrate
1 tablespoon unsulphured
   molasses
1 large egg
1 teaspoon pure vanilla extract
1/3 cup coarsely chopped
   walnuts

1. Strew seeds across a nonstick skillet. Over moderate heat, toast, shaking pan from time to time, until seeds pop and lightly brown. Let cool.

2. Sift flour, carob, baking powder, baking soda, spices and salt into a bowl.

3. In large mixing machine bowl, combine shortening, oil, sugar, concentrate and molasses. Beat on high speed to blend, scraping down sides of bowl twice. Beat in egg and vanilla.

4. Add half the dry mixture, a tablespoon at a time, blending on low speed after each addition. Combine seeds and nuts with batter. Then spoon in remaining dry ingredients. Beat on fairly high speed for 10 seconds.

5. Tear off a sheet of wax paper. Scrape dough onto paper and shape with hands into a ball. (Dough will congeal and will be soft to the touch.) Divide in half. Shape each half into a 7-inch-long smooth log. Place each log on a 12-inch length of wax paper and tightly roll up, twisting ends to secure. Freeze overnight on a flat surface.

6. Preheat oven to 375°F. Remove 1 log from freezer and let stand at room temperature for 5 minutes (do not defrost entirely). Cut with sharp knife into 1/8-inch slices. Arrange 20 cookies on an ungreased cookie sheet in 5 rows, 4 cookies to a row. Bake for 11 to 12 minutes until lightly browned. Transfer cookies to a rack and let cool completely before serving. Repeat procedure with second frozen log. Store in tightly closed tin; they'll stay fresh for up to 1 week.

Yield: About 70 cookies

Chocolate/Carob
Brownies *(Dairy)*

Light and tender crumb, chocolate-satisfying and made *without* eggs.

1²/3 cups unbleached flour
2 teaspoons baking powder
1 teaspoon baking soda
2 tablespoons cornstarch
¼ teaspoon salt
¼ cup unsweetened carob powder*
½ teaspoon each ground cardamom, cinnamon and ground ginger
¼ cup sweet butter/margarine blend
2 tablespoons corn oil

¼ cup each granulated sugar and firmly packed dark brown sugar
2½ teaspoons pure vanilla extract
1 cup unsalted low-fat buttermilk
6 tablespoons Hershey's chocolate syrup
1 cup coarsely chopped walnuts or almonds
2 teaspoons confectioners' sugar (optional)

*Available in health food stores and some supermarkets.

1. Preheat oven to 375°F. Sift first 7 listed ingredients into a bowl. Set aside.

2. Combine shortening, oil, sugars and vanilla in mixing machine bowl. Beat on medium-high speed until well blended, scraping down sides of bowl when needed.

3. On low speed, add buttermilk alternately with sifted ingredients, blending well after each addition. Then using medium speed, beat in 3 tablespoons chocolate syrup and nuts. Mixture will be thick.

4. Spread evenly into a butter/margarine-greased 8- or 9-inch square pan. Drizzle all over with remaining syrup, smoothing out with spatula. Bake in center section of oven for 35 minutes. Put pan on rack for 15 minutes. Put confectioners' sugar in a fine-meshed strainer and shake over cake, if desired. Cut into 9 or 12 pieces. Serve slightly warm or at room temperature.

Yield: 9 to 12 servings

Variations:
 1. Use ¾ cup buttermilk and add ¼ cup reduced-fat sour cream.
 2. Add 2 teaspoons finely minced orange zest from navel orange in step 3.
 3. Ice with Honey Frosting (page 201): When cake has completely cooled, remove it from pan by cutting into quarters, then lifting out pieces with a spatula (it may stick to the pan if it's inverted whole). Reassemble on a flat serving plate. Prepare Honey Frosting and spread over and around the sides of cake.

Banana/Carob Fluff (Pareve)

A rich and creamy-tasting froth, made without milk or egg yolks, that can be a delightful finale to a meat meal.

2 cups unsweetened apple juice
1 package unflavored gelatin
1 tablespoon cornstarch
2 tablespoons light brown sugar
1 tablespoon unsulphured
 molasses
2 tablespoons unsweetened
 carob powder*
¼ teaspoon each allspice,
 ground cardamom and
 cinnamon

½ teaspoon pure vanilla extract
1 ripe banana, well mashed
3 large egg whites
1½ teaspoons granulated sugar
Pinch cream of tartar (see note)
2 tablespoons thin-sliced
 blanched and toasted
 almonds
Shaved or grated chocolate for
 garnish (optional)

*Available in health food stores.

1. Pour apple juice into a medium heavy-bottomed saucepan. Sprinkle with gelatin and let stand for 5 minutes to soften. Whisk in cornstarch. Then whisk in brown sugar, molasses, carob and spices. Cook over low heat, whisking often, until mixture starts to simmer. Continue whisking while cooking until lightly thickened and smooth.

2. Pour into a large bowl. Whisk in vanilla and banana. Chill for 30 minutes. Whisk for 30 seconds (or beat with portable electric or rotary beater). Return to refrigerator until mixture thickens but does not set. Whisk or beat again for 30 seconds.

3. Beat egg whites with sugar and cream of tartar until stiff but not dry. Whisk ⅓ into fluff; fold in remainder. Pour into a chilled 1½–2-quart soufflé dish; strew almonds over top. Cover with a sheet of plastic film. Refrigerate until set (about 3 hours). Top with shaved chocolate, if desired. Texture will be soft and moist, resembling that of the Italian dessert zabaglione.

Yield: 6 servings

Variation: For the consistency of soft ice cream, place in freezer for 3 to 4 hours.

Note: For Passover, omit cream of tartar; substitute 1 teaspoon finely minced orange rind for vanilla extract.

Hamantaschen with Apricot/Prune Filling

(Dairy or Pareve)

These fruit or poppy-seed pockets, which are said to resemble Haman's tri-cornered hat, contribute to the festive holiday of Purim. In New York City, hamantaschen are a daily offering in many ethnic bakeries with such filling choices as lekvar (prune puree), apricot and, most traditionally, poppy seed—and even honey-coated chopped fruits and nuts. The texture of the cookie-like dough varies from crispy to crumbly. My version of the dough is easily prepared with a food processor, and is the perfect foil for the soft, sweet apricot/prune filling, or the uniquely textured poppy-seed filling. The cookies freeze beautifully and are delicious when reheated after freezing. A trayful can brighten any buffet display.

FOR THE DOUGH:
¼ cup 1-minute quick oats
About 2⅓ cups unbleached flour
1 teaspoon baking powder
½ teaspoon each baking soda and salt
¼ teaspoon each cinnamon, ground ginger and ground coriander
3 tablespoons each firmly packed light brown sugar and flavorful honey
4 tablespoons sweet butter/margarine blend or sweet pareve corn-oil margarine, melted, plus 1 teaspoon for pans
2 tablespoons Italian olive oil

2 large eggs
¼ teaspoon pure vanilla extract
3 tablespoons ice water or chilled cognac
About 2 teaspoons confectioners' sugar

FOR THE APRICOT/PRUNE FILLING:
½ pound dried unsulphured apricots
1 pound soft pitted canned prunes (2 8-ounce cans)
2 cups unsweetened apple juice
2 tablespoons light brown sugar
1 teaspoon cinnamon
½ teaspoon ground coriander
1 teaspoon minced lemon zest
2 tablespoons flavorful honey
1 teaspoon pure vanilla extract

1. For the dough, fit food processor with steel blade. Put oats in workbowl and pulverize. Stop machine. Add 2¼ cups flour, baking powder, baking soda, salt and spices. Combine in 2 on/off turns.

2. In measuring cup, combine sugar and honey with melted shortening and oil, beating with fork to blend. Beat eggs and vanilla into mixture. With machine running, drizzle mixture through feed tube. Process for 30 seconds. Then drizzle in water or cognac. Process until mixture forms into 1 or 2 balls. (If dough doesn't congeal, sprinkle with remaining flour and process briefly.) Gather up and shape into 2 balls. Put each ball on a sheet of wax paper. Gently press each piece into a 6-inch circle. Fold up paper around each circle. Lay flat on plate and chill for 2 hours or until firm.

3. To prepare filling, put apricots in strainer. Rinse under cold running water, separating each piece. Transfer to medium heavy-bottomed saucepan. Add prunes, apple juice, sugar, spices and lemon zest. Bring to a boil. Reduce heat to simmering. Cover and cook for 20 minutes. Uncover. Raise heat to slow-boil and cook until liquid is reduced by half (about 8 minutes), stirring often. Remove from heat. Cover and let stand until cooled. Puree through food mill into medium bowl. Stir in honey and vanilla. (May be prepared a day ahead and refrigerated in tightly closed jar. Bring to room temperature before using.)

4. Preheat oven to 350°F. Roll out each circle of dough on lightly floured board to ⅛-inch thickness. Cut into 3-inch rounds with lattice-edged cookie cutter or wine goblet. Re-roll scraps after briefly chilling. Place a teaspoonful of puree in center of each circle. Fold up edges by thirds, leaving an opening at center and pinching edges together where they meet. Finished shape should be triangular. Place on lightly greased cookie sheets about 1 inch apart and bake in center section of oven until lightly browned (13 to 15 minutes).

5. Cool on wire rack for 20 minutes. Put confectioners' sugar in small strainer and sprinkle over cookies. Serve while filling is still slightly warm.

Yield: About 30 hamantaschen

Note: To keep fresh after bake day, freeze without crowding in tightly covered container. To serve, preheat oven to 350°F. Place cookies on cookie sheet. Loosely cover with sheet of aluminum foil and bake until heated through (10 to 15 minutes). Cool on wire rack.

Hamantaschen with Poppy-Seed Filling

(Dairy or Pareve)

*Dough from recipe for
Hamantaschen with
Apricot/Prune Filling (page
208)
1 cup poppy seeds
1 cup unsweetened apple juice
¼ teaspoon each ground ginger,
ground cardamom and
freshly grated nutmeg
3 tablespoons honey*

*2 teaspoons finely minced
orange zest
¼ cup dark seedless raisins or
chopped dates
1 tablespoon fresh lemon juice
2 tablespoons unsweetened
seedless raspberry jelly
2 teaspoons sweet
butter/margarine blend or
sweet pareve margarine*

1. Prepare dough following steps 1 and 2, page 208.

2. While dough chills, prepare filling. Pour seeds into a sieve and rinse under hot running water. Fine-grind, or break up in a mortar and pestle. Transfer to a medium heavy-bottomed saucepan. Add apple juice, spices, honey, zest, raisins or dates and lemon juice. Bring to a boil. Reduce heat to simmering. Cook, uncovered, stirring often, until all liquid evaporates and mixture thickens. Stir in shortening and jelly. Refrigerate until well chilled (may be prepared 2 days ahead up to this point).

3. Follow instructions in steps 4 and 5 of pastry recipe (page 209) for rolling out dough, filling and baking.

Yield: About 30 hamantaschen

Variation: Instead of raisins or dates, use ¼ cup soaked, then drained and chopped dried apricots, add ¼ cup coarsely chopped blanched almonds and ¼ teaspoon almond extract at the end of step 2 of this recipe.

Date and Oat Cookies *(Dairy)*

A happy wedding of the old and the new: dates, a natural confection of the ancient Holy Land; and oats, a current favorite of nutritionists. Together, with the aid of a mixture of tempting ingredients, dates and oats make cookies designed for the sheer delight of munching: crisp, satisfying and always with just the right amount of sweetness.

2¼ cups unbleached flour
1½ teaspoons baking powder
½ teaspoon baking soda
1¼ teaspoons each cinnamon,
*   ground cardamom and*
*   allspice*
20 pitted dates, halved
½ cup shelled almonds or
*   walnuts*
1 cup 1-minute quick oats
¾ cup firmly packed dark

*   brown sugar*
⅓ cup corn oil or peanut oil
2½ tablespoons unsulphured
*   molasses*
¼ cup frozen apple juice
*   concentrate*
2 teaspoons pure vanilla extract
1 large egg
¼ cup unsalted low-fat
*   buttermilk*
Unhulled sesame seeds*

*Available in health food stores.

1. Preheat oven to 375°F. Sift together into a large bowl the first 4 listed ingredients. Set aside.

2. Put dates, nuts and oats in workbowl of food processor that has been fitted with steel blade. Process until mixture is crumbly. Set aside.

3. In large mixing machine bowl, put sugar, oil and molasses. Beat on medium-high speed until blended, scraping down sides of bowl once. Add concentrate and vanilla and blend.

4. Drop egg into batter and beat until well blended. Scrape down sides of bowl. On low speed, beat in date mixture. Then add dry mixture alternately with buttermilk and beat until well combined.

5. Grease 2 cookie sheets lightly with sweet butter/margarine blend. Drop cookies by spoonfuls onto pan, flattening to ¼ inch with moistened fork. Sprinkle with sesame seeds. Bake in center section of oven for 15 to 17 minutes, shifting position of pans midway to assure even baking. Cookies are done when tops become lightly brown (do not overbake). Transfer to a wire rack to completely cool before serving. Repeat procedure with remaining batter. Cookies will remain crisp for a week in tightly closed tin.

Yield: About 4 dozen

Mandelbrot (toasted almond cookies) *(Pareve or Dairy)*

Some classic recipes for these time-honored tea cookies call for 6 eggs and 1 cup of sugar. Considering that my Russian Jewish grandmother drank her tea with a sugar cube clamped between her teeth, mandelbrot and tea meant a heavy dose of sugar per swallow. My Mandelbrot is far less sugary (and eggy) than the traditional versions, but still sweet enough to satisfy—even without a sugar cube.

1 cup dried apricots, preferably unsulphured*
1 teaspoon fine-minced orange zest
1 tablespoon, plus ¾ cup sugar
About 4 cups unbleached flour
2½ teaspoons baking powder
1½ teaspoons cinnamon
½ teaspoon freshly grated nutmeg
2 large eggs
⅓ cup corn oil
¾ teaspoon almond extract

1½ teaspoons pure vanilla extract
⅓ cup fresh orange juice
3 tablespoons honey
2 tablespoons cognac or sweet sherry (optional; see note)
¾ cup blanched almonds, coarsely chopped
2½ teaspoons sweet pareve margarine or sweet butter/margarine blend, melted

*Available in health food stores and some supermarkets.

1. Preheat oven to 325°F. Put apricots in a cup. Barely cover with boiling water and soak for 10 minutes. Drain, squeezing out liquid; cut apricots into small pieces and place in a bowl. Toss with orange zest and 1 tablespoon sugar. Set aside.

2. Sift 3¾ cups flour into a bowl with baking powder, 1 teaspoon cinnamon, and nutmeg. Sift remaining ¼ cup flour onto a sheet of wax paper. Set both measured ingredients aside. Combine balance of cinnamon and 1 tablespoon sugar in a cup. Reserve for topping.

3. Put eggs and remaining sugar into mixing machine bowl. Beat on medium speed until well blended. Add oil and extracts and blend. Combine orange juice with honey, and liquor if desired. On low speed, add liquid mixture alternately with flour/spice mixture, using all but ¾ cup of the flour mixture. Beat in nuts. Batter will be sticky.

4. Remove bowl from base of machine. Stir with wooden spoon, then work in with hands the remaining ¾ cup of flour mixture, apricot mixture and some of the plain sifted flour (see step 2), if necessary, to make a soft dough that's no longer sticky. Divide dough in half. Shape each piece into a 1-×-7-×-3-inch rectangle.

5. Place mounds on lightly oiled cookie sheet. Brush with melted shortening; sprinkle with topping. Bake for 35 minutes. Remove from oven. Raise oven heat to 400°F.

6. Place mounds on cutting board. With sharp serrated knife, cut into ⅜-inch slices. Lay slices flat on baking sheet in 2 or 3 separate batches, and bake for about 7 minutes to toast. Cool on wire rack.

Yield: 36 to 38 cookies

Note: If liquor is not used, increase orange juice measurement by 2 tablespoons.

Farfel and Fruit Candy   (Pareve)

This confection is built around matzoh farfel, small pieces of matzoh, which greedily absorb the sweet liquid, swell up and hold the candy together. Packed with the essence of dried fruits, this is an unusual and intriguing sweet.

½ cup dried apricots (preferably unsulphured),* well rinsed
½ cup unsweetened apple juice
½ teaspoon each cinnamon and crushed coriander seed
¼ teaspoon each freshly grated nutmeg and crushed cloves

1 cup commercial matzoh farfel
12 dried pitted dates, halved
12 soft pitted prunes, halved
½ cup firmly packed dark brown sugar
½ cup shelled walnuts
2 tablespoons honey

*Available in health food stores and some supermarkets.

1. Put apricots in a small heavy-bottomed saucepan with apple juice and spices. Bring to simmering point. Cover and cook for 8 minutes (most of liquid will have evaporated). Let cool.

2. Fit workbowl of food processor with steel blade. To bowl, add farfel, dates, prunes, sugar and nuts. Coarse-chop in 10 on/off turns. Remove cover from processor and add honey and cooled apricots. Process until mixture forms a chunky mass that holds together (do not puree to a paste).

3. Turn onto a large sheet of wax paper and compress into a 2-inch-thick long log. Bring ends together to form a 6-inch wreath. Transfer to a flat plate; cover with plastic film and freeze until firm (3 to 4 hours). Bring to the table and cut into ⅜-inch slices.

Yield: 12 servings

Dried Fruit Tzimmes:
A Dessert   *(Pareve or Dairy)*

Textured, moist and irresistible!

½ pound pitted prunes
¼ cup dark seedless raisins
¼ pound dried apricots
   (preferably unsulphured)*
½ teaspoon ground cardamom
1 teaspoon cinnamon
2 cups unsweetened apple juice
3 tablespoons firmly packed
   light brown sugar
3 tablespoons water
1 large egg

2 tablespoons fresh lemon juice
½ teaspoon finely minced
   lemon zest
2 cups commercial matzoh
   farfel
2 teaspoons sweet
   butter/margarine blend or
   sweet pareve margarine
1 tablespoon honey mixed with
   1 tablespoon warm water

*Available in health food stores and some supermarkets.

1. Put prunes and raisins into a medium bowl. Rinse apricots under hot running water. Add to bowl with spices. Heat 1 cup apple juice to the boiling point. Pour over mixture. Stir and let stand for 45 minutes, stirring once, midway.

2. Put sugar and water into a small saucepan. Over medium-high heat, cook until mixture bubbles up and begins to caramelize. Stir in remaining apple juice. Cook over medium heat until any solids that have formed are dissolved. Stir into fruit.

3. In cup, beat egg and lemon juice with fork. Add to fruit with lemon zest. Fold in farfel (tzimmes will be thick). Let stand while oven preheats to 375°F.

4. Grease an 8-inch square baking pan with ½ teaspoon shortening. Spread dessert evenly into pan. Cut remaining shortening into small pieces and strew over all. Cover with sheet of aluminum foil and bake in center section of oven for 30 minutes. Uncover and return to oven for 10 to 15 minutes longer (confection is fully baked when it sets and is lightly browned). Remove from oven and immediately drizzle with honey mixture. Let cool for 10 minutes before cutting with a sharp knife into 8 or more serving pieces. Serve warm or at room temperature.

Yield: 8 or more servings

Variation: Add ½ cup coarsely chopped walnuts or blanched almonds in step 3.

Apricot Pound Cake   *(Pareve)*

To lovers of sweets, pound cake usually conjures an image of a butter-tasting yellow confection on which to heap fruit and ice cream. This lighter version—just 2 egg yolks—derives its moistness from apricot puree rather than butter. It stands on its own—deliciously—as a gratifying after-dinner treat.

½ pound dried apricots
   (preferably unsulphured)*
1½ cups water
¼ teaspoon crushed cloves
3 tablespoons honey
1½ teaspoons fresh lemon juice
2 cups unbleached flour, plus 1
   teaspoon
2½ teaspoons baking powder
½ teaspoon baking soda
½ teaspoon each cinnamon and
   freshly grated nutmeg
3 tablespoons sweet

butter/margarine blend, plus
   1 teaspoon
2 tablespoons corn oil or peanut
   oil
⅓ cup sugar, plus 1 tablespoon
½ teaspoon pure vanilla extract
4 large eggs (use 2 yolks and 4
   whites)
¾ cup plain low-fat yogurt
3–4 tablespoons finely chopped
   blanched almonds, lightly
   toasted

*Available in health food stores and some supermarkets.

1. Preheat oven to 350°F. Put apricots in colander and rinse under cold running water. Transfer to a heavy-bottomed saucepan. Add water and cloves. Bring to a boil. Reduce heat to slow-boil (a little hotter than simmering). Cook, uncovered, stirring from time to time, until fruit is soft and almost all the water has evaporated (about 12 minutes). Remove from heat. Cover and let stand for 15 minutes. Puree through a food mill into a bowl. Stir in honey and lemon juice. Cool to room temperature before using. (Mixture may be prepared several days ahead, refrigerated in tightly closed jar and brought to room temperature before using.)

2. Sift 2 cups flour, baking powder, baking soda and spices into a bowl. Set aside.

3. Put 3 tablespoons shortening, oil, ⅓ cup sugar and vanilla in large mixing machine bowl. Beat on medium speed until well blended, scraping down sides of bowl once.

4. Separate eggs, dropping 2 yolks into batter and 4 whites into another large mixing bowl. Blend yolks with batter. Spoon in ½ cup of the puree and combine. Then add yogurt alternately with sifted ingredients, beating on low speed until mixed, and then on medium speed until smooth.

5. Using whisk attachment of mixing machine, beat egg whites on medium speed until foamy. Turn up to high and sprinkle in remaining tablespoon of sugar. Beat until firm and glossy peaks form. Stir 1 cup into batter; fold in remainder.

6. Grease an 8-inch springform pan with a teaspoon of shortening. Sprinkle bottom and sides of pan with a teaspoon of flour, shaking off excess. Pour batter into pan, spreading out evenly. Drop balance of puree by spoonfuls across top of cake; then gently spread mixture over surface, expecting that some of it will mix with the batter. Bake in center section of oven for 40 minutes. Cover loosely with a sheet of aluminum foil and return to oven for 10 to 12 minutes. Cake is done when toothpick inserted in center comes out clean.

7. Place pan on a rack. Immediately sprinkle cake with almonds. Let stand for 15 minutes before removing rim. Cool completely before transferring to a serving plate.

Yield: 8 to 10 servings

Rice Pudding with Fruit   *(Dairy)*

Rice pudding is an American dessert, adopted wholeheartedly by the New York Jewish community—perhaps because rice was virtually unknown to the Jewish immigrants from Eastern Europe; and because of the pudding's luxurious richness, so unlike the austere day-to-day fare of the Old Country.

The recipe that follows is "lighter" than the rice pudding my husband's mother made, which he remembers ecstatically from his childhood; but variation 2, he affirms, captures all the sensual whipped-creaminess— "with very little," I remind him, "of that old-fashioned fattiness."

1¾ cups water
¼ teaspoon salt
½ cup raw rice
1⅓ cups each skim milk and whole milk
½ cup unsweetened apple juice
2 tablespoons each firmly packed light brown sugar and honey
¼ teaspoon each cinnamon and freshly grated nutmeg
½ teaspoon ground cardamom

1½ teaspoons minced lemon or orange zest from navel orange
½ cup coarsely chopped lightly packed dried dates
3 large eggs (use 2 yolks and 3 whites)
1 teaspoon pure vanilla extract
1 large crisp sweet apple, such as Golden Delicious or Washington State

1. Preheat oven to 325°F. Pour water into a 3-quart heavy-bottomed saucepan. Add salt and bring to a boil over high heat. Sprinkle in rice. When water returns to a boil, reduce heat to simmering. Cover and cook for 13 minutes. All water should be absorbed. If not, drain off residue. To rice add milks, apple juice, sugar, honey, spices, zest and dates.

2. Break eggs into a cup. Add vanilla and beat with a fork. Stir into rice mixture. Place saucepan over low heat and heat until liquid is just under simmering point. Pour into a lightly greased 3-quart ovenproof casserole dish.

3. Spread a dishcloth across an ample-sided broiling pan. Place casserole atop cloth; pour 1½ inches of boiling water around it. Bake in center section of oven for 1 hour, stirring once, midway.

4. Peel, core and coarse-chop apples; fold into pudding. Bake for 10 minutes longer. Then reduce heat to 300°F and continue to bake for 50 minutes. Top will be lightly browned. Serve warm or cold.

Yield: 6 servings

Variations:

1. Substitute almost-ripe chopped bosc pears for apples. Dark seeded raisins or dried cherries may be substituted for dates. When using cherries, taste for sweetness, adding 1 tablespoon granulated sugar, if desired, in step 1.

2. Mimic whipped cream by pouring ¾ cup of canned Pet light evaporated skim milk into a mixing machine bowl. Put in freezer with whisk attachment until milk is almost frozen. Beat on high speed, sprinkling with a tablespoon of sugar and ½ teaspoon vanilla, until mixture is as stiff as whipped cream. Serve immediately or place in freezer for 1 hour or longer before serving.

For dessert strudel and dessert blintzes, see pages 135 and 124.

Index

ABOUT THE AUTHOR

Francine Prince is the author of the path-breaking *The Dieter's Gourmet Cookbook, Diet for Life,* and eight other popular cookbooks that comply with the Surgeon General's recommendations for better health. Her first-of-a-kind cooking approach was developed in response to a family crisis. In 1974 she helped save her husband's life by innovating a save-the-heart diet that is as delectable as it is nutritionally correct. The diet's unprecedented style has been the foundation of all her books.

Francine Prince has appeared on more than a thousand television and radio programs demonstrating with dramatic simplicity how quick and easy it is to prepare foods that are good for you—and *delicious.* Her healthy-heart cuisine has been endorsed by some of the nation's foremost medical experts and praised by food critics nationwide. Accounts of her achievements have appeared in *Vogue, Cosmopolitan, Self, Working Woman, Essence, Mademoiselle,* and *The Saturday Evening Post,* among other major periodicals. She is frequently the subject of newspaper and magazine features.

Francine Prince and her husband, Harold, live happily and healthfully in Manhattan.